T0381547

COMPLETE
TEACHINGS OF
WICCA

BOOK TWO: THE WICCE

THE WITCH OF OZ

BALBOA
PRESS

A DIVISION OF HAY HOUSE

Balboa Press books may be ordered through booksellers or by contacting:

Balboa Press
A Division of Hay House
1663 Liberty Drive
Bloomington, IN 47403
www.balboapress.com.au
1 (877) 407-4847

Print information available on the last page.

ISBN: 978-1-5043-1213-4 (sc)
ISBN: 978-1-5043-1214-1 (e)

Balboa Press rev. date: 02/06/2018

TABLE OF
CONTENTS

RECOMMENDED READING

The Complete Book of Witchcraft	Raymond Buckland
The Complete Teachings of Wicca Book 1 The Seeker	The Witch of Oz
Tarot and Initiation	Lady Tamara Von Forslun
Spiral Dance	Starhawk
An ABC of Witchcraft	Doreen Valiente
Goddess in my Pocket	Patricia Telesco
The Goddess Path	Patricia Monaghan
To Stir a Magick Cauldron	Silver Ravenwolf
Teen Witch	Silver Ravenwolf
The Witches Calendar	Llewellyn
Dreaming the Divine	Scott Cunningham
The Goddess Companion	Patricia Monaghan
Green Witchcraft 1 & 2	Ann Moura
To Light a Sacred Flame	Silver Ravenwolf
Wicca, Guide for the Solitary Practitioner	Scott Cunningham
Living Wicca, Guide for the Solitary	Scott Cunningham
To Ride a Silver Broomstick	Silver Ravenwolf
Encyclopedia of Magical Herbs	Scott Cunningham
The Truth About Witchcraft	Scott Cunningham
The Secret of Letting Go	Guy Finley
Covencraft	Amber K
Earth Magic	Marion Weinstein
Family Book of Wicca	Ashleen O'Gaea
Natural Magic	Doreen Valiente
Principles of Wicca	Vivienne Crowley
365 Goddess	Trish Telesco

FOREWORD -
THE SECOND
BEGINNING

I have now been involved in many Covens and with many Circles not only in Australia but also around the world. I have taught many hundreds of Students and Seekers of the Old Path known as Wicca. During my 50 odd years of being involved, and I do mean odd. I have put together all my notes and studies and created this series of books titled *"The Complete Teachings of Wicca"*. This is book 2 of the series of books subtitled *"Book Two – The Wicce"*

I realised that we as humans had removed ourselves from Mother Nature's embracing and loving arms, and turned to the new foundation of society and their life structures of the present industrial and technological revolution against Nature and man. Including false heat and cooling, fake lighting, GMO food and the like. We forgot to look at our greatest asset and teacher MOTHER NATURE. She has given us everything we have ever needed, and we have always wanted more. Man has not looked at what he needed, but at what he has wanted.

We dream of always having more than what we have, we all desire our own home, car, family and a good job to support our family and give us what we desire. But much of man has become ignorant and selfish in that we want more and more. With each generation we want more than our parents, and so we look at ways of obtaining them. The problem is that we have become considerably lazier than our ancestors, and with each generation society has found ways for us to do less, but still with the ability to want more. Objects that are worthless upon our demise at the end of our life, we have become like Bowerbirds collecting to make ourselves shine and stand out among our peers.

In noticing all these changes in mankind and our greed to have more and more, we have forgotten our First Mother, THE EARTH. We are no longer in harmony with Her and Her ways to teach and guide us by being One with the Seasons and Her Sacred Lunation's. We have forgotten and pushed aside what our ancient ancestors learnt and taught us. Remember She is not only our First Mother, but She is our HOME, the only one we have.

Let us awaken our ancient etchings and look again to the stars and to the Seasons, and get back in touch with our true selves both within and without. If we become One with Nature again, we will no longer need anything else except what She has to offer us, for we will need no more. This second book comes as a form of study and lessons to help you connect back to Mother Nature, by noticing all that is happening in Nature, the Seasons, the wind, the weather, the insects, the birds, the animals, mankind, our families and friends, and most importantly ourselves. My first book "The Complete Teachings of Wicca – Book One – The Seeker", gives you all the basics that is needed when starting in Wicca, and how to progress with this knowledge in using it for the betterment of yourself, and the very world around you, Nature.

Start to open your eyes and notice what you have either forgotten or not seen before and learn from Nature, as She is our greatest Teacher, and will teach us much if we just stop long enough and listen. Each section gives you a few symbols and associations for each of the Zodiacal months and learns more about the stars and what you will learn more about yourself. To be connected and understand real Magick, you have to firstly connect and get to know your real self, and the very world around you, its nature, seasons and astrological changes that happen on a day-to-day basis. It will take a moment to really notice Nature and what the animal can reveal to us, it may just save our very lives.

Each Zodiac month has between 28-31 days, except February, which varies. So, this must be divided into your circle. Each day notice in Nature what is revealed to you, both within and without? What colour stands out the greatest in Nature, what emotions are showing within you and outside of you, which are strongest, what actions both positive and negative have been taken this day, also If you want to divide each day into morning, afternoon and evening, as events change from hour to hour. Some of us are morning people some are night people.

Keep a Nature Diary on everything that occurs daily; physically, mentally, astrally, psychically and spiritually. The Astrological Zodiac Wheel is divided into 12 spans or some may say 13, (representing the hidden or thirteenth sign Arachne) each representing a sign of the Zodiac and an association with a particular Goddess and God. On each of your Zodiac sheets, there is a Circle, which is divided into 31 sections representing 31 days of your month. (Just omit a section if there are fewer days in that month).

When each day of the zodiac comes into being, fill in the appropriate span as noticed or happened in and on that day. Colour it in the appropriate colour that stood out the most during the day. On each sheet within the circle and section, write all that is noticed in that span of time, each day; what Nature has shown and revealed to you; i.e. weather pattern changes, animal's life, colours etc. Notice everything both within and without and see how it affects you. What changes are happening in your life and those around you, and the whole world of major events that stands out?

"Knowing Nature Is Knowing Yourself,
And Knowing Yourself
Is Knowing the Great Mother Goddess"

Wicces Portal for the Meditational/Trance Journey to Taurus

Wicces Portal for the Meditational/Trance Journey to Gemini

Wicces Portal for the Meditational/Trance Journey to Cancer

(Insert Image 6 Art Leo as the Goddess Sekhmet)

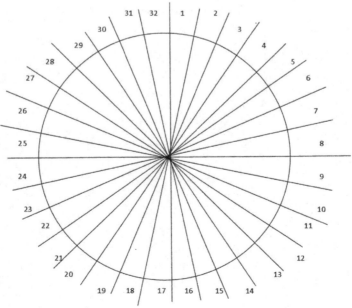

THE GODDESS SEKHMET AS LEO
22ND JULY — 21ST AUGUST

In the Temple Zodiacs of ancient Egypt, the sign Leo appears as a Goddess with a Lion or as a Lioness, signifying, dignity, royalty and respect. The Egyptian Goddess Sekhmet, (The Powerful One) ruler of Fire and Solar Power; had the body of a beautiful woman, and the head of a lioness. She was a warrior Goddess and also a Healing Goddess, and the Protector of Her people. The ancient Temples of Sekhmet say that Her Sacred Breath formed the desert. Her symbols are the Sun Disk, Red Linen and the Lion, as She was pictured as the Lioness, the most feared of all animals. Her Consort was the God Ptah and Her sacred Temple still resides in Egypt called the Temple of Kom Ombo.

A lion accompanies the Sun Goddess Wurusemu of Arinna of Anatolia, whilst Ishtar and Atargatis rode astride their lions or were drawn by chariots pulled by lions. In India and Tibet, the Goddess Tara is shown not only riding the Cosmic Lion representing Solar Radiance, but also holding the Sun in the palm of Her hand.

The Sun, ruler of the sign Leo, was in earlier times regarded as feminine, as the female principle representing the Great Sun Mother. The story of Amaterasu, Sun Goddess of Japan, brings out both the self-reflective and playful qualities of the Leonian nature. In protest against the torments of Her jealous and spiteful brother, Amaterasu retreats into a cave, depriving the world of Her Light and warmth. Amaterasu was eventually coaxed out by the playful antics of another Goddess Ama No Uzume; and Her attention was captured by Her own brilliant reflection in the polished bronzed Magickal "mirror of eight hands".

Playfully independent creatures, such as cats are often seen as the Goddesses companions, especially in maternal matters as the 'she-cat' was considered a great and gentle mother. Black cats pulled Scandinavian Freya's mighty chariot, whilst light and heat shone from Her necklace of the Sun.

Bast, the Cat Mother Goddess of Egypt, was associated with both the Sun and the Moon. She was a dual Goddess of pleasure and fertility, who loved music and dancing, and was known as "The Lady of Life" and "Mother of all Children".

CORRESPONDENCES:

Archangel:	Michael.
Alchemy:	Digestion.
Animal:	Lion, all felines.
Birthstone:	Citrine, Cats Eye, Jasper, Peridot Star Sapphire, Fire Opal, and Red Coral.
Colour:	Orange, Purple, Red and Yellow.
Day:	Sunday
Direction:	South
Element:	Fire
Fish:	Salmon, and Sturgeon.
Gods:	Apollo, Helios, Horus and Ra-Hoor-Khuit.
Goddesses:	Arinna, Amaterasu, Atargatis, Helinaehu-Ku Mask, Sekhmet, and Tara,
Metal:	Gold.
Mode:	Leadership and Creation.
Plant:	Hazel, Holly, Lily, Safflower and Sunflower.
Perfume:	Olibanum and Copal.
Quality:	a Fixed Sign.
Represents:	King, Ego inflation, very dramatic, impressive and protective.
Ruler:	The Sun
Season:	Summer.
Tarot Card:	Strength/Lust.
Tree:	Cypress.
Weapon:	Sword.
Personality:	Adaptable, Faithfulness and Strength.

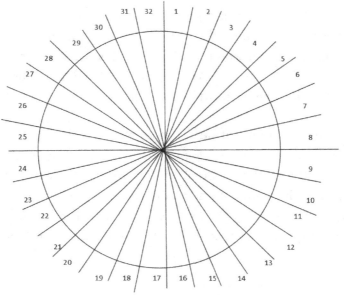

THE GODDESS CHICOMECOATL OF VIRGO
22ND AUGUST — 22ND SEPTEMBER

The Goddess of Virgo gives the life-sustaining gift of the worldwide symbol of food, which are grain, vegetables and fruit. The Corn Mother Goddess Virgo (her symbol is three cobs of corn), which has been revered since the days of early agriculture. The word Virgo means "Self-Sufficient". Also, the story of the Labor of Hercules who dealt with two women in the divine task of Virgo, where he takes the emerald girdle of the Amazon Queen, Hippolyte, and rescues Hesione from a horrific monster sea serpent.

Chicomecoatl was an early Aztec or Maize (Corn) Goddess. Her Triple Aspects of Maiden (the sprouted seed), Mother (the growing sheaf), and Crone (the harvested grain), were celebrated by great processions to Her Temple at each and every stage of the cycle throughout the year. The cosmic Virgo is situated in the skies of the Southern Hemisphere.

Corn Goddesses in North America were also central deities for the people, ancestor Goddesses Somagalags and Queskapenek, taught the secrets of food gathering, collecting, and eventual agriculture and also harvest production to their people, and again return the seed to the earth for next seasons food. To the Keres Indians, the Goddess Irriaku or Yellow Woman gifted the sacred corn through Lyatiku, the Earth Mother to Her people.

In autumn of each year, the women of early Greece observed the Thesmophoria, a three-day agricultural fertility ritual in honor of Demeter (Roman Goddess Ceres) of the Eleusinian Mysteries. Another quality of Virgo is that of the virgin, it had its meaning corrupted in Roman times. Originally the word Virgin, meant a woman who was independent and free to express her sexuality as she chose. Sex WAS a sacred act, as expressed by the Hearth Goddess, Vesta, and the Vestal Virgins, who tended Her Fire, the Spirit of Life itself.

CORRESPONDENCES:

Alchemy:	Distillation.
Animal:	Brown Bear, Wombat, Koala and all Solitary animals.
Archangel:	Auriel.
Birthstone:	Amethyst, Peridot, Garnet Red Emerald and Sardonyx.
Colour:	Green and Yellow.
Day:	Wednesday.
Direction:	North.
Element:	Earth
Fish:	Brim and Trout.
Gods:	Mercury and Narcissus.
Goddesses:	Astraea, Cares, Ceres, Demeter, Irriaku, Ishtar, Isis, Justitia, Lyatiku, Mary, Pele, Persephone, Queskapenek, Somagalags, and Yellow Woman.
Metal:	Platinum
Mode:	Perfect and Analytical
Perfume:	Narcissus, Honeysuckle and Cypress
Personality:	Warm, cultivates tolerates.
Plant:	Hazel, Narcissus and Sage
Quality:	Mutable sign
Represents:	Worry, anxiety and craftsmen.
Season:	Winter and Harvest.
Tarot card:	The Hermit
Tree:	Pine, and Elder

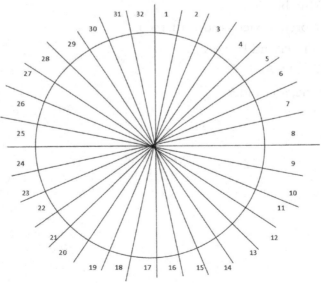

THE GODDESS ISIS OF LIBRA
23RD SEPTEMBER — 22ND OCTOBER

The guiding principle of Libra is personified in the Egyptian Goddess Maat as the Spirit of cosmic law and justice. Holding the Scales of Balance (Libra). She was known as "The Eye", in recognition of Her clarity of perception and seeing of the Truth in all situations. Maat was a compassionate Goddess. There was no sense of recrimination or eternal damnation in Maat's judgments where She held the Ankh of Immortality in Her hand and weighed the hearts of humans after death against the lightness of an ostrich feather (Her symbol). Thoth as the judge of men's souls always oversaw this ceremony. If the heart was too heavy, the soul was reincarnated for further Karmic lessons on Earth until it became light enough for the next stage of evolution.

Libra is also situated in the Southern Hemisphere near Scorpius and Virgo, and is the only one of the twelve zodiac signs not to be represented as an animal but a set of scales that weigh the balance of man and the progression of one's soul.

Both Semitic Goddesses Ishtar and Sumerian Inanna were known as The Queen of Heaven. The Priestesses of these Goddesses were the Oracles and interpreted the divine order of the Goddess and passed down justice from the Goddess to the people. In Greece She was known as the Goddess Themes, who gave birth to Dike, whose name survives in the Greek word, 'dynasty', meaning judge. Themis also birthed the Horae, the Daughters of Time who made the Seasons come and go; and the Morea, the Three Sister Fates. The first Sister Klotho spun the threads of each life; the second Lachesis allotted each year's portion; and the third, Atropo, cut the thread at the end of each life.

All these aspects of the Goddess, gave structure to the Libran principles of Justice, Harmony and Balance. She reveals Herself around the time of the Autumnal Equinox, the time of weighing and balancing our past and divining our future by a letting go of things gone by.

CORRESPONDENCES:

Alchemy:	Sublimation
Animals:	Elephant, Eagle and Otter
Archangel:	Raphael
Birthstone:	Rose Quartz, Moonstone, Beryl, Emerald and Opal
Colour:	Green, Pink, And Purple
Day:	Friday
Direction:	Southwest
Element:	Air
Fish:	Stingray, Seahorse and Sea snail
Gods:	Eros, Hephaestus, Vulcan Chonsu, Thoth and Zeus
Goddesses:	Aphrodite, Astraea, Dike, Gaia, Hera, Inanna, Juno, Psyche, Themes, Themis and Venus.
Metal:	Brass
Mode:	Diplomat and negotiator
Perfume:	Galbanum Vanilla, and chamomile
Personality:	Good natured and the need to calculate
Plant:	Aloe Vera, Ivy, Mullein and primrose
Quality:	Cardinal Sign
Season:	Spring
Tarot card:	Justice
Tree:	Willow, Oak, and Rowan
Weapon:	The Wand

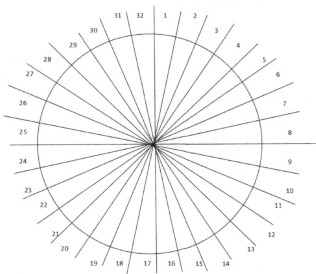

The Goddess Pele of Scorpio
23rd October – 22nd November

Scorpio's symbols are the Scorpion, the Snake and the Bird, linked with the Goddess, appearing among the earliest evidence of human life on Earth. Formerly, Death was seen as a natural benevolent force, part of the maternal aspect of the Goddess. She brought forth life at birth, and at death received it back into Her Womb (tomb) to be reborn. Selket, the beautiful Scorpion Goddess of Egypt, was painted on the insides of coffins. Her arms, usually wings, were extended protectively, welcoming the dead to the Underworld.

Statues from the ancient Palace Knossos in Crete show the Goddess with Her snakes twisting up Her arms. The snake like the Moon, changes and transforms itself by shedding its skin, it releases and dies off the old and slithers forth reborn, shiny and renewed. Another Scorpio image is that of the volcano. Pele, the Goddess of Mt. Kilauea on Hawaii, appears stamping Her feet just before an eruption. She expresses Her Scorpio repressed energy in an explosive release of great power.

Her volcanoes produce Obsidian, black glass; the Amazons in ancient Anatolia where the Goddess Hecate was worshipped venerated black stones. Hecate, like Persephone and the Norse Hela, was known as the Queen of the Dead. Hela was associated with the volcano Mt. Hekla in Iceland. Her name which was later corrupted into the fires of Hell, originally meant HOLY, HEAL and WHOLENESS, affirming the regenerative powers of death.

CORRESPONDENCES:

Alchemy:	Separation
Animal:	Birds, Eagle, Scorpion, Thunderbird and Snakes
Archangel:	Gabriel
Birthstones:	Malachite, Olivine, Moonstone, Amethyst, Black Glass, Jet, Obsidian, Snakestone and Topaz
Colour:	Browns and red
Day:	Tuesday
Direction:	West
Element:	Water and Long Snows
Fish:	Eel, Sea Snakes, Sea Slug and Octopus
God:	Hephaestus, Pluto, Ptah, Set, Typhoon, and Vulcan
Goddess:	Ereshkigal, Hecate, Hel, Hela, Persephone Pele and Selket
Metal:	Steel
Mode:	Spontaneous
Perfume:	Benzoin, Hyacinth and Pennyroyal
Personality:	Most intense, passionate, judging, loyal and tenacious
Plant:	Cactus, Ivy and Water Reed
Quality:	Fixed Sign
Represents:	Jealousy, Ingenious strategist
Ruler:	Mars
Season:	Autumn
Tarot card:	Death
Tree:	Chestnut and Walnut
Weapon:	Conch and Triton Shell

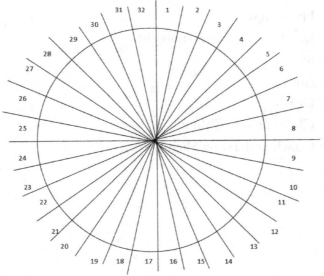

THE GODDESS RHIANNON OF SAGITTARIUS
22ND NOVEMBER — 20TH DECEMBER

The Sagittarian symbol of the Horse and the Archer appears as a manifestation of the Goddess all over the ancient world. Cretan Leukippe was a white mare and Indian Saranya the mare-mother. The Great Mare Goddess of the Celts was Epona whose image endures on the chalk hillside at Uffington, England, carried with Her a bag of abundance. Much like the Welsh Goddess Rhiannon who rode a white horse and carried a similar bag. Rhiannon combines compassion with a wild, independent spirit that typifies Sagittarius.

Like the Finnish Mielikki and the Norse Skadi, she was a Goddess of the Forrest who both protected and took the form of many different animals. One day, in the shape of a hare, she was being hunted by a pack of dogs. A lad, Cian, rescued the hare and for his kindness, the Goddess invited him to her home on the Magickal Island of the Sidhe (pronounced sheee). Months later Rhiannon was enjoying the beauty of one of Her sacred groves when Cian crept up and tried to rape Her. The Goddess, in rage, took the form of a great white mare and with one forceful kick of Her massive hind hoof broke his leg.

The Amazon Goddess Artemis (Roman Goddess Diana) was honored at the Great Temple of Ephesus. She was both hunter and protector of animals, aided women in childbirth, and was worshipped on the New Moon. The Goddess always shows a strong young vibrant warrior woman with bow and arrows, reminiscent of Algerian rock paintings dating back to Neolithic times. As champion of freedom, many stories are told of Artemis helping woman escape from rape and abusive marriages into independence.

CORRESPONDENCES:

Alchemy:	Incineration
Animal:	Hare, Deer, Dragon and Wolf
Archangel:	Michael
Birthstone:	Lapis lazuli, Peridot, Emerald, Pearl and Topaz
Colour:	Light Blue and Purple
Day:	Thursday
Direction:	Southwest
Element:	Fire
Fish:	Red Emperor, Coral Trout and Snapper
God:	Bellerophon, Chiron, Jupiter, Nerigal, Odin, Pegasus and Thor,
Goddess:	Artemis, Athena, Bona Dea, Danu, Diana, Epona, Leukippe, Minerva, Neith, Nephthys, Pandora, Rhiannon Saranya, Sophia, Tyche and Yemen
Governs:	Hips, thighs, sciatica, sacral areas and rheumatism
Metal:	Tin
Mode:	Spiritually impetuous
Perfume:	Aloes, Calendula, Hyssop and Saffron
Personality:	Optimistic, sensual desires, freedom loving, jovial, humorous character, honest, intellectual and philosophical
Plant:	Rush, Dragons Blood, and Mullein
Quality:	Mutable sign
Ruler:	Jupiter
Season:	Summer
Tarot card:	Temperance
Tree:	Oak, Birch and Grasstree
Weapon:	The Arrow, Spear and Athame

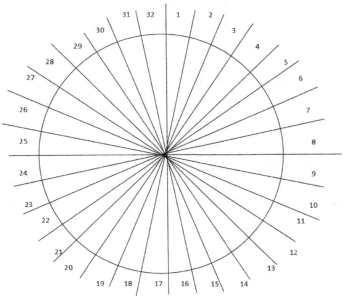

The Goddess Amaltheia of Capricorn
21st December — 21st January

Amaltheia is one of the many named Goddesses who created the Earth out of Her own body substance. Capricorns constellation in the heavens is that of Amaltheia, and the early tribal Goddess replaced by the Olympian Gods like so many of the older matriarchal deities. Amaltheia survived as a Divine Goat who was held in awe by the immortals. One of Her horns became the Cornucopia or Great Horn of Plenty, signifying infinite abundance.

Gaia was another of Her names, who molded the mountains along Her spine and created valleys out of the hollows of Her flesh. In compassion for the ignorance of humans, Gaia formed caves on Her body as entrances into Her deepest secrets. Delphi is the most famous of these Oracle power caves where Priestesses as active Oracles have sat for millennia. The Romans associated Capricorn with the Goddess Vesta, who guarded the Hearth and protector of all women. She embodied the ancient persevering quality of Capricorn, passing Earthly wisdom down through the generations.

In Arnhemland, Australia She is known as Kunapippi, the First Mother. Only the Initiated can enter Her sacred cave, Her womb/tomb. The tribal medicine man would swing above his head the mighty bullroarer fast enough that he may hear Her voice and learn from Her wisdom. North American Paso wee (Great White Buffalo Woman) and Athena of Greece both show practical Capricornian skills and knowledge. They were wise in the ways of material creation and gave form to ideas. Paso wee received Sacred Knowledge from the Buffalo Spirit. She taught the women of Her tribe how to build the first tipi and what herbs to use for medicines.

CORRESPONDENCES:

Alchemy:	Fermentation
Animal:	Ass, Goat, and Water Serpent
Archangel:	Auriel
Birthstone:	Amethyst, Malachite, Ruby, Garnet Red, and Sapphire
Colour:	Black, Dark brown and Grey
Day:	Saturday
Direction:	Northwest
Element:	Earth
Fish:	Cod, Cobbler and Tuna
God:	Bacchus, Chronos, Khnum, Khem, Pan and Saturn
Goddess:	Amaltheia, Athena, Gaia, Kunapippi, Makalii, Paso-wee and Great White Buffalo Woman
Governs:	stomach, genitalia, bowels and kidneys
Metal:	Lead
Mode:	Illumination
Perfume:	Lilac, Mimosa, Musk, and Vetivert
Personality:	Admirer of excellence and feminine energy
Plant:	Indian Hemp
Quality:	Cardinal sign
Ruler:	
Season:	Winter
Tarot card:	The Horned God
Tree:	Elm, Silver Birch and Ghost Gum
Weapon:	horns, tusks and the Pentacle

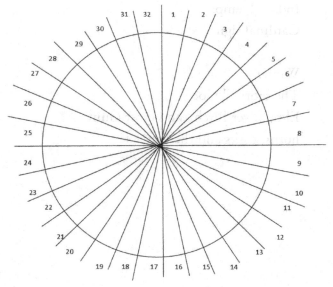

The Goddess Nut as Aquarius
22nd January – 20th February

The Goddess as Aquarius makes a bridge between the Earth and Sky, connecting the Spirit of Earth to the Spirit of Heaven, the rainbow bridge to the Gods and Goddesses. In Egypt She was named Nut, Mistress of the Celestial Ocean, who forms an arch over the Earth giving birth to the Sun each day, and accepting it back into Her body each night. Tears from Her eyes, formed the stars of the cosmos and milk from Her breasts flowed down to nurture the Earth

Both the powerful Goddesses Ishtar and Ashtart were known also as the Queen of Heaven, and were associated with the planet Venus. Ashtart descended to Earth as a fiery falling star, and the sacred stone at Her Shrine was said to whisper prophecies for those who could understand, or at least open their heart and soul and listen in the wind. Hebe, the Goddess of Youth, was the original cupbearer of the Greek Gods. When She fell and exposed Her genitals, the Gods were so disgraced and decided to give Her Sacred Grove to Ganymede. This attitude is in striking contrast to those of earlier times. Where in Egypt, Britain, Ireland, Norway, South America and Sumer, the sight of the sacred vulvas of the Goddesses including Hathor and Ninshursag healed people. In Sumer, Gula, the Goddess of Healing and Childbirth carried the water jay of Aquarius.

In Africa She is known as Mawu, Goddess, and Creattrix of supreme power who birthed and created all on Earth. She breathed life into Sekpolis' soul, and into all beings, thus giving them life. When challenged in heaven by Awe (the monkey who believed he could also create life), Mawu sent him back to Earth ashamed. Awe carried with him the seeds of Death to remind all beings of Mawu's ultimate power

CORRESPONDENCES:

Alchemy:	Multiplication
Animal:	Man, and Peacocks
Archangel:	Raphael
Birthstone:	Amethyst, Garnet red, Chalcedony and Crystal Quartz
Colour:	Blue and Turquoise
Day:	Saturday
Direction:	East
Element:	Air
Fish:	Coral Trout, Wrasse, Rainbow Trout, and Trevally
God:	Ahephi, Ganymede, Hapi, Kaelo Janus Zeus and Uranus
Goddess:	Anumaki, Chandra, Ea., Enke, Hebe, Mother of Waters, Pachamama and Varuna
Governs:	Lungs, heart and spleen
Metal:	Aluminium
Mode:	Gentle natured
Perfume:	Costmary, Galbanum, Lavender and Star Anise
Personality:	Friendly, humanitarian, honest, loyal, inventive, intellectual, attractive personality, sensitive and patient
Plant:	Olive
Quality:	Fixed sign
Ruler:	Saturn and Uranus
Season:	Spring
Tarot card:	The Star
Tree:	Birch and Elm
Weapon:	Thurible and Incense

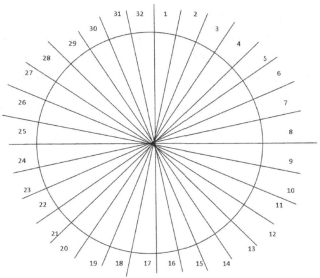

THE GODDESS NAMMU AS PISCES
21ST FEBRUARY — 19TH MARCH

Nammu means "Ocean" and is the earliest recorded name of a Universe creating Deity found on Earth. In Sumer, the Goddess Nammu was known as the oldest of the old, the Primeval Sea who created all above and below. Nina was another of Her ancient names from Sumer. Of truly Piscean Nature, Nina had a fish or serpent tail and swam in the sea. She was known as a compassionate prophetess, an Oracle of unfathomable depths who interpreted dreams. Other, slightly later fishtailed Goddesses of the Sea are Atargatis of Syria and Nu Kwa of China. The story of Nu Kwa is of Her restoration of Peace and Harmony on Earth after a period of chaos and suffering.

The essential theme is of the universal benevolent laws of Nature, the patterns of the Tao-The I Ching. These Goddesses are associated with Venus, the planet of love and harmony, as is the later Greek Aphrodite who also emerged from the Sea. To the Navajo people of North America, she is Estsan Atlehi, Changing Woman. To walk the Trail of Beauty is to follow Her patterns and cycles, the flow of life in birth, death and rebirth. The Goddess as Pisces is the whole within which everything constantly shifts and changes. From night to day, summer to winter, seed to mature tree, back to seed, and from waxing to waning Moon, she is indeed Changing Woman.

CORRESPONDENCES:

Alchemy:	Projection
Animal:	Boar and Buffalo
Archangel:	Gabriel
Birthstone:	Bloodstone, Amethyst, Pearl and Sapphire
Colour:	Red and Violet
Day:	Thursday
Direction:	West
Element:	Water
Fish:	Dolphins and Whales
God:	Anubis, Neptune and Poseidon
Goddess:	Aphrodite, Atargatis, Atlehi, Changing Woman, Kaulua Nu Kwa, Nina, Venus and Varuna
Governs:	Womb, genitals, liver and gall bladder
Metal:	Platinum
Mode:	Indecisive
Perfume:	Ambergris, Jasmine, Lily and Sandalwood
Personality:	Indecisive, charitable, caring and maternal
Plant:	Opium Poppy
Quality:	Mutable sign
Ruler:	Moon
Season:	Autumn
Tarot card:	The Moon
Tree:	Weeping Willow and Twisted Willow
Weapon:	Cauldron and the Chalice

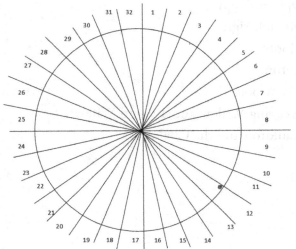

THE GODDESS BRIGID OF ARIES
20TH MARCH — 19TH APRIL

The original name of the sign/constellation of Aries in Egypt was Seret, the Ewe. She symbolized fertility. The compassionate Goddess Rachel of the early Hebrew tribes was also revered as "The Divine Ewe" Aries, the first sign of the Zodiac, and symbolizes the will to action, energy in process. The Goddess Mahuika of Aotearoa, (New Zealand) discovered fire and taught the Maori people how to create and use it. Fire flamed from Her fingertips and Her flashing eyes could be seen far across the islands.

The Celtic Goddess Bridget was born at Dawn when the Sun kissed a good morn to all, a Pillar of Flame reaching from the top of Her head into the heavens. The Ingheau Aundagha, the Nine Daughters of the Flame, tended this fire. Later, Christian sisters worshipped Her as St. Bridget, and continued to tend the Flame, until members of their order who knew of its 'pagan' origins eventually extinguished it.

The Goddess as Aries in Her warrior aspect many times resisted the onslaughts of patriarchy. Celtic queens such as Maeve, Cartimandua and Boudicca were sexually independent warriors. They were known for their strong wills both in their powerful diplomatic and battlefield leadership and in their choice of bedmates. Macha, an aspect of The Morrigan, Irelands Triple Goddess, dealt with attempted rape by binding Her assailants to forest trees and teaching them to be faithful servants of the Goddess. They later built the Temple Emain Machu serving Her there for the rest of their lives.

CORRESPONDENCES:

Alchemy:	Calcification
Animal:	Ram and the owl
Archangel:	Michael
Birthstone:	Hematite, Diamond, Ruby and Sardonyx
Colour:	Red
Day:	Tuesday
Direction:	Southeast
Element:	Fire
Fish:	Marlin, Porpoise and Sailfish
God:	Ares, Chnoum, Mars and Onouris
Goddess:	Bridget, Boudicca, Cartimandua, Maeve, Mahuika, Morrigan, Rachel and Seret
Governs:	Heart and Throat
Metal:	Iron
Mode:	Courage, strength and control
Perfume:	Dragons Blood, Frankincense and Neroli
Personality:	Ego inflation, very dramatic, protective,
Plant:	geranium and Tiger Lily
Quality:	Fixed sign
Ruler:	Sun
Season:	Autumn
Tarot card:	The Emperor
Tree:	Cypress
Weapon:	Spirit Candle and Fire Wand

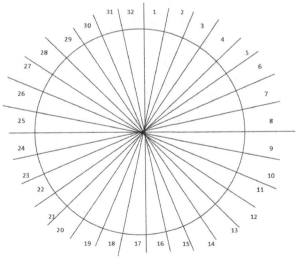

THE GODDESS HATHOR AS TAURUS
20TH APRIL — 19TH MAY

The arrival of spring and Bloddeuwedd was the Spring Queen Goddess and Lady of the Flowers and was celebrated when the Sun was in Taurus in the Northern Hemisphere. Sensuality and merriment were the way of the Goddess religion that saw human love and sexuality as sacred rather than profane. The Taurus Constellation, which includes the Pleiades or Seven Sisters as the Australian Aboriginals call it, was one of the earliest named by man. Classical poets wrote of the Constellation under the Moon-Cow Goddess named Io, as well as Taurus.

Many early Goddesses such as Sumerian Ninshursag and the Goddess Asherah took the form of the Divine Cow. Asherah was known for Her wisdom and as 'She who builds" because She taught the people how to make shelter from timber and from mud bricks. Her symbol was the Sacred Tree. In Egypt, the cow was the most ancient form of the Goddess Isis, Hathor and Neith. The Cow-Mother's milk splashed the sky with stars creating the Milky Way. Greek Goddesses Io, Europa and Hera also appeared as the White Moon-Cow. The symbolic association between horns and the crescent Moon may go back as far as the last Ice Age. Depictions of cattle were common in cave paintings of the time. The bull motif, celebrating life, is found in early shrines to the Goddess at Catal Huyuk (Anatolia) and Knossos (Crete). Cows symbolizing the nurturing aspect of the Goddess are still treated as Sacred in India today.

CORRESPONDENCES:

Alchemy:	Congelation
Animal:	Bull and Buffalo
Archangel:	Auriel
Birthstone:	Rose Quartz, Rhodonite, Carnelian, Emerald and Topaz
Colour:	Orange and red
Day:	Friday
Direction:	Northwest
Element:	Earth
Fish:	Shark and Barracuda
God:	Osiris
Goddess:	Hathor, Hera, Juno and Venus-Aphrodite
Governs:	Hands and feet
Metal:	Gold and copper
Mode:	Earthiness, fecundity, growth and incarnation
Perfume:	Patchouli, Rose and Storax
Personality:	swiftness, faith, steadfast, and earthiness
Plant:	Mallow and Mint
Quality:	Fixed sign
Ruler:	Earth
Season:	Winter
Tarot card:	The Hierophant
Tree:	Pine and Yew
Weapon:	The Pentacle and Salt

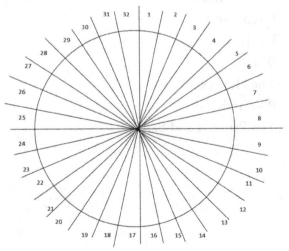

THE GODDESS DEVI AS GEMINI
20TH MAY - 19TH JUNE

In the legends of the Hopi people of North America, the Creation of Earth and Life was accomplished by Sister Goddesses of the same name. When the whole universe was the great Sea, the sisters Huruing Wuhti lived in the houses of the West and East Oceans. They created the Earth and met on the Rainbow Bridge between East and West to survey their work. When the tiny bird they had sent out, returned to report no signs of life, they then created many creatures to populate the land. Lastly, they made a woman, Tuwabontum and then a man, Muing WA who became the first ancestors of the Hopi people.

There are many other sister Goddesses throughout the world. Often, they seem to share different aspects of the one deity, such as Isis and Nephthys of Egypt. Both Goddesses were known as Nature Goddesses with life-giving powers and underworld deities who helped guide human souls through Death. Isis was of the Dawn and giver of the west wind, and Nephthys was of the evening and giver of the East wind.

The Indian Goddess Devi has many names and aspects - Parvati the beautiful, Tara the compassionate, awesome Kali whose name literally means time, and Durga a name taken from the Buffalo Demon She conquered. The Goddess as Gemini is of the Air Element, she is mutable and changeable, a communicator, messenger and birther of ideas.

CORRESPONDENCES:

Alchemy:	Fixation
Animal:	Bowerbird and Magpie
Archangel:	Raphael
Birthstone:	Citrine, Agate, Topaz and Tourmaline
Colour:	Orange
Day:	Wednesday
Direction:	East
Element:	Air
Fish:	Flathead, Flying Fish and Garfish
God:	Apollo-Diviner, Castor, Janus Mercury, Pollux, Sam-Taui and Twin Murti
Goddess:	Devi, Huruing Wuhti, Kali, Isis, Nephthys, Parvati and Tara
Governs:	Lungs, throat and Third Eye
Metal:	Electrum and Quicksilver
Mode:	Communication, sensuality and sexuality
Perfume:	Bergamot, Lavender and Wormwood
Personality:	Artistic, expression and inventor
Plant:	Orchid
Quality:	Faithfulness and adaptable
Ruler:	
Season:	Spring
Tarot card:	The Lovers
Tree:	Palm and Elder
Weapon:	The Air Wand and Thurible

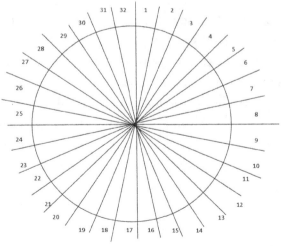

THE GODDESS YEMAYA AS CANCER
20TH JUNE — 21ST JULY

The Goddess as Cancer is a nurturer and fierce protector of the life she had created. In Hercules' fight with the Hydra, the Crab joined in and pinched him on the foot. Rewarding Her support of the Goddess, Hera then placed the Crab, the Cancers symbol in the heavens. The Moon rules the sign Cancer, and the Moon Goddess has been revered under many names throughout the world, throughout time - African Yemaya, Goddess of the Full Moon; Greek Artemis of the New Moon and birth; winged Selene who drove the chariot pulling the Full Moon across the sky, and the Crone Hecate of the Waning and Dark Moon; Pacific Island Hina; Mayan Ix Chel; Jezanna of Zimbabwe. Both in the stories of Ix Chel and Hina, the Moon are highlighted as a symbol of Woman's freedom. These Goddesses both fled from abusive husbands to dwell in the night sky, coming and going in their own rhythms, their loneliness eased by the connection with women on Earth.

Moon Goddess Jezanna of the Moshona people, showed the life protecting quality of Her Nature when She put an end to child sacrifice in Her honor. Notambu, Her Priestess, had the courage to stand-alone and oppose the yearly ritual, trusting more in the love of the Goddess than the Traditions of Her culture. At Notambu's cry, Jezanna appeared in the sunlit sky making Her well known. The child was spared and the Goddess' tears of joy rained down on the crops in great abundance. The Moshona rejoiced in the compassion and wisdom of the Goddess and Her Priestess.

CORRESPONDENCES:

Alchemy:	Dissolution
Animal:	Crab, Sphinx and Turtle
Archangel:	Gabriel
Birthstone:	Moonstone, Carnelian, Amber, Chalcedony and Ruby
Colour:	Orange and yellow
Day:	Monday
Direction:	West
Element:	Water
Fish:	Swordfish, Tuna and Crabs
God:	Dionysis, Khepri, Khepera, Bacchus and Pan
Goddess:	Artemis, Hecate, Hera, Hina, Hydra, Ishtar, Ix Chel, Jezanna, Selene and Yemaya
Governs:	Pancreas and Kidneys
Metal:	Quicksilver and Silver
Mode:	Baptism, Birth, Motherhood and the womb
Perfume:	Jasmine, Onucha and Myrrh
Personality:	Artistic, expression and inventor
Plant:	Lotus
Quality:	Halo and spirituality
Ruler:	Moon
Season:	Autumn
Tarot card:	The Chariot
Tree:	Ebony
Weapon:	The Water Wand and Chalice

THE WICCES
TRANCE
PORTALS

The next pages are from visions that I have had during intense meditations and Trance states that have given me these visions as doorways to a different dimension of thinking/feeling. They seem to aid me through the 4 different stages of the Moon energies, and attuning with myself, give me the energy and assistance that I need on my journey to self-realisation and the connecting with all that is Pachamama (the Great Mother Earth). So, for each phase of the Moon please separate the sections into quarters and tune in at those Moon phases to see what it reveals to you. Fill in the section with the appropriate insight that is revealed, each year tune in again and rewrite what it reveals if you see a pattern of growth then you know you are on the right Path to self-knowledge and Enlightenment. Be honest with yourself, as Truth will reveal the greatest Mystery of all "Self-Divineness" in other words the Goddess within shall be awakened.

TRANCE PORTAL OF LEO

Trance Portal of Virgo

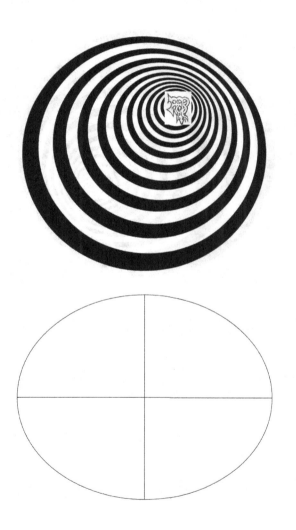

TRANCE PORTAL OF LIBRA

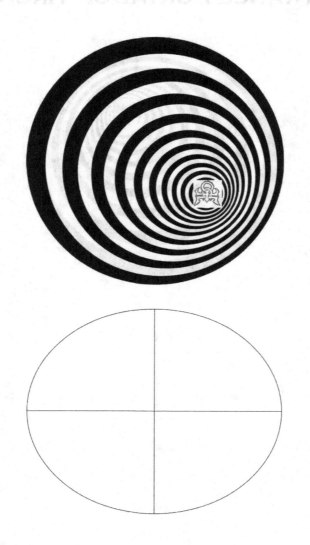

Trance Portal of Scorpio

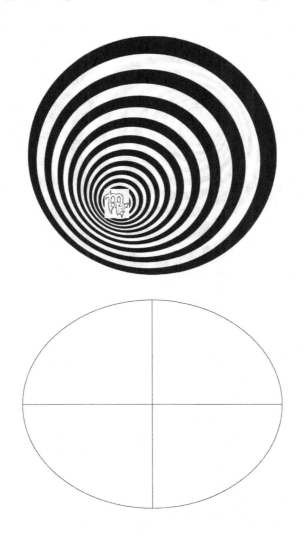

TRANCE PORTAL OF SAGITTARIUS

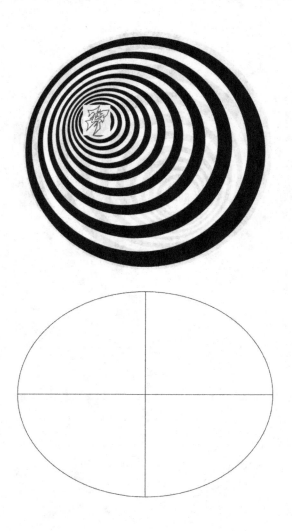

TRANCE PORTAL OF CAPRICORN

TRANCE PORTAL OF AQUARIUS

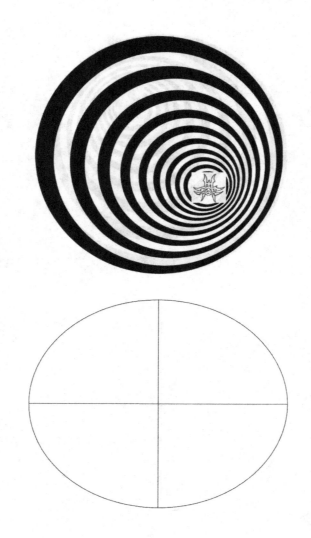

Trance Portal of Pisces

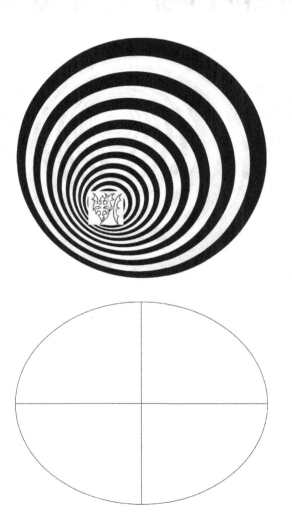

Trance Portal of Aries

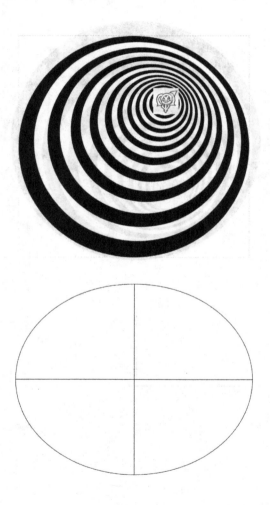

TRANCE PORTAL OF TAURUS

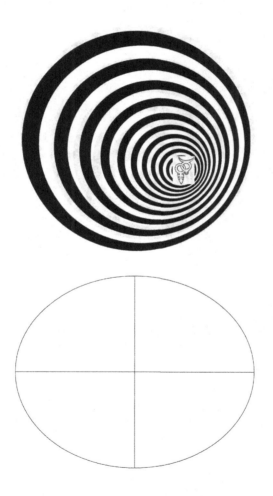

Trance Portal of Gemini

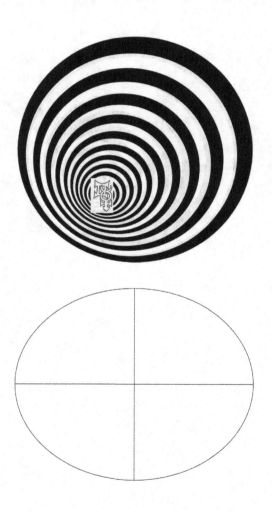

TRANCE PORTAL OF CANCER

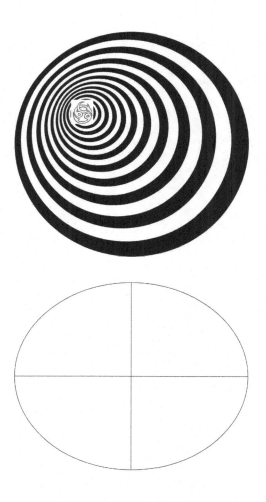

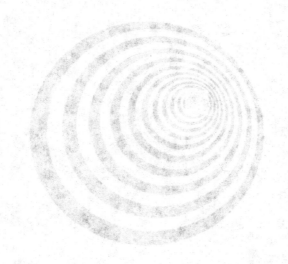

OUR RIGHTS!

Have you ever heard of combustion engines? Carburetor's that can get hundreds of kilometers to the litre have been put aside. An old friend of mine from Perth, Western Australia - Ralph Sarich, designed the Combustion engine. His prototype was offered to the Australian government to invest in this great invention, but they did not take up the offer and, so he had to go overseas to sell the idea and designs to foreigners. These may have made him hundreds of millions of dollars but again will be buried until a time that man declines in using normal petroleum engines because of the power of petrochemical companies. We have created engines from electric or magnetic engines that can practically run forever.

You don't know much about them because if they were to come into use, they would put all oil companies out of business, there are a few on the market thanks to companies such as Toyota who have brought this concept into reality, but still we are not doing enough to educate the masses into understanding and learning about these new ideas, as we are still brainwashed in the old fuel run vehicles. The concept of the "Internal Combustion Engine" has been obsolete for 50 years. But because of Oil Cartels and corrupt government regulations, the rest of the world have been forced to use petrol for over 100 years, and will continue using petrol and Deosil run engines until we have exhausted all the resources and choked our planet and ourselves to death. We are slowly destroying our planet and using more and more fossil fuels, man has bred beyond what the Earth can sustain us. Big business is primarily responsible for destroying the Water we drink; the very Air we breathe; and the very food we eat, our water now costs more than soft drinks, the food that we eat is mostly GMO (Genetically Moderated Organisms). Through this GMO our food has lost so much of the natural nutrients that Mother Nature placed into everything for our benefit. Man has no care for the world that they are destroying, only for their own immediate families and the money they make in the process.

HOW MANY OIL SPILLS CAN WE HONESTLY ENDURE?

Each year we constantly hear of millions and millions of gallons of spilt oil that are now slowly destroying the oceans, and the many forms of life that it supports, including mankind. Among things that are being destroyed in the oceans is Plankton. Plankton is a common seaweed that supplies 70-90 percent of the Earth's oxygen. Most of us believe it is the rainforests of the world that supply a majority of our atmosphere, but that is incorrect they only offer between 20-40% But it too is diminishing through big business at a massive destructive rate of thousands of acres of rainforest being destroyed daily. Both Plankton and the Rainforests support the

ECOSYSTEM, which forms the very basis of our food supply and life as we know, how about us starting to support this ecosystem and save our planet and our very lives before it is too late.

THE PLANKTON IS DYING!
AND SO IS OUR PLANET!

Let us go to any remote state or country, anywhere on the planet Earth, and in doing a little research we will find that these huge companies broker out their toxic waste all over the world, and governments are quickly taking up the offer because of the big money they are offering in taking their toxic refuse. These billion-dollar companies control legislation; in fact, they CONTROL the Law and many governments. The law says that NO Company can be fined more than $25,000 per day. This is ridiculous as these companies are making $10 million a day by dumping lethal toxic waste into our oceans and then governments are offering up our land and burying this toxic refuse in our deserts, away from society. But everything within the Earth, moves, shifts and travels, toxic refuse does the same. It is only good business to continue to do this because as we are all aware MONEY is more important than our HEALTH? These companies influence the media, so that they control our minds. They have made it a crime to speak out, and if we do so we are called conspiracy nuts, and we are laughed at. I am angry because we are all being chemically and genetically damaged. Unfortunately, this will affect our children's children (if we have any, as it is a scientific fact that men are 50% less fertile than they were 20 years ago. We go to work each day blind and not giving a second thought to the demise of our planet, and right under our noses we see our car and the car in front of us spewing out noxious and poisonous gases. They are accumulative poisons. We are being poisoned with everything that big business has to offer.

THESE POISONS ARE KILLING US SLOWLY,
EVEN WHEN WE SEE NO EFFECT.

None of us would have believed 20 years ago that on a certain day that we would not be able to see 20 feet in front of us; that we would not be able to take a deep breath because the Air would be a mass of poisonous gas; that we would not be able to drink out of our taps due to the chemicals they place in our water systems and that we would have to buy water in a bottle. Our common given rights as creatures of the Earth and as humans has been taken away from us.

Unfortunately, the reality of our lives is so grim, that nobody wants to hear it! We argue every day with people that either do not want to face the reality that we are headed for a doomed place, if we continue to treat the Earth as our ongoing source to take as much as we like, through abuse and ignorance. There is an Australian saying "She'll be right mate". What a load of rubbish. We have turned our paradise into a rubbish tip without remorse or even the concept that enough is enough. When are we going to wake up and realise that time is running out.

What can we do?

We need a responsible body of people (not the E.P.A. "Environmental Protection Agency" which is government run) who can actually and genuinely represent us and the planet as a Natural whole, and not big business. We need a knowledgeable organization funded by the community and governments as a body of people who are free from the government and corporate bullying. This body of people must not allow the introduction of anything into our environment that is not absolutely Biodegradable, or able to be chemically neutralized upon production.

And finally, as long as there is profiting to be made from the polluting of our Earth, companies and individuals will continue to do what they want. Fines should be representative of the damage that they are doing. Fines that will make them stand up and think, instead of just laughing the matter away. We must FORCE these companies to be responsible and to operate safely and responsibly with all our best interests in mind. So that when they don't, we can take back our resources and our hearts, and our minds, and

Do what is right!

JUDAISM HAS
A GODDESS

If you go back far enough you will see that all religions have their roots in ancient systems of Pagan cultures, they start with a cosmogony, which explains to their followers how the Universe and our world was created. In the Hebrew Haggadah Bible, they also conform to this pattern. The belief system of both Jews and Christians have their views of the ultimate feminine as the Divine Mother of Jesus, but conform their own ideas about Genesis.

In Genesis 1:1-2 it is written *"In the beginning, God created the heavens and the earth. The latter was a formless void; there was darkness 'on the face of the deep' and God's spirit moved on the waters."* * But there is another scholastically acceptable way where it reads: *"In the beginning a number of Gods (Elohim) began to give birth to the heavens and the earth. The earth still belonged to Tohu and Bohu (Goddesses of formlessness and ultimate space), and darkness was on the face of the mother creator the Goddess Tiamat, and a huge wind flapped its wings over the face of the water".* This is the true translation from the original Hebrew writings of the Bible before being translated into Latin then Greek, and then being lost into English.

The Hebrew word Elohim, is explained further as "The Gods", and can be accepted, but there is an ancient truth of the word God that encompasses both male and female aspects of deity. In all of Nature we see the resemblance of everything that is birthed being of a creation of a male and female principle that comes together to create new life. Why is it so hard to presume that deity is also a Goddess and God, and together they formed and created the Universe and all within it?

It is far easier to picture a mother god giving birth to all life than a father god giving birth. This will need a lot of enormous changes within our consciousness of the relationship of all women and men to the divine. You have got to remember that the winner always writes history, and the winners have been patriarchal in every aspect, there is no way that they would allow the feminine to be accepted above that of their own male status and ego.

Since the birth of the New Religion, which is only two thousand years old, they have slowly removed the importance of the feminine and created a very Patrifocal uneven religion that only answers to the needs of the male within their path and Androcentric (male dominated) attitudes. When a man writes, he writes through the eyes of a male, and when a female writes she writes through the eyes of a female. Much of what has been written has been by men, since women were not allowed to enter the schools of learning, they were forbidden and banned from word knowledge in all its forms, so it cannot be truly trusted. Feminist Judith Plaskow affirms that the:

"Deep resistance called forth by naming the Goddess in Judaism indicates the needs she answered are still with us for a God who does not include Her is an idol made in man's image acknowledging the many aspects of the Goddess among the names of God becomes a measure of our ability to incorporate the feminine into a monotheistic religious framework".

We need to bring forward an historical perspective in Judaism and educate the world, not just those following the Judaic system of belief but for the Goddess. The sad thing is that many cannot conceive nor even give it any thought at all, because of the brainwashing that we as humans have had over the past two thousand years, that there is only ONE God, the Christian God. The difference is that when we talk of the Goddess we talk of the masculine side of Her as God, we see both sides within the one. How can we ever prove the original truths, as they have been buried, destroyed and changed hundreds of times to suit the many dreams and visions that priest, messiahs and prophets had, before taking note and writing them down as the "Word of God". The old saying is that "If god is male, then male is god", has little comfort to women the world over who have been forced into a lesser importance than man.

The Goddess (God with an ess) is the Supreme Ultimate Creattress of the Universe as sustained and provider for all life. Unlike the male God of the New Religion She is not a Goddess of War; she is a mother aspect of the divine. She is not separate from the world, She is the world, and with Her Consort, Her counterpart the God of Nature, they are not separate but dance eternally as One entity and are "prima-inter pares". Inscribed on the Temple walls at Sais at her Temple of Aset in the inner chamber it says: *"I am all that is, was or ever will be".*

Because the Judaic faith saw sexuality as dirty, especially within women unless married, they also became misogynistic and believed that all women carried sin, and that they were creatures of filth and pleasure, whereas they saw men as the redeemer and conqueror of sin. They had to create a divine virgin to conceive the Son of God, instead of allowing the loving act of God and woman to conceive a gift to the world. But still they did not give Mary a place of pride as Goddess of the Earth born God Jesus, but instead as just a carrier, or receptacle of the divine spirits gift to man. Women need to develop the insight and acceptance of an ultimate Feminine as the Goddess as it will assist women to become stronger and more empowering instead of one with guilt and being inferior to men.

The original writers and editors were Deuteronomists who struggled against the concept of the Goddess figure being a part of the Hebrew Bible. So slowly throughout millennia they have tried to banish her and remove her importance from history by brandishing her as an evil creation of the devil, but the true originals concepts of the Goddess run deeper and through every part of the original writings of the Hebrews. Beginning with the original wife and consort of God (Yahweh) who was (Hochma or Sophia) as true Goddess in her own right. But then they changed her names and her titles slowly throughout the Judaic history of the Catholic Church into the Holy Spirit within the Divine Trinity. Originally it was The Father, The Mother and Divine Child, but was later changed to suit the more masculine was of foreword thinking as the Father, Son and Holy Spirit. Gradually instead of being given the right place alongside her consort God as Goddess, she was changed to a lessor symbol to become the Virgin Mary and the Mother of Jesus, instead of correctly The Great Mother Goddess Mary, Mother of Jesus.

Many ancient stories come out of the Euphrates Valley where the ever-flowing rivers the Tigris and the Euphrates made these lands very fertile and attracted people from afar to settle in these Magickal lands. These small settlements became some of first and largest civilizations that had ever been built. It was here that the greatest Goddess Tiamat (The Dragon Mother) was both loved and feared, two of Her poems are the 'Epic of Creation' and the 'Epic of Gilgamesh':

> *"When on high were not raised the heavens,*
> *And also below on earth a plant had not grown up.*
> *The abyss had not broken its boundaries*
> *The chaos of Tiamat was the producing Mother of all of them."*

The Goddess Tiamat was the living principle of the primordial sea and of Chaos. She is often seen either as a great dragon or riding one. Tiamat is the Primordial Dragon who lives under the deep oceans until needed and then spreads her Magickal wings and flies to the Earth with the power of her legs firmly on the Earth. Tiamat is a culmination of all the Elemental powers, Dragon of the Sea (Water), Wings to fly (Air), Walks with power on land (Earth, and breaths fire (Fire). Tiamat is the essence of all creation and through the Elements that dance within Her being; she is ready to bring forth all Creation just buy Her sacred breath. Her name is spoken in Genesis 1:2 where the Hebrew *'Tehom'* is traditionally translated as *'the deep'* and recalled that the Sea Goddess Tiamat lives in the deep abysmal reaches of the oceans, as the Great Mother she is assisting in the birth of life from the womb of Her bitter sea.

Returning to Genesis 1:2 *'who is it that flaps its wings like a bird'* over the face of Tiamat? *'Merachepet'* is the Hebrew word for *'hover'*, which gives the impression of vast wings being able to float or hover. As we continue throughout Judaic history, who else had wings?

In the Garden of Eden was the first creation by Yahweh; this was Lilith, she who had the beauty of all women and with great wings of flight. Lilith has always been depicted as a beautiful naked woman with outspread wings. She had the feet and claws of an owl, and always had several owls attending her every need (this was a symbol of divine wisdom). Sadly, in time too, she like all the others was degraded from a celestial Goddess of beauty to the defamed "Night Hag", where it was written in Isaiah 34: 8-14:

> *"The land shall become burning pitch,*
> *Thorns shall grow over its strongholds.*
> *It shall be the haunt of jackals,*
> *Yea the night hag shall there alight*
> *And find herself a resting place."* *

The beautiful Goddess Tiamat was later debased into a 'night-jar' or 'night monster', termed Lamia *"The Dirty Goddess"*. For Wicces of the 21st century who have reclaimed the Goddess know the truth, and revel in Her original concept as an empowering Mother Goddess, who became *"The Queen of the Wicces"*. *Mother* of all knowledge, and from whom all creation comes forth from her very primordial womb of eternal life and death.

* *Scripture quotations taken from the 21st Century King James Version, copyright © 1994. Used by permission of Deuel Enterprises, Inc., Gary, SD 57237. All rights reserved.*

She was the first of Creation by the Judaic God Yahweh as the original Earth Mother, who made love with Adam, but he saw Her as less than he, and so She invoked the first Magick of the land and freed herself from Adam and the Garden of Eden, where she flew away into the far unknown, to the land that lies to the East. Yahweh, it is believed by many scholars had a consort; the belief is that the ancient Goddess Asherah was his consort and wife. Many of the houses of the time had inscribed above the entrance to their homes as sign saying:

> *"May all who enter be blessed by*
> *Yahweh and Asherato".*

In truth both Yahweh and Asherah were both adored and worshipped together as a complimentary deific couple to their people. They would still be loved and honoured today if it was not through the pride and egos of the male priesthood of the Judaic faith. Way before the time to the Judaic belief system, were many stories all the same as the new, just with different names. As Yahweh was the *"King of Heaven",* although he was originally named Baal, and Asherah was the *"Queen of Heaven",* who was originally named Ishtar (Astarte). One of the oldest Hymns to Ishtar of a ritual baking of the ceremonial cakes for the "Queen of Heaven" included these lines:

> *"I am Isis, I am she who is called goddess by women*
> *I gave and ordained laws for humans which no one is able to change*
> *I divided the earth from the heavens*
> *I ordered the course of the sun and the moon*
> *I appointed to women to bring their infants, to birth in the tenth month*
> *I made the beautiful and the shameful to be distinguished by nature*
> *I established punishment for those who practise injustice*
> *I am Queen of rivers and winds and sea*
> *I am in the rays of the sun*
> *Fate hearkens to me*
> *Hail Egypt that nourishes me.*[19]

This shows a Goddess who is divine and creative, a Mother of Nature who is ethical in teaching humans how to live in harmony and how to love unconditionally. In the Hymn above, we see the name Isis, as she was the most widespread of all the Goddesses throughout the then known world, and seen as a different face of the same Goddess that was revered.

Alongside her was the Goddess Maat; both have been identified as similar deities of the old Judaic faith. In 1945 in the deserts of Egypt hundreds of ancient scrolls were found covering a period of over 400 hundred years and they all speak of the powers of the Goddess and the connection to the Earth and the people. One of the scrolls states this:

> *"I am Protanopia, the Thought that dwells in the Light.*
> *I am the movement that dwells in the All, she in whom the All*
> *Takes it stand, the first born as among those who came to exist.*
> *I am invisible within the thought of the Invisible One.*
> *I am revealed in the immeasurable, ineffable.*
> *I am the head of All, since I exist in everyone.*

I am perception and knowledge, uttering a voice by means of thought
I am the real Voice. I cry out in everyone".

These words call out to my soul and make me listen they do to me. But one of the more profound and the most beautiful of scrolls ever found is by a female deity who was un-named but merely called *'Thunder Perfect Mind'*, this widely revered Goddess seems to have been all over Egypt and Asia as her writings have been found everywhere.

"I am the first and the last,
I am the honoured one and the scorned one.
I am the whore and the holy one; I am the wife and the virgin.
I am the mother and the daughter; I am the member of my mother.
I am the barren one and many are her sons.
I am the one who has been hated everywhere and who has been loved everywhere.
I am the one whom they call life and you have called Death".

Is it not acceptable then to Judaic and Christian women that their very own Virgin Mary was and is 'God the Mother' as well as 'Mother of God'?

THE GODDESS OF THE 21ST CENTURY

After being involved in the Craft and Goddess movement for over 5 decades, I have seen a massive change in the women of the Earth and their desire and need for a Female Deity; a Goddess that answers to females needs, without repressing women and female spirituality. The Goddess movement has grown and changed in so many ways, and in answer to the prayers and needs to suit the ideals of the 21st century woman. She has been awakened by women the world over, who have been calling her forth from the Shadows of their own subconscious minds to a world that needs the ultimate feminine, the Mother. She has been called and She has heard their prayers and is now reforming the Old Religion into the New Age Religion of the present, the past has been awakened and remembered, and will take us into a Matrifocal future, or at least a world where the masculine and feminine are a compliment and a balance to the world of today.

No matter what land, culture, country or faith, the Goddess is alive and well and attracting not only women to Her many paths but men who have realized the feminine within and without is needed in this time of great uncertainty. It is time not to suppress the feminine, but Empower it, so the world can see the true beauty in everything that She stands for and represents. She is not separate from the world, she is the world, and everything has a little light of the Goddess within them, if they only take off their blinkers and let Her shine forth. Let us all now honour the Great Mother and in this great hour of need for a Mother, let us honour all Mothers throughout women's forgotten past and listen to Herstory not history. The Patriarchal religions of the world have created a world of uncertainty, imbalance and fear. Let us through the feminine remove the imbalance of the patriarchal warring world and assist our own community in EMPOWERING women to awaken to a world of harmony, peace and equilibrium.

"None Greater than the Triple Goddess"

FESTIVAL
BLESSING OF
THE CAKES
AND WINE

1. N:_____ "Blessed Goddess, Blessed God, Mother and Father of all life, we thank you for your bounty on this night of N: _____ and we offer you all the adoration, love and respect that grateful children have to give".

(All call out their praises; we give you our love, we honor you etc.)

2.N: _____ "Tonight we your children who are gathered to Consecrate and consume the Sabbat Cake of harvest of the Earth and the sacred Wine of your heavenly Blood-Mana, so that we can carry your eternal Light within us. May we carry your Love and Light into the world of Man? By this sacred sharing and Unification may we also hold firm the bonds, which bind us together in Spirit on the Path of Wicca? Blessed Be the cake of the Living Earth".

3. N: _____ *(Takes the Sabbat Cake and holds it high in their power hand and says)*

4.

"Great Mother and Horned Father, we thank you for your bounty from your Earthly body which sustains all of creation with the sacred seed and fruit of your Divine being. From your Earthly womb comes forth all life and all of life's sustenance. Allow us to use this sacred symbol to ourselves with your limitless presence. Be in and of us always, as your child may you always be a part of our lives as Great Mother and Horned Father".

4.N: _____ *(Pass the cake around to everyone)*
"We are all linked, one to another, kin to kin. Bread sustains all human life. It is the giving of total sustenance for all of life. It is this giving and taking of sustenance that we continue the sacred, never-ending chain of eternal life. May you never hunger my sisters and brothers".

5.N:_____*(Takes the bread, holds it in their receptive hand high and says)*
"Blessed Be the Wicca, the microcosmic path to the Triple Goddess. We stand unified in a world between all points of time and space. In this loaf is a small amount of life-giving grains from the eternal womb of the Great Living Earth, our Mother. We give back to you know Great Mother in humble thanksgiving. May you and all the creatures of the wild and tamed world partake and enjoy and be nourished. May you never hunger my Great Lady and Lord".

6.N:_____*(Holds up the Wine in their receptive hand)*

"Great Mother and Horned Father, we thank you for your Mysteries of your Realms of water and fire, they sustain our spirit and our imagination. This wine is the blood of your Divine Womb, which brought forth all life. By your Divine Blood all livings creatures are truly blessed and made sacred. Through your womb all things are born, and by it shall we all return to you, from Womb to Tomb. Allow us to use this sacred symbol to fill ourselves with your boundless and divine presence. Be in and of us always. May your never thirst my sisters and brothers".

7.N:_____ *(Holds the Chalice in Power hand)*

"As a river blends with the great ocean, we are not alone. We start as a small pool but become one with the cosmic ocean, we are never alone. We are part of the sacred ebb and flow of the vast ocean of the cycles of life, death and rebirth. These sacred and precious drops of your life-giving waters that come from your great womb, we devoutly give back to you now in humble thanksgiving. May this sacred symbol of your womb and your blood give life eternal to all who partake with pleasure and love?"

8.N:_____*(Chalice is then passed around to all, as all honor)*

"We are all connected, one to another. The divine blood of the Great Goddess and Great God, which were the first primordial sea womb from which all life, swam when life began. It will be to them that we shall return when our mortality has ended. In the sacred sharing of this divine Blood do we now affirm that we are all sisters and brothers in the never-ending sacred chain of life, death and rebirth? Joining one to the other, Moon after Moon, generation after generation, forever and always. May you never thirst my sisters and brothers. None greater than our divine link".

(Chalice is now passed around the circle person to person each saying)

"May you never thirst my sister or brother".

9.N:_____*(Dips a piece of cake into the wine holds it high and says)*

"Behold the unity of the Goddess and God. They are all they are One. May their Earthly Womb and heavenly Blood be united and manifested in us. Ready always for any and all acts of positive creation. (East some) Behold the Goddess and God is now within me and within all. The Sacred Lady and Lord dance within me always".

10.N:_____"By this sacred act of unification we are signifying our willingness to be Earthly vessels for the manifesting creative power

of the Great Mother Goddess and Great Horned God. As we depart
our Sacred Circle, and move back into the world of Mortals".

11.N:_____ *(All repeat)*

"Heaven and Earth are one
Goddess and God are one
Female and Male are one
Night and Day is one
Light and Dark are one
Fire and Ice are one
All life is now balanced and in harmony.
So Mote It Be.
"ALL LIFE IS NOW BALANCED. SO, MOTE IT BE".

The Circle is now formally closed with song:

"May the long time Sun shine upon you?
All love surrounds you.
And the pure Light within you, guide your way home".

THE
ALEXANDRIAN
TRADITION

The Alexandrian tradition of Wicca was named after Alex Sanders and was established in the 1960s and joined later with his wife Maxine, who was considerably younger than he was, as she joined his coven when she was only 16 years of age. Originally Alex claimed to have been Initiated by his grandmother when he was seven years old (*The King of the Witches* by June Johns), but later realizing his untruth openly admitted that this was false, as he was originally Initiated into a regular Gardnerian coven, run by one of Patricia and Arnold Crowther's Initiates, a lady by the name of Pat Kopanski.

When Alex began to publicize and promote Wicca, he was met with much animosity and personal attacks from the traditional mainstream members of Wicca. Many saw him as nothing more than an egotistical man wanting fame and personal notoriety, he was also attacked as giving away and divulging the secrets of Wiccecraft to the public, which at the time was a no-no. It is strange because 20 years later in Australia when I was trying to legalize and publicly get recognition for Wicca, I too was attacked and accused of many of the same accusations for trying to get the "Church of Wicca" federally accepted as a legal religion.

Whatever may have been his or my motivation? It does not matter, as it was time for the world to know the truth about Wiccecraft and Wicca, and realise that it was a growing interest to many of the public, wanting to find their own truth in relation to the earth, nature and Magick. Publicity, (the correct sort of publicity) was needed, as it made people aware of his existence, and the existence of Wicca. This helped to open the interest in the Old religion and people found their ways to Alex and Maxine, seeking Initiation. The 1960s and the 1970s saw the Initiation of many people, including the likes of Stuart Farrar, a well-known author at the time, and Janet Owen who eventually became Janet Farrar. Also initiated by Alex and Maxine was My High Priest Imhotep (Jeff Camm). Imhotep and I worked together running our Coven in Victoria Park and he was my Craft partner, for many years and he also Initiated me into the level of Third Degree that of the High Priestess.

I eventually traveled to England to visit with Alex and Maxine at his home in Bexhall, and met with his Coveners at a festival. He was very entertaining, and his coven was quite dedicated in the Craft. There are now many hundreds of Alexandrian Covens around the world, as well as many Gardnerian Covens. There is not a great deal of difference between them as they are all from the same tree, adopted by Alex and changed a little for the Wiccan Community.

It is, of course, hard to quantify just what makes the essential *"Alexandrian Tradition,"* as every coven varies in many ways, even from the same birthed lineage. Each High Priest and High Priestess will change and rewrite their rituals and ceremonies, especially the festivals as they vary depending on whether they are Northern or Southern Hemisphere. Here in Australia our land is honored greatly and so are the first peoples and their Magick.

Generally, though, Alexandrian unlike Gardnerian covens focus strongly upon a stricter and more disciplined manner of training, which incorporates areas more generally associated with Ceremonial Magick, such as the Kabala, Angelic Magick, and Enochian Magic (these are of course on a higher level). The typical Alexandrian coven has a hierarchical structure, and generally meets weekly or whenever the coven is in decision for the Seekers at a lesser level and sometimes Lesser Festivals, and Initiates and Priesthood meet at Full Moons, New Moons and Festivals. Most Alexandrian covens will allow non-Initiates to attend some Lesser Festivals, usually as a Neophyte or Seeker who undergoes basic training in Coven Outer Courts, and completes many projects, prior to being accepted by the coven for Initiation to the First Degree, the level that makes you a Wicce. Some, though not all, Alexandrian covens will also welcome certain genuine non-initiated "Guests" at certain meetings. My own experience of Wicca was as a guest of an Alexandrian coven, the "Coven of the Acorn" which was run by the High Priest Simon Goodman and his High Priestess, Michelin.

Alexandrian Wicca uses basically the same tools, regalia and rituals as Gardnerian Wicca, though in some cases, the tools are used for different purposes, and the rituals have been adapted. Another frequent change is to be found in the names of their Goddess and Gods (Aradia and Cernunnos) and the Guardians of the Watchtowers or Quarters of the Magick Circle. In some ways these variations are merely cosmetic, but in others, there are fundamental differences in philosophy.

That said, over the last sixty years, the two traditions have moved slowly towards each other, and the differences, which marked lines of demarcation are slowly fading away. In reality all forms of Wicca and Wiccecraft are the same except for our own personal touches that we add to make them personal and more connected to our way of thinking, and our places where we live. Individual covens certainly continue to maintain different styles and working practices, but it is possible to speak today of "Wicca" encompassing both traditions without thought of whether they are Alexandrian or Gardnerian.

SOME SPECIAL DATES

- Alex and Maxine married and moved to London in 1967 (they were Hand-fasted in 1965).
- "King of the Witches" by June Johns was published in 1969.
- Stewart Farrar met Alex and Maxine in 1969, when Stewart's publisher sent him to interview them for a magazine article. Stewart was initiated into their coven in London on 21st February in 1970.
- "What Witches Do" by Stewart Farrar was published in 1971?
- Alex Sanders died in Sussex on 30 April 1988.

"Hecate, Cerridwen, Dark Mother, take us in; Hecate, Cerridwen, let us be reborn."

The King of Wicces is dead but not forgotten. He has entered the Summerland's of Lyonesse. The tomb is a passage and not a grave, and at the end of the dark earth barrow we find ourselves once more walking beneath the waxing crescent Moon of Isis Urania, the Star Goddess, in the Isles of the Blessed. So, we who love him say:

"Blessed Be and Hail and Farewell,
Merry Meet, Merry Part and Merry We Meet Again!"

CHURCH OF
WICCA'S FIRST
GATHERING

Sunday 1st October 1989 at 11.00am.

11.00 a.m. All are brought in and seated silently.
Light meditation for 10 minutes Lead by our Bard Lord Ariston. Followed by the Middle Pillar Exercise.
Wicca the Way is then lead by the Bards and sung by all!

WICCA THE WAY

*"Wicca the way the powers that be, for the young and the old,
the bold and the free. The Path is to know, the Path is to see,
The way of the Ancients as it used to be.
CHORUS:
Gathered together those of the kin,
In freedom and love beyond any sin.
Merry Meet, Merry Part, 'tis union for all,
Blessed the friendship that answers the call.*

*All be Earth's children of Sun and of Moon,
Down through the ages we've danced to the tune.
The flow of all life through Goddess and God,
None shall forsake thee, the Sword and the Rod.
CHORUS
Holy the star that is worshipped in truth,
Morgaine and Merlin forever-in youth.
All is the Horned One Fertility Rite,
Blessed Be Diana in Love and in Light.
CHORUS
Candles and Incense and tools of the trade,
For Magus and Wiccans all debts are paid.
Praised be the elements, fire, earth, water and air,
Celebrations and Sabbats, you'll find us there.
CHORUS
Blessed ye the Power and bind ye the Cord,
Blessed the union, Love the reward.*

The song of the ages it echoes again,
Blessed the knowledge, long may it reign.
CHORUS
The Path of the Wicca, the Path of the Wise,
In Power and Glory all truth shall rise.
We stand united through ages long past,
The truth that is Wicca forever shall it last.
CHORUS
Gathered together those of the kin,
In freedom and love beyond any sin.
Merry Meet, Merry Part, 'tis union for all,
Blessed the friendship that answers the call.
Blessed the friendship that answers the call.
So, mote it be!"

The Road Begins *lead by Lady Tamara*

"Let no man dare to ride the wind as Mother's Children do,
Let no man dare to tempt the fire his way,
Let no man think the waters will obey him and be true.
Nor order up the earthquake in his day.
For the Children of the Goddess walk a very Special Road.
To speak the Truth, it's not an easy way, but no one who hears Her
Calling and has felt the gentle good, there is no other Path and he is JOY.

So filled with JOY he follows Her and though the Road is long,
He hums an ancient lay on Merry Tune,
And his burden grows much lighter for he knows he is not wrong.
And his Children's, children's, children, saying the Ancient Witches Rune.
He's the one to ride the wind that answers his command,
And he'll force the fire that others say is wild,
And its waters will obey him, and the earthquake will seek his hand.
And then he smiles, for now he knows He's Mother's Child."

Blessed Be!"

Lady Margaret *addresses all saying:*

"Merry Meet and Blessed Be!

Welcome to the first of many gatherings at The Church of Wicca. For although we have many ways of worshipping the Mother Goddess, we all have one thought and faith in common, this is the Mother Goddess, our Earth. Though She has been given many names we know that there is only the One, and through Her strength and faith we have prayed for the day when we can at last worship in peace and openness. Today we do this, and I shout HURRAYA! This will not be a church of politics and we will not judge any who come to worship with an open and loving heart. For we have been the Hidden Children of Our Lady for too long, we shall hide no more and I say unto you I am a WICCE; I am a WICCE:

Many of us have learnt through our teachings, that there is nothing that can harm us except our own ignorance of self-ego, for too many people walk around every day and fear everything in life whether it be, rejection, denial, worrying about money, losing a loved one or just crossing the road. Remember this is only our mortal body and if we must live in fear of what is to be then we are no better than the Ostrich that hides his head in the ground, so he doesn't have to face reality. Let us stand tall and together not as only a religion but as a family, for if we stand alone in this saddened world of depression then we become a small branch from the Great Oak tree, and we can easily be broken, but if we stand together then we become the Great Oak and we cannot be broken.

Let us now pray not for us but for the rest of humanity, that they too can discover the wonderment, and perceive the true beauty of the Mother Earth."

Prayer by Lady Neith:

"Gracious Goddess, come thou among us, A Boon we ask for our Australia.
Fill our hearts with gladness; cleanse our minds of all envy, Hatred and greed.
Give us knowledge and the wisdom to use it.

As we walk the Ancient Pathways, guide our footsteps lest we fall by the wayside.
When we stumble, lift us up.
Let us never forget, that as we receive of thee, we must share with our Brothers and Sisters.
Gracious Goddess, show us the way to bring peace and prosperity to our people
And grant to our Australia strength in peace.

And in this peace, show all of mankind of the beauty of the Mother Earth and teach them to appreciate what you have given unto us, but what they yet do not see or understand. Help them understand that the earth is our life. Gracious Goddess we are thy children. As we will it."
So, mote it be!"

Lord Manannan says: *"Let us now sing in praise of the Lord of the Earth."*

Lord of the Dance:

"When She danced on the waters and the wind was Her horn,
The Lady laughed, and everything was born.
She fled to the Sun and the Light gave him birth,
The Lord of the Dance then appeared on the Earth.
CHORUS:
Dance, dance, wherever you may be,
For I am the Lord of the dance said He.
I'll lead you all wherever you may be,
I'll lead you all in the dance said He.
CHORUS
I danced in the morning when the world was begun,
I danced in the stars, and the Moon and the Sun.
I crawled through the darkness by the song of the Earth,
I joined in the singing and She gave me birth.
CHORUS
I danced at the Sabbat when you chant the spell,
I danced and sing that everyone be well.
The dance is over do not think I'm gone,
I live in the music, so I'll still dance on.
CHORUS
They cut me down, but I did not hide,
I am the light that will never ever die.
I'll live in you if you live in me,
For I am the Lord of the Dance said He.

Dance; dance wherever you may be,
For I am the Lord of the dance said He.

I'll lead you all wherever you may be,
I'll lead you all in the dance said He.
I'll lead you all in the dance said He!
HURRAYA!"

Lady Tamara leads the Ritual of Acknowledgement:
Man in Black - Aaron and **Maiden** - Kerry; hand out assorted grain for harvest.
Lady Tamara then says:

"Out of all that we can be a single seed must be selected to help us grow
into the rightful Children of the Earth. Let us now in silence
CHOOSE - CUT - CHERISH (here we all select a few seeds, then choose them, cut them
away from the rest, and hold them in the palm of our hand and cherish, discarding the rest.)
Place half of the seed in the palms of both hands; hold up the left hand closed and say:

"BLESSED BE THE HAND PUT FORTH WITH MIGHT"!
Place the other up high but open and say,
"BLESSED BE THE HAND PUT FORTH WITH MEANING"!
Then rubbing them together and spitting into your palms saying as you do!
"BLESSED BE WHAT WE MUST DO WITH MIGHT AND MEANING, THAT
OUR HANDS MAY HOLD THE HARVEST OF OUR HIGHEST HOPES".
Then in order each to plant their seed into the cauldron filled with damp soil.

Prayer of Dedication:

"Great Goddess, when I entered weeping into this world of men.
I was helpless, a child, naked, incapable of treading a Path or accomplishing
a purpose. Now I have grown, finding a Path to thee.
Freely acknowledging your Power, to dedicate myself, and any skill
Learnt on the way, now here am I free of pretense.
And if I bend my knee, it is my choice, for your magnificence.
O Ancient Ones that dwell in fire, water, wind and desire,
Grant us leave that we may be, one song in total harmony.
And though our Paths may intertwine, we're different vessels of your wine.
So, in softness of Loves name collect our sparks to make one flame.
And spread your love, O Ancient Ones, amongst your daughters and your sons.

And grant us grace that we may know, our shrine reflects the others glow.
And grant us peace and let it be, as deathless as the Pagan tree.
And the entire Circle's where they are cast.
Behold us Mother
We are home at last.
So, mote it be!
Merrily we have met, and merrily we part.
Hail and Farewell!"

All then celebrate with a great feasting and singing and dancing into the night with great Fellowship.

BEING IN
BALANCE!

THE HEAD: The forepart and left side of the head is electrical, and so is the inside of the head. The back of the head is magnetic and so is the right side.

THE EYES: The forepart of the eyes is neutral and so is the background. The right side is electric and, so it is with the left side. The inside is magnetic.

THE EARS: Forepart of the ears is neutral, back part also. Right side magnetic left side electrical, inside neutral.

MOUTH AND TONGUE: Forepart neutral, back-part as well as right side and left side both neutral, inside magnetic.

THE NECK: Forepart, back-part and right side of the neck are magnetic, left side and inside electrical.

THE CHEST: Forepart electromagnetic, back part electrical, right side and inside neutral, left side electrical.

THE ABDOMEN: Forepart electrical, back-part and right side magnetic, left side electrical, the inside neutral.

THE HANDS: Forepart neutral, back part also, right side magnetic, left side electrical, the inside neutral.

THE FINGERS OF THE RIGHT HAND: Fore and back part neutral, right side electrical, left side also the inside neutral.

THE FINGERS OF THE LEFT HAND: Fore and back part neutral, right side electrical, left side as well, the inside neutral.

THE FEET: Fore and back part neutral, right side magnetic, left side electrical, inside neutral.

THE MALE GENITALS: Forepart electrical, back part neutral, right and left side also, the inside magnetic.

THE FEMALE GENITALS: Fore part magnetic, back part, right and left side neutral, the inside electrical.

THE LAST VERTEBRA TOGETHER WITH THE ANUS: Fore and back part neutral, right and left side as well, the inside magnetic.

EXERCISE: 4 x 4 breathing.

(This is where you breathe in to the count of 4, then hold to the count of 4, then exhale to the count of 4. Keep this up for at 5-10 minutes)

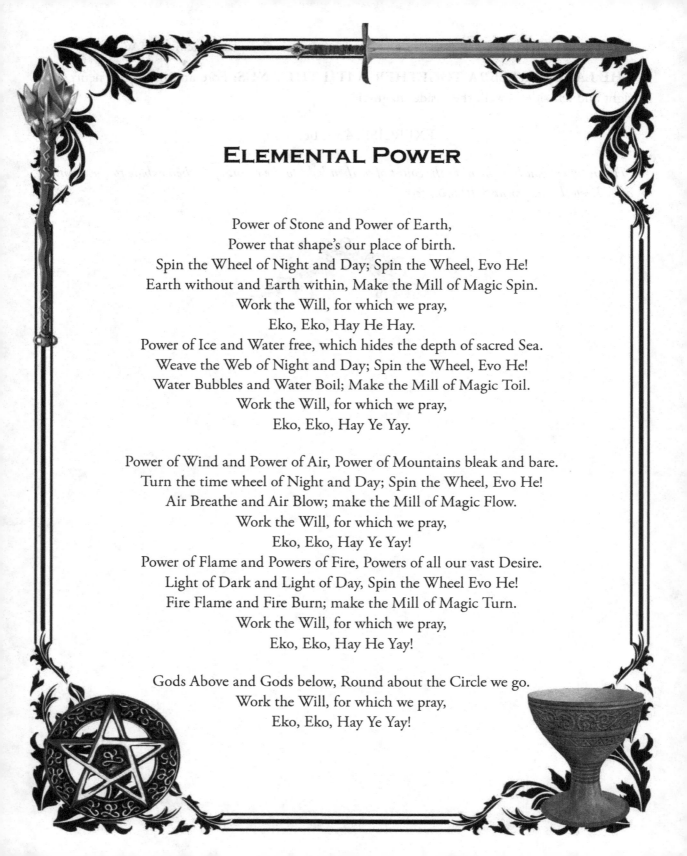

ELEMENTAL POWER

Power of Stone and Power of Earth,
Power that shape's our place of birth.
Spin the Wheel of Night and Day; Spin the Wheel, Evo He!
Earth without and Earth within, Make the Mill of Magic Spin.
Work the Will, for which we pray,
Eko, Eko, Hay He Hay.
Power of Ice and Water free, which hides the depth of sacred Sea.
Weave the Web of Night and Day; Spin the Wheel, Evo He!
Water Bubbles and Water Boil; Make the Mill of Magic Toil.
Work the Will, for which we pray,
Eko, Eko, Hay Ye Yay.

Power of Wind and Power of Air, Power of Mountains bleak and bare.
Turn the time wheel of Night and Day; Spin the Wheel, Evo He!
Air Breathe and Air Blow; make the Mill of Magic Flow.
Work the Will, for which we pray,
Eko, Eko, Hay Ye Yay!
Power of Flame and Powers of Fire, Powers of all our vast Desire.
Light of Dark and Light of Day, Spin the Wheel Evo He!
Fire Flame and Fire Burn; make the Mill of Magic Turn.
Work the Will, for which we pray,
Eko, Eko, Hay He Yay!

Gods Above and Gods below, Round about the Circle we go.
Work the Will, for which we pray,
Eko, Eko, Hay Ye Yay!

THE MIDDLE
PILLAR!

The ancient Middle Pillar Exercise is a deep meditation of the ancient Hebrews that work with an ancient Mysticism called the Kabbalah, its origin is far older and has its roots in Egypt. Reference, to the *'Middle Pillar'*, being of course to the Holy Kabbalah. We use it as a doorway to enter our main microcosmic world. As a vacuum cleaner it removes spiritual stains and tunes us in, to ready us mentally for further work either with a group, as in a Magick Circle, or even as a solo Wicce. After you have made yourself completely comfortable, loosen any tight clothing. Taken your shoes off for grounding, and turn down any bright lights and mute any unwanted noises. You then commence in the 4 x 4 breathing exercise, that you should maintain this for at least 3 to 5 minutes to purge your mind of distracting thoughts and to fill your bloodstream with oxygen and to hold your concentration.

Visualize floating just above your head a sphere of soft, but warming white light 4 inches in diameter even though this light is so vividly bright it is not blinding nor uncomfortable to your eyes, feel the light move down slowly into your chest radiating. When it gets there explode the sphere of light so that a soft but brilliant white light fills your whole body, try to feel the light reaching out to all your extremities then slowly bring the light back together as a ball again and reform the sphere in your head.

Now move the sphere of light into your throat and at the same time change its Colour to a light sky blue feel the blue sphere, then explode it as before and feel the blue light permeate your whole neck region with good health and communication. Feel it push out any traces of negativity or ill feelings about anything at all. Feel it in your skin, bones, blood, and vessels and feel it cleansing out your whole system.

Now reform the Sphere into your head again and then when ready, move it down to your breast bone or Heart Chakra and at this time change the colour to rose-pink and repeat the explosion of light through every fiber of your chest and heart region once more, the health and vitality should almost leave a taste in your mouth as your upper torso glows so, so pink. After you have basked in the warm pink reform the Sphere and move it down your torso to your genital region and lower abdomen region and change the Sphere to a russet reddish brown colour repeat the exploding, permeating and reforming the Sphere after your genitalia region.

After your genitalia region move it down to your feet region where all the negativity has been forced by the previous explosions. Watch the dirty black colour slowly brighten as it absorbs your negative vibrations. Now rather than reforming the Sphere push all your negative, dark events to your feet out of your life drain it out of your body so there is no blackness left at all anywhere in your body just a clean peaceful glow. Now spend a few minutes just feeling the Spiritually clean body you may also choose to thank the Goddess and God, the Elementals of the Earth for helping.

THE ROAD
BEGINS

In the name of the Gracious Goddess and Her Consort The Horned God, I give you greetings and say, "Blessed Be", and welcome you to the teachings of Elphane with open arms and an open heart to you who are seeking the Old Ways to become a true Wiccan and maybe even a genuine Wicce. I hope that you may have read my first book the prequel to this titled "The Complete Teachings of Wicca Book One-The Seeker". As it leads onto the writing of this book giving you the basis required to advance yourself and your knowledge of Wicca and Wiccecraft.

It is essential that to develop to the full your powers when you will eventually work within a Magick Circle, which is the ancient Temple of the Wicces that you commence in the study of metaphysics and Magick. The Wiccan training that follows throughout this sacred Book of Shadows has been kept secret and hidden from the gaze of the profane and mortal eyes for millennia, until recently within the last 60 years when our world has opened up to the world our faith, our ways and our rituals. It does include some of the secret Lore of Wiccecraft.

If you have read my first book, then you would already be aware of many things, as it helps you to understand the basics of this book and what follows, as they are in order of training and knowledge leading into structure. What follows is a related form of theory and practices, which conditions and trains the mind, body and soul, to understand the very essence of what The Craft, the True Craft is all about.

Think inwardly, Wicca is a community of love and generosity; it is a philosophy and a religion of Nature, being the Earth Mother. It is a way of life, a living religion. We must learn to follow the laws of the land and of Nature. Freedom is the very essence of what Wicca is all about, we believe in the freedom of expression of individual's rights, and everything is acceptable if it does not hurt anyone or anything, or create hang-ups. We must use our knowledge of the Craft for personal benefit, and to help others and NOT for personal gain. I help rather than exploit, as it is often the want of the practitioners of black magic that has always been confused with Wicca and its Craft. They are NOT the same and never will be how can they be. We aspire to become One with Deity in its purest form in every way possible. Black Magick or Satanism is a cocoon; a dimensional shelter for introverts and is greedy and shallow, and very anti-Christian. Whereas Wicca is not anti-anything, except maybe anti-anti, as it is open and honest and fights to be a Warrior of the Earth and all of Nature. Black magic and Christianity both thrive on Mystery and ritual. Christianity is open prudery, and therefore Satanism always tries to be exactly the opposite, which leans towards sexual excess, for both have sexual hang-ups, whereas Wicca treats sex as a normal, natural and pleasurable experience.

Birth and death are the two factors, which have always intrigued man, and in his search for the answers, he has embraced sex with religion, which has been common in all branches of mankind since the beginning of time. This is whereby man assists god in the Creation of life. We do not exactly how life is created but we do know that a man and a woman are drawn together in a moment of ecstasy, and thus a new life is created. During the moment of orgasm, the two lovers are elevated briefly from the Mundane Plane to the Fool Stool of the Gods.

Wicca is a Fertility religion, but this does not mean that we have sexual orgies to better our sexual pleasure. Quite the opposite as sexuality is very private and we believe that it should be kept private between the two adult lovers at home and away and definitely not within the confines of our Circles or Temples. Wicca is a Fertility religion whereby we honour all creation and the very act of creation as the essence of the Goddess and God lending us for a brief moment their very light force and assisting in our creation of life.

WORDS OF THE MIGHTY ONES

Keep your silence amidst the noise of the world
for there is my Peace in that silence.
Keep peace between yourself and all other
beings and listen to all mankind.
For even the ignorant among mankind may
perceive a Truth we do not see.
Surrender not your Spirit to any other, yet seek not battle,
But rather seek to avoid those who trouble your Spirit
and spread vexation about them.

Seek not ambition too closely, for the most
humble work must also be done,
This pleases the Lady and Lord.
Those of the Wicca are as your Sisters and Brothers.
Speak not of the Wicca to the outsider,
for the world is plagued with misunderstanding.
Remember that the world also has its virtues and ideals,
And its people have their right to seek for Deity.

Strive to be gentle and understanding with your fellow man,
And be tolerant of their emotions, even if you do not understand them,
And regard the passing of years without despair.
Surrender the things of youth without sorrow,
For age shall bring you deeper Wisdom and greater understanding.
Study then the secret ways and cultivate the Spiritual Strength
To shield you in unexpected misfortune.

Seek not to harm your own body,
nor the body of any man, woman, child or animal.
For all bodies are made of the substance of the Earth,
And you shall not harm the Earth Mother.

Therefore be gentle with yourself
for you are a child of the Goddess and God.
Therefore care for your body keeping it clean and healthy.
Disgrace not the Craft before your fellow man,
And bring not disrepute upon its followers.
Remember that you have walked this world before
And you shall walk it again in time.

You may fill this world with broken dreams and sadness,
And these may stay with you for many lifetimes,
Yet this world is beautiful, tough you are blind to its true beauty.
Therefore be careful, Seek and be happy
And you shall find the Path of Truth, which is the Path of Divine Love
And perpetual Happiness,
Which is the Goddess!

KNOWING
YOUR HEALTH

To Wicces we recognise eight signs to show your true health, and these correspond to the Eight Mystical Paths of Enlightenment, the Eight Directions of the Magick Circle and the Eight Tools of Wiccecraft.

1. **Vitality**   this means having a life full of energy. It should show in the way you walk, and in the condition of your eyes, called Iridology. There should be a spring in your step and you should have the energy to do whatever is required of you, it is about utilising your day's energies with gusto.

2. **Appetite**   this means not only having an appetite for food when you are hungry but also an appetite for new experiences, and for sex. Perhaps a better term would be a lust for life.

3. **Deep Sound Sleep**   I believe that you only need between 5-6 hours of sleep a night. This does not mean a way to health is to start cutting down your sleep hours that you need. Rather, it indicates that as you get healthier you will need less sleep. If you need 10-12 hours of sleep per night, on a regular basis, you might want to see a doctor as this indicates a medical problem. Notice too, that it is not the quantity of sleep, which is recognised, but also the quality of sleep. In my Tradition good sound sleep indicates a dreamless sleep. This of course I mean un-disturbing dreams.

4. **Good Memory**   this is fairly clear and indicates that you should have both a good short-term memory and a good long-term memory.

5. **Humour**   we should all have a good sense of humour to be healthy. We should especially be able to laugh at ourselves, and the world immediately around us. As a friend once said to me:

   "Don't take life seriously, as you will never get out alive."

6. **Infinite Giving**   No, this does not mean giving away all your possessions and money. Rather it means to be healthy you should be able to give of yourself freely to your friends and those in need. Also, you should give time and effort to yourself.

7. **Clearing, Thinking and Precise Action**   This indicates a sign of good health is the ability to quickly see through a problem, decide, and act on that decision without any undue length of time. Procrastination and fear are types of diseases associated with imbalances to the bodies energy system. There is also the implication that part of being healthy is having intuitive and psychic abilities, which are correct often.

8. **Realisation of Oneness**   this is a state of utmost health. It is indicated by the having of all your dreams instantly realised, perhaps another way is that the healthier person is a "Natural Person".

WATCHTOWER
SYMBOLS
AND SIGNS

EAST - INNER SIGHT

There are many symbols associated with the East and the Element of Air. Whatever you can picture in your mind associated with the Air and flying is typically what can be used as a symbol such as: fans, birds, feathers, wind musical instruments, hunting horns in particular.

The East is the Portal of the Sun at Dawn, and all Dawn symbols are associated with this realm. The Wand is the Weapon of Air, as it is made from a branch that never has been earthed or touched the ground. The Staff of the Hermit is a powerful tool, such as the Djed of Osiris, the Caduceus on the Staff of Thoth, even the lance or Spear of Longinus, and even the pointed finger are all symbols of the East and of Air.

Colours: associated with this realm are sky blue, amber, pale gold, turquoise and white.
Gods: Osiris, Khepera, Aurora, Apollo, Orpheus, Hermes, Mercury, Prometheus, Quetzalcoatl, Freya and Iduna.
Enlighteners: Merlin, Nerada, Serapis, Jesus, Imhotep, Khamua-Set and Buddha.

If you are about to do a ritual or Spell, make sure you research every possible thing about it, as it will make your Magick true and effortless, as Nature guides the Invisible if the knowledge and heart is true. Understand what you are doing and all its deep meanings. Never presume you know everything, because we never know everything. Know also that women bring Power into the Magick Circle; she is the strongest on the Inner Levels and in deeper touch with the Astral Plane of the East. A man is best at directing that Power once it has been raised and passed to him. He is at his fluid worlds and strongest on the Physical Plane. This power alternates through the different Planes. There have been and are good female Magi, but in general it is best for a male to take the East and be Warden of this Realm. The High Priest (HP) must hold all things together within the Magick Circle, dignity of bearing, and calmness of mind are the attributes to cultivate in this realm. He is also responsible for the behaviour in the Magick Circle and without, always assisted by his Man in Black.

INNER LEVEL: 4 X 4 BREATHING.

With the God Hermes walk through the Portal in the East, look carefully and open your inner vision, try to remember all that you will see, hear, and do. Walk through the Portal with Hermes and take your place in a large chair, see the Portal gates close with Hermes behind them. Let your mind adjust slowly to the very world of the daytime. Just notice everything, relax and enjoy.

(Record your journey in your BoS)

SOUTH - THE WILL POWER:

This Realm is the power of the Noonday Sun at its peak; its Warden should be a male and has the task of mediating the Powers of love, honour and courage to all these within the Magick Circle. The symbols are strength, The ceremonial Sword, the Athame, Shield, Bow and Arrow, Chariot, the Torch, Hammer and Anvil, Double headed Axe, the Winged Disk, the Eye of Horus and the Lyre.

Gods:	Mars, Helios as the Sun God, Ra, Athene, Brigid, Bran, Sekhmet, Vulcan and Hephaestus.
Colours:	Reds, oranges and gold's.
Enlighteners:	Arthur, Aesculapius, Chiron, Hercules, Gawain and Llew.

The Warden of the South should be loyal and courageous, he should not be easily scared or upset as he is responsible for the safety of all those within the Magick Circle.

INNER LEVEL — 4 x 4 BREATHING

Through the Southern Portal, build up a great figure of Apollo. The gates to the Portal open up and the golden figure holds out his hand, and you are drawn towards him as you arise and move towards him in the southern Portal. You enter the Southern landscape and explore this realm with the Sun God, taking your time to notice and learn as much as is offered. Remember all that is offered and store well in your memory. Apollo brings you back safely. You settle and see the Portal close with Apollo behind them.

WEST — FAITH:

The West is the place of the Setting Sun, and the point of contact on the Inner Levels. The Warden should be a woman who has some Psychic Power; her task within the Magick Circle is to mediate the influence of the Inner Levels to become the point of communication using the polarity of the East and West to achieve this.

Symbols:	Water, the Chalice, Cauldron, Shells, Caves, Oceans, Lakes, Scabbards, the Moon, and the Womb.
God:	Isis, Nephthys, Artemis, Sin, Thoth, Selene, Hecate, Diana, Arianhrod, Ishtar, Neptune, Manannan and Poseidon.
Colours:	Indigo, Royal Blue, Dark Red Wine, purple, grey and lavender.
Enlighteners:	Oannes, Ea., Dagon, Hypatia - the Virgin.

The Warden of the West is the Seer of the Magick Circle; she must be honest and truthful with herself and with others on all levels. Of all the Portals this is the one through which the power of the Magick Circle enters.

INNER LEVELS:

Warden sites before the Western Portal and builds up in her mind the gates, seeing behind them a beautiful night sky full of radiating stars. They open to reveal the Moon Goddess Artemis. She wears a short hunting kilt of white and silver, with leather sandals winding up her legs. She carries a bow, and on her back, is a quiver of arrows. Beside her are two great wolfhounds waiting patiently. She holds out her hands and beckons you to rise and come to her. You follow her through the Portal and explore its regions and what it has to offer. When you return take leave of the Goddess Artemis and record what you have seen and sensed.

NORTH — UNDERSTANDING:

The Portal of the North and of Earth is the Gateway to the Midnight Sun. The Warden should be a woman with an affinity with the Earth, of growing things. Here the emphasis is on growth, both active and spiritual, on benevolence and understanding of the needs of all life.

Symbols:	Basket, Cornucopia, Flail, Scourge, Boline, plough, horn, seed, furrow, spindle, corn dolly, bread, wheat sheaf, corn cobs, scythe and a Sickle
Gods:	Changing Woman, Ceres, Cerridwen, Demeter, Kore, Persephone, Hades, Pluto, Rhea, Ge, Geb, Gaia, Rhiannon, Hathor, and Isis.

Colours: Amber, green, russet, brown and black.

Enlighteners: Thoth, Merlin, The Fae and Moses.

INNER LEVELS:

Sit and build in your mind's eye the Northern Portal and through the gates reveal the Goddess Persephone, crowned with flowers and carrying a basket of fruit and grain. She offers you her hand and you step through and follow her into the Garden of the North. Learn all you can for it will help the Earth Mother, when you have learnt all you can return through the Portal and write of your journey.

BOOK OF
SHADOWS

Keep your Book of Shadows (BoS) in your own handwriting. You can let others in your Coven copy what they will, but never lend your BoS or give it to someone else, as it is your personal Magickal and Spiritual diary, and can never be replaced if lost or damaged. If they are found by the wrong people they can bring a lot of negativity and conflict into your life, asking questions that you may or may not be yet ready for. You should guard your BoS and keep it out of sight from prying eyes, so wrap your BoS in a nice cloth and hide it away until you next need it.

Your BoS should be learnt and known as much as you can by heart, as many of your rites and spells will be repeated and it shows that you know your knowledge and your writings which makes you feel more sure and unwavering when you perform your rites. Your BoS is one of your most important tools that you as a Wicce may ever have, so if you have a Will, write in it where you wish your writings to go, or if you wish them to be cremated or buried with you. I have two Wills one for all my normal life, and a spiritual Will for all my Magickal items, knowing that other family members may not see how special your tools really are, and just discard them into the rubbish without any hesitation or thought.

> *"Eight Words the Wiccan Rede Fulfil,*
> *And it Harm None, Do what you Will".*

Be sure in your faith along the Path of Wicca, and always trust in your Higher Self and The Great Mother and Her Consort, the Horned One. Remembering that one day you who know so much in whichever ways you have been taught, knowing that one day you who know so much, know but very little. For as much as we learn, we realise that there is so much more to learn, and that in reality we know but very little in the grand scale of things. Know that the Great Mother Goddess gives all, teaches all and guide us, even though we may be blind, deaf or ignorant to what She is bestowing on us. Let us open our ears, eyes and hearts and hear in the whispering winds the voice of the Great Mother and Her divine teachings. If we do this with an open heart then we will find our Truth and then know that we are on the Path to Wisdom. Blessed Be!

PROPERLY PREPARED
I MUST ALWAYS BE!

This means that not only must you be prepared and clean in body but most importantly in mind and heart, and definitely in Spirit. You must never enter the Holy Temple or Magick

Circle, with any form of negativity, or emotions of that day's contents, you must only enter with a happy, peaceful heart, and with love and truth in your every thought and attitude. Therefore within the Wicca we take on a new Name; this is our Sacred Spiritual Name, which helps us become the Spiritual Beings we wish to become (we usually take the simple names of herbs, plants, trees or crystals, something that is reflected in nature and for our learning) This is why we also wear Ceremonial Robes and regalia. These do not have to be elaborate, but can be as simple as you like for they are to help you do their job in allowing you to flow freely, and not dressed in normal civilian clothing. They are not for vain purposes. We all have the same style robes except for their colours, which represents the individuals level within The Church of Wicca. These must be kept clean, ironed and neat always. Usually for your first robe I suggest the colour green or brown, never black as it has negative connotations.

Always before placing your Ceremonial Robes on, you must always bathe or shower properly, as you wash yourself imagine the water being like a waterfall, cleansing and purifying your body but cleansing you on every level. Whilst I bathe or shower I usually say this little prayer:

"O Gracious Goddess who hast formed me, your unworthy servant in your image.
Bless and sanctify this water for the cleansing of my body, mind, and soul,
And let there be no deceit, stupidity or negativity here. Gracious Mother send me your Light that
I may be worthy to enter into the Sacred Temple and to enter in your presence. So, mote it be!"

As stated prior black robes are a colour that I prefer Wiccans to avoid, except the Man in Black who is the principal Ritualist under the High Priestess and High Priest. Most of our Brethren work barefoot so we can feel the Earth beneath our feet, weather permitting. When you are Properly Prepared you may now enter your Temple, but always bow from the waist before entering to show respect, then bow at the Altar, this is a subconscious awakening that makes us aware that the Goddess and God are always present, and here it is a sign of dedication and respect. The Altar should always be placed in the North, except in rare occasions, as this is the realm of the Earth and the Goddess and God. You must never turn your back to the Altar or point your feet towards the Altar, as this is a sign of disrespect.

When you enter the Magick Circle you bring with you the Spirit Candle, this is the Light of which you will light all Inner Candles, this in our Fellowship is called 'The Warming of the

Temple' and is done usually by the Man in Black. Starting with only the Altar Candles, left (representing the Goddess) and the right (representing the Horned God), we then light the Thurible of Incense. After this small preparation you would then continue to the South then sit or stand and meditate facing the North for at least 10-15 minutes.

Here is a little Rune Prayer that we say as we go into meditation:

"Gracious Goddess, come thou among us,
A boon we ask for our Australia.
Fill our hearts with gladness,
Cleanse our minds of all envy, hatred and greed.

Give us knowledge and the wisdom to use it,
As we walk the Ancient Pathways.
Guide our footsteps, lest we fall by the wayside,
When we stumble, lift us up.
Let us never forget that as we receive of Thee,
We must share with our Sisters and Brothers, in every way.

Help the Wicca to be strong that we can come together
without politics and egotism.
Gracious Goddess show us the way to bring
Peace, Harmony and Prosperity to our people.
Grant to our Australia, strength in Peace!
Gracious Goddess we are thy children, as we Will it,

So, Mote it be!"

CONSECRATION OF WATER & SALT

In nearly all-Religious paths, they have what is termed Holy Water or Consecrated Water. It is because firstly, salt is the purest substance on our Earth and is ruled by the Spirit. It has absolutely no negative energies about it at all, it is a fighting agent for all wounds, and it preserves and heals.

Secondly water is the most precious resource of the planet for man's existence, in fact they are both needed for the survival of mankind and in general, life itself will cease to be without them. So, if we combine them, together they become a potent mixture and in themselves become a Sacrament. This Sacrament is that all life came forth from the deep Abyss of the ocean, and in this act, we are re-creating the act of Creating for our Magick Circle.

Touch the water with your Athame saying:

"O wondrous Waters of Life, with this sacred tool do I exorcise you of all impurities that may harm us, with the power of Creation do I transform you into the clean and sacred essence of life on all levels. With the aid of our Great Mother Aradia and Her Consort, Cernunnos do I bless you"?

Then place the salt in the middle of your Magick Altar Pentacle, (refer to Book One) and touching the Salt with the tip of your Athame charging it say:

"By Light and Love do I Bless this pure Creature of salt, let all malign forces be cast out and let only pure forces enter herein. I Bless you and Consecrate you to be a sacred power to Create only pure form in the names of the Goddess Aradia, and the Horned God Cernunnos."

You now mix the salt into the Water Chalice mixing it with your fingers in a Deosil manner saying:

"Be ever mindful that as water cleanses the body, and salt purifies the mind, that only the Goddess purifies the Soul".

PREPARING THE TEMPLE OF THE WICCA

First you must find an area that is big enough for a nine-foot Magick Circle, preferably outdoors and somewhere private where you can't be distracted or disturbed, away from gazing eyes. With our Temples it has taken many years to get them the way we want, and it will probably take more years to complete it and make it as beautiful as I can, without moving too far away from Nature. I have used everything that was removed from that sacred space whether it was trees, rocks, whatever. All have been used, the boundary of the Circle is the natural rocks from the land, and they have been placed accordingly.

Surrounding the whole Temple are gardens of many Magickal and Healing herbs and a pathway of cobblestones, river rocks and path lights to illumine the way to our Sacred Space. At the four quarters (The Watchtowers) are placed large monolithic Pillars 10 feet high, which have Ivy growing up them. The Magick Circle is covered with a beautiful carpet of lawn, and in the centre, is a small circle of river rocks for the Bale Fire, which is where we light our beacon to guide the Spirit energies in.

The Altar is placed in the North, the realm of the Earth, and the Goddess and God. Our Altar is of natural wood and is waste high and an arm's length deep and width. Covering this is a beautiful Altar cloth of green and gold, with two Ancient Bacchus Urns from the 12th century Greece, used as Altar candleholders, which are placed either side of the Altar. And then of course are the appropriate Tools of the Craft that are to be used during the ceremony.

The Sacred Temple, which is to be the Magick Circle, is measured by your Singulum, which is worn around your waste, this giving the diameter of the Magick Circle. During the first-degree Initiation you are taught the 360 degrees of the Magick Circle, as against the Cycle of Nature, and the 365 days of the year, with this system you must use your tarot cards for ritual use and much meditation.

Being measured exactly 9 feet, it has the same measurement of the Moon on a 1" to 1-mile ratio, and the centre of the Circle is another small Circle which is the beacon and represents the microcosm within the macrocosm in all things. When you first enter the Sacred Space you must prepare, and anoint yourselves on the points of your body as in the Self Blessing Ritual of the Goddess.

THE ELEMENTAL
JOURNEYS

The Journey of Earth

"Of whirling gases and clay,
Did the ancient primordial creative spirit form the flesh and bones of man?
Our physical bodies were made up of the rich clay of the Earth,
With particles of divine dust.

By the Magick of creation we will manifest within this matter
Our true Wills so we can rise up from the duct of the Earth to be the
eventual and Rightful rulers and students of the Outer Kingdoms.

To experience ordinary life and meaning,
We call upon you by your most sacred and ancient of names,
Our primordial Pachamama, The Sacred Earth.

You are the fields of beauty of our present life, and by your unlimited giving
and guidance do we remain the human children we surely are.
Enter into this your sacred Element of Earth, and stabilize us with your solid
physicality. (The Earth Invoking Pentacle is done over either salt or soil)

Manifest for us Great Mother the true meaning of all your wondrous secrets that we
as your divine Children lust learn in order to observe and obey your Laws.
Help us to reveal our true Divine purpose for being in this our Earth.

Aid us Great Mother that we may truly grow from being just Children of
the Earth into you're loyal and devoted Divine Children of Spirit.
Through your Great Divine Power,
and in the deepest service to all of life as we know it.
Help us to realise that we are not Solitary creatures, but part of your
divine Spirit whose single atoms we most surely are.

We know that the Earth is our Great Mother, whom we call Pachamama,
From your great belly of creation, from the womb to the tomb we shall return.
Knowing that we will pass the ordeals of the Living Earth,
Our feet are free to walk upon the sacred ley-lines of this sacred Earth.

Grant that we may walk it with truth, acceptance and pride, and
always under your divine guidance. So, Mote It Be!"

THE JOURNEY OF WATER

"Great Mother amid the sacred Waters of Life, let there be a Firmament,
so that the Great Sea and the Sky shall separate unto themselves.
For we know that which is above is likened unto that which is
below, for the Magickal appearance of a single wonder.

The Sun is our Divine Father who gives light and life to the Earth, and the
Moon is our divine Mother who shows light in the greatest darkness.
The Winds of time and space of the east have carried this all into conception.
This Magick ascends from earth to the Stars, and then
descends back unto the Earth when it is due.

By Life and Love do we call upon the Great Mother, whose ancient
and yet timeless womb brings forth all everlasting life?

Maiden of Great Mysteries you are, and curse of all that lives by Nature.
Enter this your sacred Element of Water, with your electro-magnetic ebb
and flow, move for us the cosmic tides of compassion and love.
(Here salt is added to the water in the Chalice with the Water Invoking Pentagram).

Manifest for us Great Mother, your potency and deep Magick,
Open unto us the hidden depths of thy primordial Watery wisdom.
Whatever we experience therein may we succour the appreciative Salt of good
sound sense to open our mind that we sense and know true knowledge

Allow all our tides and waves to be in balance with your Cosmic Tides
of the Great Oceans, open our deep consciousness towards the anchors
of our respectful and appreciative illumined attainment.

Great faithful Element of Water, Consecrated Elementals of the ebb and flow of life, through the Magickal rhythm of the Sacred Waters of Life and Death, and always in the divine service of the Universal Sea of the Spirit of the Great Mother, whose divine and scattered drops we surely are.

We know that here we must face the Ordeal of Water; here we must be brave, for Water is the Element of our Heart and our Emotions, of true love and compassion. We have lips and voices that are open to truth that we are able to speak honestly of our emotions and of our hearts physically, mentally, psychically and spiritually."

THE JOURNEY OF AIR

"In the very beginning, did the Great Spirit of the Mother Goddess issue from the void and with Her sacred breath did breathe forth an illumined soul into man. May we as your Divine Children also breath forth-sacred words that will resonate throughout all realms to bring forth new life to our divine rights and latent qualities.

Great Mother we call upon you to send forth your breath, which is the source of all inspiration, may it fill us with strength and hope, that as your divine children we shall find our true inheritance as immortals in the freedom of the sacred spheres of Spirit.

Speak unto our Souls Great Mother that we may hear your voice, and that we will carry through the echoes of your harmony.
Enter this your gentle but strong ambient Element of Air, that it will carry your vibrant voices always across the winds of time and space.
(Here do the Air Invoking pentacle over the Thurible of Incense)

Great Mother manifest for us your true purpose, and meaning, that the sacred Winds of Time and Truth will awaken within us your divine words of guidance May the Shining Ones, our Ladies and Lords become visible to the world and our divine eyes of Inner Vision?

Be Consecrated Faithful Element and servant with your nimble Elementals of Air, through the divine Power and always in the sacred service of the One Eternal Great Mother whose single breath we surely are.

For we know that we must brave the ordeal of Air, for Air is the Element of the Mind, of creating, and of the wild and free ideas that haunt us. Our hands are strong and free, so we can grasp all that we need to by taking hold firmly yet with strength."

THE JOURNEY OF FIRE

"Great Mother, you are a Light that no darkness can extinguish, that has
and will burn evermore through time and space, A sacred Fire of absolute
love that illumines and births each and every spiritual seed

In the sacred Separation of your ancient and sacred fertile Light and your
Divine powerful source which lies within the total of all your great and ancient
knowledge and wisdom. You are the strongest of the strong overcoming all
darkness and with your great Light interpenetrating all solidity.

Within your great adaptation is the Arcane and Esoteric Arts
of the sacred divine Mystery of true Magick.
We call upon you Great Mother; we call upon you Great Radiant Father of all life,
You, who give so freely your illuminating rays of life giving sustenance to all.
O Mighty Unseen parent of the visible Sun and the invisible Sun,
Pour forth all your powerful giving rays of divine Light and energise and
awaken your sacred divine sparks that reside within all aspects of life.

Enter Oh Great Father into this great and powerful Element of Fire, your Magickal flame
of the Invisible Sun and make it agitated by the sacred breath of the most Holy Mother.
(Here light the flame and do the Fire Invoking Pentacle).
Manifest Great Father your hidden yet divine Power, and illumine and open for us
the Sacred Hidden Temple that is Magickly concealed with this sacred flame.
May we all become regenerated and eternal by your sacred Light, through
the breadth, height and fullness of your Crown of Solar radiance as our
Lord God, may you forever shine forth within and without.

Faithful Element of Fire, by divine right be truly Consecrated, may the Elementals
dance always by all flames. May we always be devout in your divine service of
the Power of the One supreme Light whose single sparks we surely are.

*Here, we must pass the ordeal of Fire, the Ordeal of the Heart and the Mind,
For Fire is the Element of our Will, our eyes are open so that we can
truly see what lies ahead on our divine quest as a Spiritual warrior of
the Great Mother Goddess and Her Consort The Horn One."*

SEALING THE
PORTAL

SEALING THE EASTERN PORTAL

(This is done on any New Moon of Aquarius, Libra or Gemini)

Face the East and open your Third Eye and visualize a beautiful Greek Temple built of white marble. Holding your visualization and your thought firm and solid, now in your mind's eye see a great figure of the Greek Sky God Zeus, ruler of Olympus. See him as a tall elegant and powerful looking man with radiant gold skin, and his eyes of sky blue. His hair and beard are the colour of honey with flashes of red. He is in the prime of his life. He is adorned with a robe of white with a blue sash over his right shoulder, and in his hand, he carries radiating Golden electric blue Lightning Bolt. At the Portal he stops and looks at you as he waits for you to invite and invoke him:

"Great Zeus, King of heaven and of Gods, Ruler of Olympus and the Ear, the divine Son of Chronos. You are the mighty overseer of Justice and the great Protector of mankind, Hero of man as your children as their great Father. Hear me Great Father! Look upon this sacred Portal and grant us your sacred Seal to the Eastern Portal, with your Powerful and Magickal thunderbolt that all your Children within may be safe and true."

The Great God Zeus raises his arm and with the Lightning Bolt strikes the ground, a great drumming sound echoes and as dust disappears, there in its place is a flat white stone with a sacred Sigil of Zeus that helps unlock his power. Take notice of it and when you are able copy it down into your BoS. The Seal of Zeus is now set into the threshold of the Eastern Portal; thank Zeus and bow from your waist:

"Many thanks Great Father, thank you for this sacred favour Great Zeus. May there always be peace and harmony between us, and May you always be welcome here in this our Sacred Temple."

(Zeus smiles and raises his Lightning Bolt into the air and turns away into the beautiful landscape of Dawn.)

You are still facing the East. But close your thoughts down from the previous visualization. Take a deep breath and again relax and open your Third Eye, and see with your Inner Sight a great Throne carved of red sandstone, seated upon it the Great Egyptian God Osiris. His skin

122

is of a reddish hue with his dark black raven hair flowing beneath a white linen scalp cloth and gold Crown with a large white orb placed on top. He wears a simple white kilt with a gold belt with a sword hanging from it; he wears plain gold sandals in the shape of an ankh. Around his neck is a pectoral necklace in layers of turquoise, jet, emerald and rubies, interlaced with yellow gold. He holds in his right hand a gold crook and in his left hand a flail, both symbols of his power and authority. You stand in awe of this powerful God of Egypt and you invoke him:

"Great Lord of Upper and Lower Egypt, God of all Egypt and the unseen
world, Father of all Life, of the Sun-Hawk, Horus and the Jackal.
Hear me Great God of life and death, grant to this sacred place, our Holy Temple
and to all those who dwell within your love and protection against all foes.

Heavenly Father place your divine Seal on the Portal of the East in the name of the greatest
Magickal Mysteries of Egypt that we may work in peace and harmony under your protective eyes."

Osiris slowly rises from his great Throne and swings his great flail and strikes the ground making the sound of a great chord of a Lyre that hits our ears, and there Magickly appears a second flat white stone, this is the Second Seal of the East. You now invoke in the name of the Egyptian God Osiris and his divine Mysteries.

"Great lord and King of Amenti, Father of all Egypt in Life and Death.
I thank you for being here with us, and granting us your divine Seal of the
Eastern Mysteries. May there always be peace and harmony between us.
Be always welcome on this hallowed land and in this Magick Circle".

The God Osiris nods his head in acceptance, and he raises his crook and as he turns there is a great swirling of desert sand that hides all from view, when it clears, he is gone, but his sacred Seal remains. Take notice of this Seal and draw it in your BoS so as to know and remember and eventually work more with his Seal as a gift to you of his knowledge.

You again take a deep breath and relax, and close down the imagery, and close your thoughts and your mind. You then take a moment and then lift your head, and with your deep insight visualize a great Portal, and behind that portal is the ancient hill of Glastonbury. You visualize in the distance approaching you from his grassy Tor a figure dressed in a dark green hooded robe with a flowing cape. In his right hand he carries the Staff of Draconis, which is topped with a large Dragon with a crystal of fire in its mouth. He is the Blessed Father of Magick, the Merlin, the Arch Mage of Arthur and the Blessed Isles who comes to aid us with the ancient Seal of the Samethoi and the Druid Mysteries, as you invoke:

"Great Merlin, father of Magick, High Priest of Atlantis and our home amongst the Stars. Keeper of the sacred Seal of Pendragon, Heredity Mage of Grammarye, Master of all Magick, hear great Hierophant and grant our request that you place upon this Magick Circle your sacred Seal of Pendragon that all within shall be safe and learn of the ancient Mysteries in peace and harmony".

Merlin raises his Staff of Draconis up high and brings it down with a hard thud onto the Earth and as he does so, a large ray of light streams forth from the crystal in the dragon's mouth. Magickly the third Seal appears next to the other two Seals. A great sound of a gong is heard and there is his Magickal Seal of Pendragon in the East, you give thanks:

"Great Mage and High Priest of the Blessed Isles, we honour you great Father of Magick for this your halloed Seal. May there always be peace and harmony between us, and always guide us with your knowledge of Magick."

Merlin the Mage salutes us with his upraised Staff and as he turns a giant dragon comes to him, he climbs upon her, and together they disappear into the morning sunrise and into the distance disappearing over the Tor.

Again, you bend your head in acknowledgement, and let the vision disappear. You take a deep breath and close your mind of this image. After a short pause you lift your head and again open your Third Eye and see your Portal in the East opening, and through this Portal you see a shimmering haze of amber and rose. It slowly, like a curtain parts aside, and standing before you stands the Great Archangel of the East – Raphael. He stands there with the powerful Spear of Longinus, the Spear of Divine Light firmly in his right hand. You smell the faint aroma and fragrance of wild bush flowers that slowly fill your Temple, you now invoke:

"Mighty Raphael, Great healing Angel of the East, Guardian of the Lance of Longinus and Regent of the Element of Air. Place Oh heavenly one your sacred Seal upon this Portal that it will prove a barrier of safety and protector of all those within this Temple".

Raphael spreads his wings and raises the Spear to the Sun, and great Light hits the tip of the Lance and he then thrusts it into the ground, as he does so a beautiful sound of a trumpet is heard and divinely the 4th Seal of the East appears, you give thanks:

"Great Winged Archangel of the Present and of all Healing, we give thanks to you for this heavenly favour. May your divine Light illumine our sacred Temple, and may there always be peace and harmony between us. Be always welcome in this our Magick Circle."

The Archangel spread his wings and with the Spear on high salutes you, then turns and flies off into the distance, giving thanks.

You again close your thoughts and your mind to this image, and take a deep relaxing breath. After a slight pause lift your head and open your Third Eye and visualize in front of you beyond the Eastern Portal a great shimmering Rainbow Bridge, that leads from the Earth up into the heights of the heavens. You visualize riding over it on a great white eight-legged horse named Sleipner, upon its back of the Great God-King of the Norsemen, the Father God – Odin, who carries in his right hand a magnificent Sword emanating radiating Light, with this Magickal Sword he salutes us as you make your request and invoke him:

> *"Powerful Odin, Father of Great Magick, God of the One Eye, Keeper of the Mysteries of all Knowledge, Great God and Lord of Valhalla who sees all things, and knows all things. All-Father we ask that you set your Divine Seal upon this our Portal that our Magick Circle be made safe for all within against all evil".*

Mighty Odin upon his Magickal steed rears up and throws his Sword into the ground, and a mighty echoing war cry is heard throughout your Magick Circle, you see the final and 5th Seal of the Portal of the East, you give thanks:

> *"Mighty Father of Valhalla and Hero Warrior of Ragnarok, we thank you for your Seal which is now set by your Magick. Let there always be peace and harmony between us, and may you always be welcome in this sacred Temple".*

Mighty Odin with a great laugh rears his Steed and raises his Sword in acceptance, and he rides over the great Rainbow Bridge and disappears into the distance through the clouds. All the Seals are now set, again take notice of their Sigils and draw them down in your BoS. Now the Five Great Traditions of the world are now set: Greek, Egyptian, Celtic, Judaic and Norse. Let the visualization fade, and rise and step back to the centre of the your Magick Circle and say:

> *"By the Power and Magick of the Four Watchtowers of our Magick Circle, Ladies and Lords of the Elementals, Divine Powers of the Eastern Portal. Let Earth, Water, Air and Fire combine, to form the sacred Shield of the eastern Portal. So, Mote it be!"*

> *The Eastern Quarter of your Temple is now Sealed*

SEALING THE SOUTHERN PORTAL

(This is done on any New Moon of Aries, Leo or
Sagittarius usually the following New Moon)

After doing the LBRP and casting your Full Magick Circle you are now ready for the Sealing of the 2nd Portal, the South. Facing the South, open your mind and visualize and huge figure of Hephaestus, the Magickal armourer of Olympus, the son of Zeus and Hera. Visualize behind him the glow of a large forge of fire, with bellows pushing the flames higher and higher. See in Hephaestus' hand the Mighty Hammer of Thor; see this workmanship, request the Magickal Seal of Hephaestus:

*"Great Armourer of Olympus, Mighty Hephaestus, son of Zeus, and Mighty in
your Power of Magickal Armour. We ask that you set your Seal to our fiery Portal
of the South, make it fast and strong against all foe as a protective barrier".*

Hephaestus lifts Thor's mighty hammer and brings it down to the Earth with a large sharp crack, as he lifts it from the ground, the 1st of the white flat stones is revealed showing the Magickal Seal of Hephaestus; take note of the 1st Seal and draw it in your BoS gives thanks the Mighty Hephaestus:

*"Great Hephaestus who yields mighty Thor's Hammer, we thank you for your
sacred Seal. Peace and harmony be always between us Great Hephaestus and always
be welcome in this our holy Temple with admiration, love and respect".*

Hephaestus smiles and nods his head as he waves farewell disappears into the vast smoke of his forge.

Now close your mind and the visualization, take a deep breath and relax deeply. Pause for a few moments then when ready lift your head, still facing the South and visualise with your Inner Eye a hot, arid desert, and see coming from the sand dunes a tall beautiful slender figure of a woman, but not just any woman, she is the Lioness Headed Sekhmet, she who breathed and created the desert sands; acknowledge her and ask for Her sacred Seal:

> *"Beautiful and Powerful Sekhmet of the Lion head, Goddess of the desert sands of time, Avenger of Ra, Goddess with great strength and power. We ask for your mighty Seal, please make fast our Magickal Circle against all negative forces that approach from the South. Protect us with your sacred Seal."*

The Goddess Sekhmet gives a mighty roar then bends down to the Portal and with one of her mighty paws scores a deep trench in the sand, revealing a flat white stone which is gleaming, and upon it is Her Magickal Seal, notice the 2nd Seal and draw in your BoS Give thanks to Sekhmet:

> *"Wonderful Sekhmet we thank you for your favour of this powerful Seal. May love and peace always be between us, and may you always be welcome here in this our Magick Circle".*

Close your mind and relax with a deep breath to end this part, after a short pause raise your head and open your Third Eye and commence in visualizing beyond your Portal of the South a giant figure approaching, this figure is taller than a pine tree, with long golden red hair and a beard that shimmers with the light of the Sun bounding off it. It is Bran, the mighty hero of heroes, Protector of the Blessed Isles; ask for his Seal as a bastion and protection from all harm approaching from the South:

> *"First King of the Blessed Islands of the ancient Samethoi, Bran with the Golden Hand. And Father of the people. Grant us thy sacred Seal of safety and courage; bless us with your Magickal Seal upon this Portal of the South that our Temple be safe from all perils approaching from the South".*

King Bran gives a great laugh and his enormous Golden hand reaches down to place a flat white stone next to the other two Seals, take notice of the Sigil and draw it in your BoS, his Seal, the 3rd Seal is now set, give thanks to King Bran:

> *"Your Majesty, we thank you for your sacred Seal, father of the Blessed Isles, accept our love and prayers and with thanks be always welcome here in our Magick Circle".*

He gives a gentle nod and turns back to the Mists of Avalon. You now see three great Seals next to each other, take note of them and make sure you draw them in your BoS. Relax your thoughts and take a big breath, relaxing. After a few moments lift your head and visualise through your Southern Portal a brilliant glowing red Sun, with the light so bright, you notice stepping out through the divine Light a beautiful looking masculine figure wearing shimmering armour of Gold. He bears in his right hand a Flaming Sword, this is the Archangel Michael, ask for his Divine Seal:

"Great Guardian of the South, Archangel Michael of the Flaming sword of God,
you who stand before the Throne of Yahweh, the celestial Father and give us your
Angelic Seal that we may be safe from all perils approaching from the South".

He raises his Sword of Heavenly Flames and scorches it along the ground, as the flames die down a Third Seal appears as a chord of a harp is heard echoing across the Magick Circle, take notice of the 4th Seal and draw it down in your BoS, give thanks for his Seal.

"We thank you Magnificent Archangel Michael for your divine Seal,
be always blessed amongst your peers. May peace and love be always
between us, and always be welcome in this our Magick Circle".

Michael lifts his Sword in salute, smiles and spreads his wings and flies off into the sunset. Rest your mind and let the scenery disappear. Take a deep breath and relax, after a short pause lift your head and with your Third Eye visualise an ancient Viking hall lit with rows of fire pits. Approaching you is the giant God Thor, divine chosen Son of Odin. See hanging from his wrist Mjolnir his Magickal Hammer. See him standing at the fiery Portal of the South looking down on your Magick Circle, acknowledge him and ask for his Seal:

"Great God of Thunder, Mighty Thor as striker of the Ice Giants and
protector of Man. Great son of Odin grant us your Protection and give us
your Seal so that we may meet in safety with peace and harmony".

Thor's mighty hammer is swung over his head in a blinding arc of light, and with the sound of its howl of the Northern Winds through the air, the 5th Seal emerges, take notice and draw it in your BoS, for your Seal is now set. Thor nods his head in acceptance of our thanks:

"Mighty Thor we thank you for your Seal, may your strength never fail, and may there
always be peace and harmony between us, Be always welcome in this our Magick Circle".

The Southern Five Seals are now set, you now invoke the Watchtowers:

"By the Powers of the Four Watchtowers, I invoke the Four Elements of earth, Air, Fire and Water combine. To make this sacred Shield of the Southern Portal a barrier of divine Protection from all perils approaching from the South".

SEALING THE WESTERN PORTAL
(This is done on any New Moon of Cancer, Pisces or Scorpio)

This is usually carried out one month later, again your do the LBRP and Cast your Magick Circle. You now proceed to the West and face the Western Portal. Take a deep breath and open your inner vision and visualise a beautiful night scene of stars and the Full Moon, notice a few clouds, and stepping through them approaches the Goddess Artemis, Huntress of men's souls and awakener of dreams for woman, acknowledge her and ask for her Magickal Seal:

"Beautiful Artemis of the Mysteries of the wild forest, slender maiden and daughter
of the starlit skies and Protector of the forest and all wild life within. Great
Guardian, send forth your Mighty Arrows of the Moon and grant us your Seal
to protect us and keep us safe from all perils approaching from the West".

Artemis, the Silver Moon Goddess shoots an arrow into the ground before the Southern Portal, and the 1st stone is set with her Seal. Notice the Seal and draw it in your BoS. She does not wait and shoots another arrow into the air that sings and carried her off towards the Moon. Give your thanks:

"Great Goddess of the Forest and of the Moon we give thanks to you, sweet
Maiden of the Mysteries May peace and harmony be always between us
and know that you are always welcoming in our Magick Circle".

You acknowledge her farewell, and close down your vision of this scene, relax and take a deep breath. After a short pause you lift your head still facing the West and still see between the Western Portal the dark Starry sky but with no Moon, you see a vision of absolute beauty that outshines all others. It is the Egyptian Goddess Isis in all Her crowning glory, she holds in her right hand a sacred Ankh of Gold, ask for Her seal:

"Great daughter of the Stars and of Nut, silver footed Goddess who rules the tides of Life as the
Mistress of Magick, and the great Goddess of unconditional love. Grant us your wisdom and Seal
our temple with your divine Seal that we may be safe from all perils approaching from the West".

The Goddess Isis takes Her Golden Ankh touches it to the ground and a gust of breeze reveals the 2nd Seal at the Portal of the West, beautiful sounds of the hard echo across your Magick Circle. Notice the Seal and its Sigil and draw it in your BoS. You smile, and you notice the Goddess Isis also smiling as She raises her hands towards you and Blesses your Temple and all within, give thanks:

"Great Mother Isis, true Mother of Egypt, Mother of Magick and absolute love. Be one with us great Mother, and be always welcome in this our Magick Circle".

The Goddess bows her heads and returns to the starlit sky. Let the image dissipate, and relax your minds and your visuals. Take a deep breath and in a few moments raise your head and with your inner sight build up a scene of a Moonlit shore where stands an enormous silver glistening castle, the front of the great castle doors open and approaching you is a beautiful young Maiden dressed in greens and covered with silver trim and elegant designs. As she nears you notice that her gown is covered in millions of flickering living Stars, this is the Goddess Arianhrod, Goddess of the Stars and lady of the Moon, she approaches as you ask your request:

"Great Arianhrod, Goddess of the Starry Night, silver wheel of the night sky and daughter of absolute beauty and joy. We beseech you to grant us your sacred Seal to protect us from all perils approaching from the West".

Arianhrod smiles and looks up to the night sky as a star falls and she plucks it from the sky and places it upon your ground with the other two Seals. Behind Her in the distance we hear a mighty Conch horn sound that is calling her back to her Castle.

"We give thanks great Lady of the Stars and maiden of the Mysteries, may your Seal keep us safe and true, be always welcome in this our Magick Circle with love and joy".

Release these thoughts from your mind's eye, and relax. After a few moments take a deep breath and visualise beyond the Western Portal and beautiful waterfall, with its gentle sounds of falling like a myriad of singing voices. You notice that stepping from within the waterfall a tall glamorous figure wearing a cloak of deep indigo blue. With great deep dark brown eyes that pierce our own being. The cloak is thrown back over one shoulder and we see revealed great white wings that stretch across the sky, we now know it is the Archangel Gabriel, he stands and waits for our invocation:

"Great Voice of the Celestial Father of the living Christ and of Judaism, Archangel Gabriel of the Annunciation, grant unto us your sacred Seal to keep use and this Magick Circle safe from all perils approaching from the West".

> *"Gabriel Archangel of the Annunciation, bringer of Joy to mankind, voice*
> *of the one Father of the living Christ and of man. Grant to us and this*
> *place thy sacred Seal that we may work in peace and love."*

The Archangel Gabriel takes a single white glossy feather from her wings and it gently floats down and as it touches the Earth it turns into the 4th Seal, and our thanks go out to Gabriel as she re-enters the great waterfall.

> *"To send to our deepest thanks and prayers, be always Blessed Great Gabriel*
> *amongst your peers. May there always be peace and harmony between us,*
> *and May you always be welcome in this our Magick Circle".*

You now allow the image to fade from your inner vision, and you relax your thoughts, and after a few moments lift up your head and with your 3rd Eye visualise and build up a beautiful Maiden figure dressed in a flowing red gown and crowned with vibrant Spring flowers, she carries in her right hand a horn filled with blood red wine. This is the beautiful Goddess Freya, the giver of love, strength and joy. You now ask for her sacred Seal for your Western Portal:

> *"Great Freya, Warrior Queen and Mother of the Vikings, draw near great Lady*
> *and grant our request for your divine Seal on our Portal to keep us safe and true,*
> *grant to this our Magick Circle joy, merriment and song with your great Seal".*

The Goddess Freya smiles as a mother to her children and tilts her horn of plenty, as the wine flows it washes away the soil and reveals the final and 5th Seal of the Western Portal. With great rejoice we sing in our hearts and she joins in signing as she returns to her mountains as we give thanks

> *"Great Lady of the mountains, Goddess of laughter and merriment, we thank*
> *you for your beautiful gift of your sacred Seal to keep us safe and happy, be*
> *always welcome here great Lady Freya with peace and harmony always".*

Now all the five Seals of the West are set, we now invoke the Watchtowers:

> *"By Magick of the Mysteries of the West do I invoke the protection of the Four*
> *Elemental Watchtowers, and the Elements of Earth, Air, Fire and Water*
> *combine, to form the sacred Shield of the Western Portal. So, Mote it be".*

> *The West is sealed*

Sealing the Northern Portal
(This is done on any New Moon of Capricorn, Taurus or Virgo)

After you have Properly Prepared your Magick Circle and done the LBRP and cast the Full Magick Circle. Walk Deosil around to the North and where your Altar is situated. Sit and facing the North, relax and open your inner vision and build up in your mind's eye a beautiful mountainside covered with spring flowers. Feel a gentle but warm breeze blowing over your body. See a figure of a woman descending a mountain path. As she gets closer you notice she is a woman of maturity, but of complete beauty. Her arms are full of spring flowers, grains and fruit especially the full noodling of black, yellow and white corn. You acknowledge her and ask for her divine Seal:

"Great Goddess of the harvest, Lady of the Cornfields, Goddess and Daughter of Olympus, graceful Demeter. Grant us your sacred Seal to protect us from all perils approaching from the North that we may work in safety and harmony".

The Goddess in a lovingly manner places down an ear of ripened corn and it Magickly turns into the 1st Seal of the North. Notice the Sigil and draw it into your BoS. As she does this bird flies down to her and perches on her hand, singing with full heart. The Goddess turns gracefully walks back into the fields of high grown corn as you with respect invoke her Seal:

"Great Goddess Demeter, Lady of the Wheat Sheafs and Corn fields, we thank you for your sacred Seal. You have honoured us with your Magickal Seal of protection to keep us safe. May you always be welcome in this our Magick Circle with peace and love in our hearts".

You allow this image to fade from your mind and you relax. After a short pause take a deep breath and open your Third Eye and visualise through your Northern Portal a great ancient Temple of red stone. In the centre is a simple yet beautiful throne of stone where is seated a slender figure of a man, but with the head of a Jackal, holding in his right hand a large Gold Ankh. He is the son of Osiris and Isis, the Sun God Anubis, Guardian of the Underworld. He waits for your question:

"Mighty Anubis, Lord of the Two Worlds of Amenti, Guardian of the Great Mother of the Mysteries. Lord and Guardian over Life and Death. We ask you to place your sacred Seal at our Northern Portal to keep us safe from all perils approaching from the North".

The Great God Anubis rises from his throne and steps forward to the Portal where he lays down his golden Ankh, as he does so it melts into becoming the 2nd Seal, the sacred Seal of Anubis of the North. He bows his head and returns back to his Throne as you invoke:

"Great Jackal God, Lord of Light and Dark, Overseer of Life and Death, conductor of Souls, we ask for your great Seal to be placed at our Portal to keep us safe from all harm".

You acknowledge his offering, and open your heart to him offering peace and love always. You gradually allow this image to fade from your mind's eye, and relax. After a few moments you take a deep breath and raise your head and then through the Northern Portal you visualise and ancient Stone Circle on a grassy Tor. You notice as though stepping through the stones a tall Celtic warrior looking woman who bears a small Cauldron in her left hand, this is Cerridwen, ask for the sacred Seal:

"Great Mystical keeper of the Sacred Cauldron, our Earth Goddess Cerridwen, giver of wisdom to all mankind and Mother of the Magickal Mysteries of the Samethoi of the Blessed Isles. Grant to us your sacred Seal to keep our Magick Circle safe from all harm".

The Goddess gently tips the Cauldron onto the Earth and her Wine of Wisdom flows over the Portal washing away the 3rd Seal of the North. She smiles and turns and walks back to her Magickal Stone Circle and disappears in a fog as you send thanks:

The Goddess tips the Cauldron and the Wine of Wisdom flows over the Portal washing away the Earth from the Third Seal notice the Sigil and draw it into your BoS. Then She returns to the Stone Circle:

The scene now fades from your inner sight, and you relax. After a few moments you take a deep breath and lift your head and again open your 3rd Eye and visualise a rocky crag in the distance above a fertile green countryside. As you look passively over the fields of grass and clover, in the distance through the woods you see a tall figure in a cloak of forest green. As he gets closer you notice it is a male, and it is the Throne Archangel Auriel, Guardian of the planet Earth, as he approaches you ask:

"Great Throne Angel of God, Archangel of Terra Firma Auriel. Give of bread and honey to the hungry. You are the Comforter of the wounded animal and Protector of Divine Knowledge, and Angel who shares in Earth's Tears. We ask for your angelic Seal at our Northern Portal to keep us strong in faith and to keep us safe in humility".

The Archangel takes off his finger a Magickal Ring and place it by the other three Seals, it Magickly becomes the 5th Seal of the North as we offer thanks:

"Great Throne Angel with all your divine Grace we thank you for your Divine Seal, may there always be peace and love between us, and know that you are always welcomed in our Magick Circle".

Now invoke the Watchtowers:

"By the Power of this Magick Circle do I invoke the Powers and Protections of the Watchtowers of the Four Quarters for the Northern Portal. Let earth, Air, Fire and Water combine to form the Sacred Shield of the North. So, Mote it be".

The North is now Sealed

LESSER
BANISHING
RITUAL OF THE
PENTAGRAM

This is one of the most important Rituals in Wicca, as it teaches the Wiccan to cleanse and bless everything and every area of working, especially your Magick Circle. (PROPERLY PREPARED I MUST ALWAYS BE) So your Circle should already be cleared, cleansed and washed with Rosemary Water of all uncleanliness. The Portals or Quarters have been invoked and readied over the last four New Moons, and are now guarded by all the authorities of the Quartered Regions of your Watchtowers. Your Magick Circle is now Properly Prepared, to be used as a Wiccan Temple. What follows is the Lesser Banishing Ritual of the Pentagram, or better termed the (LBRP)?

This is one of the first things that the Seeker should learn by heart as all Wiccans learn this. Besides this they must also keep all their Consecrated Tools of the Wicca clean and polished before each rite. The Man in Black and the Maiden (if you have them) assist the Wiccan and make sure that the Wiccan sets out the Temple properly in every way. All four Ceremonial Etheric Quarter Candles that are to be used (red-south, green-west, orange-north, blue-east), the Altar Candles and the central Spirit Candle, must all be Properly Prepared and anointed with Consecrated Oil and fully charged by you.

When all is Properly Prepared before you enter the Circle, especially before the High Priestess enters, the Man in Black will ask the Wiccan to proceed with the Banishing Ritual. Here the Wiccan performs the rite assisted by the Man in Black or the Maiden, depending on whether the Wiccan is male or female. The only light in the Temple should be coming from the Altar Candles and the Spirit Candle.

THE RITUAL

The Wiccan stands facing the East, and behind her/him is the Maiden/Man in Black, always assisting with the visualisation and in case of any error. As the Neophyte Wiccan looks into the distance, they then close their eyes and breath in the vital force of the Spirit by doing the 4x4 breathing, they then invoke into themselves the Divine Light which they visualise hovering above their head in front of them about two feet away, they draw this Divine Light into their hands, and bring the Light down to the left hip and visualise the blue-white light on the left hip vibrating, saying:

Taking the light to the Forehead say:
> *"I am the Essence of the Goddess and God".*

Take the light to the left hip and say:
> *"I am the Life of the Goddess and God".*

Take the Light to the right shoulder and say:
> *"I am the Light of the Goddess and God".*

Take the light across to the left shoulder and say:
> *"I am the Love of the Goddess and God".*

Take the light down to the right hip and say:
> *"I am the Magick of the Goddess and God".*

Then bring the light back up to the forehead and down to the heart and say:
> *"I am One with the Goddess and God always".*

After doing this you hold the visualisation of the vibrant blue-white light Pentagram illuminating your body and soul, feel it vibrating, cleansing, blessing, purifying and pulsating. Now the next stage of the rite is where you walk Deosil around the Temple to the Altar and pick up the Spirit Candle and present it to Deity, whenever you take an object from the Altar present it first to Deity. Then take the Candle Deosil (sunwise/clockwise), and say as you form the Fire Banishing Pentagram in the Air:

"With this ancient and Mystical sign of the Wicce as the Power of Fire, do I banish all dark and negative Shadows of the East (then, south, then west, then north respectively). Let this Magickal realm be filled with the Light of Spirit and filled with Light and Love".

Repeat again at each Cardinal point finishing at the North, where you again present the candle and then place it on the Altar and leave it burning. Man in Black/Maiden then picks up her/his Athame and presents it to the Goddess and God. Then as with the Candle starting in the East, you now invoke the Elements and Elementals with steel, doing the Earth Invoking Pentagram at each Quarter and say:

"With this ancient and Mystical sign of the Earth and of the Wicce do I invoke and call upon the Sacred Sylphides of Air, (Sacred Salamanders of Fire, Holy Undines of Water, Holy Gnomes of the Earth respectfully). Bless and sanctify this Magick Circle aid in its Holy Consecration".

Finishing again in the North, with the same procedure, Place the Athame down on the Altar or Sheath it. Then bow and step back from the Altar and proceed again to the East. The Maiden or Man in Black is standing behind the Seeker as they face east and say:

"Before me the Sacred Sylphides of Air,
Behind me the Holy Undines of Water,

To my right the sacred Salamanders of Fire,
To my left are the Holy Gnomes of Earth.
For around me flame the Pentagrams of Fire,
And above me shines the six-rayed Star of the First Great Mother".

Here again repeat but the shortened version:

Touching the forehead:

"I am Goddess, I am God".

Touching the right hip:

"I am the Foundation of Hope".

Touching the left shoulder:

"I am Love".

Touching the right shoulder:

"I am the Light".

Touching left hip:

"I am the Magick of the Universe".

Touching the Solar Plexus in prayer position:

"Now and Forever".

Visualise a large glowing Pentagram within your body vibrating and pulsating light and energy.

"So, may it always be".

CASTING THE
MAGICK CIRCLE

The Circle is now cleansed, Properly Prepared and readied for the Fellowship and the High Priestess and Elders to enter. All who enter should meditate prior to their Esbat or Sabbat meeting. They are all anointed on the brow and welcomed into the Sacred Space. They then go Deosil around and sit in the south facing the Altar and meditate for at least 10 minutes. At this time the HPs and HP and the Elders enter and are also anointed and welcomed all bow as the HPs enters. She approaches the Altar bows and then presents the bell, and tolls the Circle 40 times in all. As all stand and acknowledge the toning and awakening of the Magick Circle.

Man in Black has already ignited the Spirit Flame, the Altar Candles, and the Charcoal Blocks for the Incense, ready for the HP who picks up the Magick Sword and presents it to the Goddess and God, with blade pointing to the East, then holding the handle and pointing the point of the Sword outwards, he starts to visualise that he is blasting a mote around the boundary of the Circle, of course going widdershins (anti-clockwise), finishing at the North, then going Deosil filling the moat with divine light.

Man in Black and Maiden approach the Altar, she on the left he on the right, both stand and face the Altar. Maiden picks up the Chalice of Water, as MiB draws his Athame, both raise them and present them to Deity, Maiden kneels facing MiB and he slowly lowers his Athame into the Chalice charging it and visualising a beam of white light saying:

> *"Sacred Waters of Life. By the Phallus of Creation do I exorcise you and*
> *cast out all impurities from the world of Water. I do this in the names*
> *of the Goddess Aradia and the Horned God Cernunnos".*

MiB then takes the Chalice from Maiden and assists her to rise, he places it on the Altar as Maiden draws her Athame and he takes up the Pentacle which has salt on it, both present it to Deity, he then kneels, and she invokes as she lowers her Athame onto the Pentacle of Salt, saying:

> *"Divine Blessings upon and within this Creature of Salt. Let all malign energies be cast out;*
> *make it clean and pure on all Realms. May it be a sacred Shield of protection to this Magick*
> *Circle? That only lets good enter and keeping all evil at bay. By this pure salt do I bless and*
> *consecrate you in the names of the Goddess Aradia and the Horned God Cernunnos".*

With both MiB and Maiden standing, they mix the salt into the Chalice of water, both hold it as the HPs approaches between them and takes the Chalice of Water with salt in it, as Consecrated Water and drinks some and says:

"As Water cleanses the Body, and Salt Purges the Mind,
Only the Goddess can purify the Soul".

HPs then sprinkles the Circle saying:

"Earth and Water of Elements fare, where you fall no evil there.
No dark powers shall in shadows hide, blessed tears of Light there to abide.
This Circle washed and cleaned of all, only Love and Light for all".

The HPs then anoints everyone by sprinkling them with the water or anointing their brow saying:

"May you be blessed with the Elements of Light and Love"?

HPs return to the Altar and takes a sip of the Water and anoints her own brow. She then places the Chalice back on the Altar. Bows and steps back from the Altar as a Wiccan steps forward and picks up the Thurible and slowly walking Widdershins and Thurifies the Temple saying: (firstly the Altar)

"Elementals of Air and Fire bright do my bidding this very night,
With this incense do I make a mighty shield, a Circle clean and strong to yield?
Fragrance attract, and odour repel, this Circle is safe as I do will".

Wiccan returns to the North salutes with Thurible and again places it on the Altar, bows and steps back as another Wiccan comes forward and picks up the Spirit Candle and presents to Deity and then carries it around the Circle Deosil saying:

"Be to me the Light of the Moon, be to me the Light of Night,
Be to me the light of Joy, turning darkness into Light".

Repeat this as many times as it takes to go around the Circle then present it to the Altar saying:

"By the Virgin waxing cold, by the Mother full and bold.
By the Hag Queen silent old, by the Moon the One in Three,
Consecrate this Circle, Blessed Be".

Whilst this is being said everyone visualises the Goddess sending her Divine love and light. All are now standing in a semi-circle in God Position (with arms crossed over chest) in the South facing North. HP then does the Conjuration of the Circle saying:

"By life and Love do I conjure this Circle, that it be a Temple of Light?
A sacred boundary between the worlds of men and the realms of the Gods.
A protection and Sacred Space that shall contain and preserve the power.
Which we will raise within it this night, may this Circle be blessed and true in
the names of the Goddess Aradia and the Horned God Cernunnos".

Now it is time to invoke the Lords of the Watchtowers, these are done by the Keepers of the Quarters; each stand in their appropriate Quarter and says in turn:

WEST:

"Hail Guardians and Keepers of the Watchtower of the West,
Powers of Water and ruler of the oceans deep,
Mover of the primordial bitter sea. Princess of the Powers of Water.
By this sacred Pentagram do we invoke you and call upon you
Ancient Serpent of the watery abyss.
Gentle rains, sacred twilight and evening star.
Be here we pray by the waters of our Mother Living Womb, send
forth your life giving flow. Be here now great Zephyrus".

SOUTH:

"Hail Guardians and Keepers of the Watchtower of the South, Power behind Lightning and eternal light of the solar orb, Lord over Fire and the Salamanders that dance with the noonday Sun. Great Flaming One who is summer's heat. Red Lion of the desert sands. Spark of all life, I invoke you and pray that you be present. Come Mighty Lord of the South, by the eternal inner fire that is Her spirit, send forth your eternal light, be here now Mighty Euras".

EAST:

"Hail Guardians and Keeper of the Watchtower of the East, Sacred Breath of the Air, powers of the tempest storms and cyclones, Golden Eagle of the Dawn power of the rising sun, and master of the vault of Heaven. Seeker of Stars I invoke you and call upon you, hold firm by the element of Air that is Her Divine Breath. Send forth your powerful light, I pray that you be here now mighty Euras".

NORTH:

"Hail Guardians and Keeper of the Watchtower of the North, castle of the Gods, living heartbeat of the Earth. O Horned One, Great Goat of the North essence of all Power, Master of the Powers of the Earth, and ruler of all mountains and fertile field, King of the outer darkness, Black of midnight, and Power of the whirling universe. Great

North Star I invoke you and call upon you. Come by the Earth that is Her body, I
pray you now send forth your mighty strength, be here now great Bureaus".

When all has been successfully invoked and completed, then you have formed the Ancient Magick Circle of the Wise, on all levels. After all this the Wiccans come together and link hands male to female, female to male, with your left hand facing down and your right hand facing up (the Magickal link) here forming a circle to do the Wicces Rune. It is now prepared for the ritual of the night.

At the end of the rite when all has been done you must always cleanse and banish the Circle, going Deosil starting in the East, and ending in the North saying:

"Mighty Ladies and Lords of the Watchtowers of the East (South, West and North
respectively) and the sacred Elementals of Air (Fire, Water and Earth respectively). I
thank you for your presence in attending our sacred Rites and ask that you depart to
your lovely Realms with love and peace in your heart. I say Hail and Farewell".

Everyone repeats:

"Hail and Farewell".

All to the Altar bow to the Altar as they leave the Magick Circle.

It is now time for sharing of the feast with drinks and food, but it should be kept simple and small on working nights such as New and Full Moons, but great to go all out on Festivals with big feasts, which are celebrations.

THE WICCES
PYRAMID

The very foundation of much of the Wicces Power is built from the ancient Wicces Pyramid. Like the oldest man-made structure ever built we have discovered that the significance of the Great Pyramid has its place not only amongst the Stars, but also in the very foundation of Magick. Although the Pyramid is nor circular like the Magick Circle as it is built with a rudimentary design of specialized Triangles and Squares, so too does the Magick Circle.

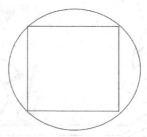

To Will - the first of the so-called four sides of the Pyramid is your dynamic, controlled "WILL".

To Know – the second side is your deep imagination, or the ability to accomplish or see your desire accomplished "KNOW".

To Dare – the third side is unshakeable and absolute faith in your ability to accomplish anything that you desire "DARE".

To Keep Silent – the fourth side is absolute secrecy, (Power shared is Power lost, Knowledge shared is Wisdom gained) "SILENCE".

You or your Coven must work in solitude, peace and harmony without the ego of discussing all that you do to others who are not enlightened enough to be involved. These four things Will Power, Imagination, Faith and Solitude are the Foundation of all the Wicces true Power.

Peace and harmony are the basic rules and absolute requirements for the working of Magick, without all four working together in harmony you're Magick Circle and your Magick will be out of balance and you will not be able to accomplish what you truly desire, and that is the integral connection with all life.

With your Pyramid, within the Magick Circle working for you, be sure that you have ample knowledge of the universal power tides, and the source and rhythm of the ebb and flow of these cosmic tides is marked by the movements of the Sun, Moon and Planets throughout the year. The Eight Great Solar Power Tides that occur are our Festivals and mark the time of our religious Sabbats. This is part of our Cosmic Calendar, they are a time to draw close to the Gods and Goddesses and receive Magickal rejuvenation from contact with these power tides known as the Solstices and Equinoxes. It is not enough to know or possess knowledge and power, you must know how to focus or aim the Power that you have raised in the desired direction and target for the genuine purpose intended.

The famous "Wicces Rune" written by the HPs Doreen Valiente, that we use when building the Magickal "Cone of Power" is raised by our very own electro-magnetic bodies and brought together and held as a beam of Light by our Will within the Magick Circle. Then with the concentration and force of your Will you then command the Power Cone of energy to go spiralling forth out of the Magick Circle and accomplish what was the higher desire of the Wicce. The Magick Circle itself acts as a lens like a torch to constrain and focus the Magickal Cone of Power. When you begin to build your Magickal Cone of Power, and cold chills of tingling determination and you feel lightly intoxicated and ready to explode. When you have experienced and expressed these things, then you will know that you have succeeded in raising the Mystical Magickal Cone of Power.

When this has been successful, and your Power has been directed and sent forth, then drop to the floor and point your hand or your Wand in the intended direction that your Power has been sent, visualising the accomplished result. You may also instead of sending this energy forth as a ball or ray of light, send it forth as a Familiar in the form of a bird or something else that you desire. You must have it report back to you often of the success of the Spell. When it reports back you will know whether to increase more energy, Will or the like, but when it is working successfully you know you have succeeded in the Magick of Wiccecraft, for it is the knowledge of, and the ability to manifest and manipulate the Metaphysical universal laws of Nature, established by the Goddess. It will elevate you from the lowest Law of the Wicca to the highest Law of the Spirit.

The Powers obtained by the knowledge of and use of the Arts is neither good nor evil, but always NEUTRAL. The Universal Laws always stay the same. It is the application of these very Laws by the Wicce and the results obtained by their use which determines what is known as Positive (+) or Negative (-) Magick. The Power that we are talking about comes from one source, and one source only – The Goddess Force. My Goddess and the Creator of all things did not create anything unclean or evil, but as either Positive or negative. It is man that gave these Positive or Negative forces, the aspects of either good or evil. The Universal Law of "Like Unto Like", upon which all Sympathetic Magick is based within Wiccecraft, has been used since time began.

Wiccecraft is used today as an affirmation throughout the world by Wiccans who would be shocked to find out that a wooden decoy duck that is set out upon the water to attract ducks from the sky, is and always has been Wiccecraft. This is a modern example of the Universal law of "Like Unto Like", or "That Like produces like", which is called the "Law of Similarity".

Another aspect of Sympathetic Magick is "Contact". Wicces believe that objects that have once been in long contact with each other, such as a person's clothing which contains their scent, or perspiration, or things that have once been a part of the person such as hair, nails, urine, blood, even jewellery, like wedding rings that has been on their body for a long period of time attracts into it the life-force energies of the person. That they will continue to act on each other no matter what the distance may be between the severed parts.

Knowing Sympathetic Magick to be an application of the Universal Law of "Like unto Like", we make use of them and the ancient knowledge in our rituals by using waxen images or clay poppets that we call Fif-faths, not voodoo dolls (this belongs to Voodoo Mysteries not Wicca).

"Yesterday's Magick is today's science,
And today's Magick is the science of Tomorrow".

THE RITUAL OF THE WICCES PYRAMID

As with the normal Casting of the Magick Circle, you must first cut the Circle Boundary usually by the HP or HPs. But after the Wardens have done their Elemental LBRP. All the Wardens approach their respective Watchtower with the HPs standing in the centre of the Magick Circle. All Wardens face outwards and bow their heads respectfully to Nature and the outer world, then turn inward and face the HPs.

The Four Wardens then draw their Athame's and present to the HPs. They then kiss their Magickal blades, stand in God Position and turn out and face their Watchtower. They each visualise their hearts rhythm and energy pulsating and slowly moving into their Athame's. The HPs then sounds the drum with 3 beats as this is done they then on the third beat point their Athame's outward and then slowly walk around the Magick Circle to the rhythm of the Drum, slowly to a half beat, saying:

"As within, so without. As without so within".

When they each arrive back at their respective Watchtower in the Magick Circle they open their minds to open the Portals of their Realm, and then after 3 more drumbeats, they slowly raise their Athame's to the Heavens forming a Pyramidal apex above the Magick Circle, still drawing power from their Portals through to the apex, when the Athame's have all reached the apex, the Pyramid Peak, 3 more drumbeats will sound after which they will then all say:

"As Above".

Now facing inwards. They all slowly lower their Athame's after three more drumbeats; they then slowly bring their Athame's down to the heart of the HPs and say:

"So Below".

All then say together:

"As Within, so without, As Above So Within".

Each Warden then withdraws their Athame into their very own hearts, and stand in God Position. Again, after three more beats of the drum all bow to the HPs as the Goddess and place their Athame's in their sheaths. All then face their respective Watchtower in turn Invoke their Watchtowers.

The Conjuration is then done by the HP. and the HPs facing each other, she to the North facing South, and he to the South facing North. As this is being done all Wicces slowly circle Deosil doing the Wicces Rune, to raise Power.

LUNA
CONSCIOUSNESS
THE DRAWING
DOWN OF
THE MOON

(Starts from the New Moon)

The new Moon is the start of the Full moon and should be performed prior to the Full Moon ritual, as the energy starts on the New Moon and builds up to the Full Moon. In our Circles we have what we call the "Meeting Dance" which is where our Bards lead us into the Magick Circle. When we have entered the sacred space we then do the New Moon dance. We place a large Turkish Tray (Altar) on top of the Cauldron, which is in the centre of the Magick Circle. On this Altar we place a large Phallic shaped crystal (The Wand), our Altar Pentacle with salt upon it, a red rose bud, a Thurible with Incense in it, a lit Spirit candle and a Crescent Moon Symbol (we use a set of ancient boar tusks bound together), and we place our Four Blue Etheric candles around the Circle at the Watchtowers, which have all been lit by the Spirit Candle.

We all form a ring around the Magick Circle and close our eyes and go into what we term the "Mother Breath" which is 7 breaths in, hold for 7, then 7 breaths out. This allows us to fully relax and release the tensions and emotions of the day, to flow from us, we continue the Mother Breath until we are all ready, until we feel alert, emptiness, and we know that we are about to commune with the Great Mother Goddess, for She is the power of all beginnings and growth.

In her Divine symbol of the Moon, she shines forth all Her phases upon us for the taking, it is for us to open in Her Tides, and as we see in Her symbol the first crescent in the High heavens, we acknowledge her strength and Power. She so freely gives to us. All Wicces rise and still forming a ring in the centre of the Magick Circle, going Deosil we all stand with right foot forward, followed by our left foot, then saying:

"We welcome you Our Lady".

As we raise our hands and head in a salute gesture

We then take our right foot back, followed by the left foot and say:

"We give you Sacred Space".

We then move outstretched bowing our heads to Her. Third, the right foot moves sideways followed by the left as we say:

"We move on with you as we become One with you".

Here we move Widdershins dancing to the Music of the Spheres. Continuing the dance steps, the dance is slow to start with but as you dissolve into it, you become aware of your body becoming very light and carefree, and you feel yourself flowing freely through the Magick Circle. The gestures become more and more meaningful as you turn the Widdershins circle saying:

"We move on with you as we become One with you".

Feel the energy tides of the Waxing Moon, her tides will pull you faster and faster, and the dance will speed up and you will feel yourself gliding Widdershins around the Magick Circle, and the movements becoming effortless. When enough energy is raised, you stop the dance holding tight to each other, and then all sit down still holding hands and meditate and Enter the Silence. Listen to what has been created. The Astral Journey should follow this Heka Ritual to the ancient 'Arch Temple to the Sanctuary of the Moon'.

THE FULL MOON
CEREMONY

There are Thirteen Esbats in the year, and these coincide with the Full Moon, the Rite must always be performed just prior to the peak of the Full Moon, and in actual fact the first stage of the Esbat is actually done on the New Moon as we have just seen in the last section. All should assemble for the Esbat. For this night the Goddess is invoked into the HPs who is the representative of the Goddess in all Her aspects of Nature Herself. This is also the night that the HPs usually cast the Circle herself.

HPs and HP consecrate water and salt in the usual way. HPs draws the Circle with her Athame, Staff or Wand followed by the HP with the Sword. HPs bears the incense, she then does the firing of the Circle. HPs. purifies the HP by using the Scourge, he then purifies her in the same manner, and all are then welcomed into the Temple and are anointed and ceremonially scourged. HPs. then invokes the Quarters, and do the Conjuration of the Magick Circle. HPs returns to the Altar and kneels facing the Altar and adores the Goddess and God in private meditation and adoration, she then ceremonially knocks three times on the Altar (this is the key to the Goddess to open the Portal between this world and the next, and the Fellowship all then dance and sing, saying:

> *"Now the sacred lady rises new within the starlit sky,*
> *Now before the Esbat meeting guard us Lady by and by.*
> *Wrap us in the cloak of darkness hide us in the Mists of Time,*
> *Ere the Spell is brewed and settled, hide till the morning chime.*
> *Guide us ere the dance commences, hide the sakes and conceal the wine,*
> *Lead us in the Age of darkness, sacred Queen and all Divine.*
>
> *Guard us Lord of hunt and forest by the powers of Fire and Air,*
> *As we come once more to worship, keep we Wiccelord in your care.*
> *By the powers of Earth and Water now the Circle spins and spins,*
> *Come unto your sacred servants guard us now the Rite begins.*
> *Thrice about the Circle go, once for Virgin pure as snow,*
> *Once for Maidens soft sweet breathe, once for Dark Moon as old as Death.*
> *Thrice about the Circle spin that the Rite shall well begin."*

After this we all continue circling slowly saying the Wicces Rune, this is to aid in building up the power within the Magick Circle. As the Coveners slowly circle and dance, the HPs goes within the ring of dancers and chants going widdershins:

"Thus, do I seek my Goddess, my Goddess, my Goddess? Aradia, Aradia, Aradia. At night I come into my Magick Circle, my Magick Circle, my Magick Circle, and with me I bear water, wine and salt, I bear water, wine and salt, I bear water, wine and salt. And my Talisman which ever I hold in my hand, my Pentacle, my Pentacle, my Pentacle which ever I wear around my neck, to remind me of you my Lady, my Lady, my Lady, and of my faith, my faith, my faith. I bless myself with devotion to implore a favour from my Goddess, my Goddess, my Goddess, Aradia, Aradia, Aradia".

HPs. returns to the Altar as the dancers all break and form a semi-circle in the South facing the HPs. HPs stands in God (Osiris) position, as does everyone. HPs. faces south. HP gives the 5/S to the HPs. HP kneels down in front of the HPs in the centre of the Magick Circle and Draws Feminine power down from the Moon into himself out through his body down his arms into the Phallic Wand and into the HPs, as he does this all are chanting the chant of the Mother:

"Shima Oma la Shima".

This continues until the Power is raised, the Coveners all standing in adoration in God Position. HP now invokes twice with Wand. Here he touches the womb, the right breast, the left breast, then the womb again with the tip of the Wand and repeats as he invokes:

"Great Mother I invoke you, eternal Light of the night sky, and living Earth beneath our feet. I call upon you Mighty Mother of us all and Bringer of all truth, and bearer of all fruitfulness and life. And by the eternal spark that is within all things, and by the sacred seed, and root, by bud and stem and flower and fruit. By life and love, by light and laughter, I beseech you to descend into this your true servant and Priestess with the Moon on her brow".

All wait as the Goddess descends into the HPs, after this the HP does the 5/s, and all men do the same, then followed by the ladies who bow with horned salute. If you wish a Boon from the Goddess, stand close and look deep into her eyes and whisper:

"O beautiful Goddess of the Moon,
By light and life grant me this Boon.
(Ask your favour in rhyme)
Hear my words addressed to thee,
As you're Will, So Mote it be".

After this the Goddess then gives Her charge in poetry to Her children:

It is appropriate for you to write your own Charge, which is the words of the Goddess to her people, her children of Wicca. It can be as simple or as elaborate as you desire, eventually it will be the Goddess who will speak through you. This takes effect after many years of trance states and opening yourself to the true energies of the Goddess. At first it is easier just to write your own words until the Goddess actually speaks through you.

Once the Goddess has been invoked and the Circles energies and power have been raised and used for some form of ceremony such as healing, Magick, ritual training, blessings and awakenings. After which the excess energies are sent forth into the Earth as a healing agent and thanksgiving. When this has all been done, it is time to end the night's ritual with the Blessing of the Cakes and Wine.

HP comes forward and kneels in front of the Goddess with the Chalice of wine should she wish to partake. After this the same with the Sabbat cakes, and they are one by one passed around the Magick Circle to all members. The Magick Circle is then closed with the Banishing of the Quarters and the cleaning up of the Magick Circle. And all Tools are put away clean and safe. Agape (supper) is then shared by all participants.

WICCANING
OF A CHILD

BLESSED LITTLE BUNNEE

"Blessed little Bunnee with a frown upon thy brow,
In your eyes a question mark that governs every how!
Rules and invocations bantered around the group,
Dizzily you take it in, thy energies recoup.

O Blessed Little Bunnee, like a child upon the shore,
When you think you've understood?
You'll find there's always more.
More to learn and understand to turn your life around,
But Blessed Little Bunnee keeps thy feet on solid ground.

The Power of your ego may take you for a ride,
But ere you know just where you are you're on a downhill slide.
So precious little Bunnee, with frown upon thy face,
Know your time comes soon enough,
When you will take the place.
Among them that stood where you are,
A-fluster and in awe,
And when you think you've got it right, aha!
You'll find there still is more!

1978

THE BAPTISM OF A CHILD
THE HOLY WICCANING

This is our method likened unto Mainstream religions, except it is done when the child is under the age of puberty. To be properly prepared they are to be bathed, they also must wear a small white robe with green trimmings and a green Singulum tied around their wastes. On their heads is a chaplet of white flowers. HPs and HP (or even the child's parents if they are Wicces) cast the Circle, but firstly the Maiden and Man in Black surround the Circle with many coloured candles or glass filled candles, 40 in all. All are brought forward and ceremonially anointed on the forehead with the symbol of the Triangle of Darkness (inverted triangle) in a Circle. HPs and HP do the Conjuration forming an Arch over the parents and child. Watchtowers are invoked as the child kneels on a green silk cushion in the North as the HPs says:

"Mighty Ladies and Lords of the Outer Spaces, Sacred Fae of the Magickal unseen world,
hear my call!" Mighty Ones of the East, South, West and North, hear my plea!
Magickal Elementals of Air, Fire, Water and Earth we call you forth to witness this
sacred rite of Wiccaning. Bring forth your Magick and guard this Magick Circle.
We are here to meet in Love and Light and ask that you keep safe and guard
this child N: _____ who is to be Consecrated and Wiccaned in
your Magickal presence under the eyes of the Goddess and God".

All Wiccans do the Wicces Rune dancing around the child. All bring white flowers and petals and scatter them on the Magick Circle floor. HPs. draws and invokes the Goddess into the Magick Circle then reads the Charge. The Elder or mother then says:

"Dear sisters and brothers, we are here tonight in this our Magick Circle to ask Blessings of the
Ancient Ones and the Goddess and God upon this child of N: _____ sister/brother of our
Tradition. We ask you to bless her/him so that she/he may grow in beauty and strength, in joy
and wisdom, in love and in light. We are aware of the many Paths out there, but we know that
each soul must find their own Truth and their follow their own Path. Therefore, we do not seek

to bind N: _____ to the Path of Wicca whilst they are too young to know and choose.
Rather do we ask the Goddess and God who know all Paths, and to whom all Paths lead? To
Bless, protect, help, defend and prepare her/him through the years of their innocence and their
childhood, so that when at last they have truly grown and understood, that shall know without
fear or doubt which Path calls out to them and their spiritual needs. We ask that they walk
upon our Path until this time freely and gladly with joy and love in their hearts, always with
an open mind to their own Truth. With the love and light of this Magick Circle do we welcome
this child N: _____ as child of the Stars and little sister/brother of this Temple.
We ask N: _____ mother/father of N: _____ to bring forth
your child that we may bless her/him with the radiance of the stars and the
Magick of this Circle, let us now anoint them and make them holy".

In Wicca everything is done male to female, and female to male, it keeps the Cosmic Balance or
Equilibrium. Unless you are in total equilibrium within yourself it can vary. So here the child
is anointed with oil in the symbol of the Wiccan saying:

"Blessed Be your feet that shall walk firmly on terra Firma and amongst the Gods.
Blessed Be your knees that shall be humble in life to all creatures.
Blessed Be your Womb/Phallus that has the Magickal Seed of creation.
Blessed Be your Heart may it be filled with love that is unconditional
Blessed Be your Lips that shall speak of beauty and always with truth upon them.
Blessed be your eyes and your inner vision that you may see true beauty in all things.
Blessed Be your mind that it may attain to knowledge through wisdom.
To you do I give the sacred Light and Love of the Goddess that you be a pure light?
And always safe by the Star of Truth that shall be both within and without to keep you
Safe".

HPs now says:

"I ask the Magickal Creatures of this Magick Circle look now down upon this child and send your
powers unto her/him;

Bestow upon N: _____ the gift of Courage!
Bestow upon N: _____ the gift of Beauty!
Bestow upon N: _____ the gift of Love!
Bestow upon N: _____ the gift of Inner Sight!

Bestow upon N: _____ the gift of Healing!
Bestow upon N: _____ the gift of Wisdom!
N: _____ raise your hands in the Air and make everyone
acknowledge you and shout out your name".

The child now shouts out her/his name, if they are too young the parents do it. The HP then says:

"I am N: _____"!

"Are there two in this Magick Circle who will to undertake and stand as Spiritual
Parents to N: _____. If so, please come forward and take your vows".

HPs then says:

Do you N: _____ and N: _____ promise to be a friend, a sister and
brother, a teacher, guide and spiritual parent to N: _____ throughout all her/
his years. To aid and guide her/him wisely as they shall require or need, and in accordance
with their parents will you watch over her/him as if they were of your own blood? Till by the
Grace of the Great Mother she/he will be ready to choose their own tradition or faith".

Spiritual parents both answer:

"I N: do so promise, so mote it be".

Child then charges the Chalice of Wine, then the Sabbat Cakes. So, ends the Rite of Wiccaning.

THE WICCES
INITIATION

The Rite of Initiation into the First Degree is the acceptance by the HPs and the HP of the Coven, and of the Coven by the Initiate. The First Degree is the Level of Power.

REQUIREMENTS:

1. The Neophyte/Wiccan must have been a member of the Wiccan Circle and Community for at least 6 months and also gone through the series known as the Outer Court Lectures.

2. She/he must have attained the age of 18 years unless special circumstances exist which allow this rule to be varied by the Committee of Elders. Or unless the parents of the child are of the Wicca.

3. She/he should have a good background of the history and origin, and the meaning of Wicca.

4. She/he must realise that this is the first stage of entering the Priesthood and must be sure of their dedication before progression.

5. After Initiation the Wicce is welcomed into the Coven of Wicca with all the privileges of the First-Degree Wicce. A Wicce is now called Sister/Brother and is taught how to cast the Magick Circle, how to draw power, methods of Healing, techniques of inducing clairvoyance, how to visualise and cast spells.

They must know the basics of Herbalism, and the various Rites and Ceremonies of the Wicca. In addition, she/he is required to copy out the Book of Shadows, and absorb and learn it by heart.

SPELLCRAFT

Spells; the exact words matter little if the intent and focus is clear, you must raise the true powers, and sufficient knowledge is known and used in protection and remembering the Wiccan Rede.

Spells should always be in rhyme if possible, as there is something Magickal about rhyme. Also, it helps you to bring out your creativity in creating ritual and Spells. I have tried many without rhyme, and they seem to lose their power if you miss the rhyme, also they are easier to forget. When in rhyme they seem to say themselves without much thought or effort, so it makes it easier to remember. As any distraction or change of thought not only loses momentum but the Magick is lost. True Magick is like a river and must flow easily and gently with love and light.

Most importantly be positive that it will work, make your belief as firm as a rock, through your will and the power of the Goddess and God. If you doubt, you have already failed, and you will never succeed.

Be sure that your Spell is for the good of all concerned, harm none and love under will. Remember the Wiccan Rede as they bind you by oath.

Cast no Spell on or around anyone without their consent and knowledge.

Spells for Gain, Love & Happiness

Candle burning is a form of Magick sometimes referred to as 'Elemental Magick,' which means that it relates to one of the Four Elements; Air, Water, Fire and Earth. As one would easily guess, candle burning comes under the ruler ship of the Element of Fire. Because of this it has as its Patron the Archangel Michael, who is Lord of the Sun. But also know that all Magick is a combination of all Four Elements to make them work. With candle Magick we create and mold the Candle (Earth) we light the candle (Fire), we express our emotions with rhyme (Water) and it is carried away into the universe to do what it was intended to do (Air).

Before doing Candle Magick at all it might be advisable to align yourself with the occult rays of the Archangel Michael for as the old saying goes: "the Angels are excellent friends but terrible enemies." As Michael rules the Element of Fire he also has dominion over the Salamanders, or Elemental spirits of the flame, who are in turn ruled by an Elemental King or Djinn named Notas. These fire spirits can aid your workings but like all beings of the Elemental realms, they can cause plenty of trouble if upset.

Invoke and call upon the Archangel Michael to avoid such unfortunate incidents I would suggest that you ask for the protection and aid of the Angel of the Sun and of Fire:

"O great Winged One, Michael Archangel of the heavenly solar orb, great protector Guide me along my path of Magick that my path is true and full of your radiant Light. Lend your divine Light and Power and mold these flames with your Magick that my Spell is true and the creative fusion of my mind with your forces to be for the Good".

Then addressing the Elemental King of Fire:

"Mighty King of the Elementals, Notas Lord of flame and power of the Southern wind. I ask your Magickal help and the help of the Elementals to strengthen my Spell. Increase my power and burn deep with the Solar Light my desires that I unleash in my Spell. Great Lord of Fire in the name of the celestial Archangel Michael of the Hidden Sun".

WICCA THE WAY

Wicca the way the powers that be, for the
young and the old, the bold and the free.
The Path is to know, the Path is to see, the
way of the Ancients as it used to be.
CHORUS:
Gathered together those of the kin, in
freedom and love beyond any sin.
Merry Meet, Merry Part, 'tis union for all,
Blessed the friendship that answers the call.
All be Earth's children of Sun and of Moon,
Down through the ages we've danced to the tune.
The flow of all life through Goddess and God,
None shall forsake thee, the Sword and the Rod.
Holy the star which is worshipped in truth,
Morgaine and Merlin forever in youth.
All is the Horned One fertility Rite,
Blessed Be Diana in Love and in Light.
CHORUS
Candles and Incense and tools of the trade,
For Magus and Wiccans all debts are paid.
Praised be the elements, fire, earth, water and air,
Celebrations and Sabbats you'll find us there.
Blessed ye the Power and bind ye the Cord,
Blessed the union, Love the reward.
The song of the ages it echoes again,
Blessed the knowledge, long may it reign.
CHORUS
The Path of the Wicca, the Path of the Wise,
In Power and Glory all truth shall rise.
We stand united through ages long past,
The truth that is Wicca forever shall it last.

PROPERLY
PREPARED I
MUST ALWAYS
BE IN FULL

This means that you must not only be clean in body, but in mind, heart and soul. You must never enter the Magick Circle with any forms of negativity; you must be happy, alert and ready for the Magick of the Goddess to be invoked. This is why we are trained carefully so as to know when and what to do when negativity enters our mind. We also take on a Wiccan name to aid us in leaving our mortal lives behind and when we don ourselves with our ritual regalia, we take on our Higher Wiccan Self.

We should all have a separate set of ritual regalia or robes that are only used when we take on our higher persona and do Magick especially when entering the Magick Circle. We prefer Seekers or Wiccan Neophytes to wear natural colours of nature such as greens and browns. This helps us in being Earthed or grounded. Once you are initiated as a Wicce you then start wearing higher vibrational colours especially white with green borders and green capes. This shows your rank within the Wiccan movement, as you enter the Priesthood then your colours range through the vibrational colours of the rainbow. We prefer only the Maiden and Man in Black to wear black robes (there is a protective reason for this which will be discussed at a later stage). Your robes and regalia should be clean and ironed not all wrinkled as this shows disrespect.

Before donning yourself with your Consecrated Robes, always make sure you have bathed or showered and prepared yourself mentally. I prefer showering before ritual when I imagine that the water from the shower is a waterfall of pure light, which is cleansing and purifying my body, mind and soul. While I shower I say this prayer:

"O Gracious Goddess who has formed me in your image,
By the blessing of these flowing waters
Bless me and make me clean on all levels of body, mind and spirit.

Remove all deceit and stupidity and ignorance.
Gracious mother send forth your divine Light that I be worthy to enter your Magick Circle".

We should if possible always be barefoot when entering the Magick Circle. In Winter I recommend special shoes only worn in ritual and the Magick Circle. Do not wear any deodorants; talc or perfumes/after shaves etc. as they connect you to your mortal life and your lessor personality. When bathed and clean take up your Robe and as you dress say:

"I wear this sacred vestment robe to awaken my Higher Self, may I truly become the Wicce that I am within. May this robe awaken my soul for the journey that lies ahead on the Path of Light".

Take up your Consecrated Tabard, which goes over your Robe, and say as you dress:

"I wear this sacred vestment Tabard; may it be a shield of faith to protect me and keep me safe? May it be a symbol of strength and calm"?

Take up your Consecrated Pentacle that is worn about your neck and say as you place it on you:

"I wear my Consecrated Pentacle as a symbol and a shield of my chosen Path of Elphane to the world. May it be a magnet to attract all positivity and a shield to repel all negativity"?

Taking up your Cape as you wrap it about you say:

"I wear this vestment Cape to keep me warm, to raise my Spirit, and if need to become the Cape of Invisibility when and if danger threatens".

If you have a Coronet or Crown, as you place it on your head say:

"May this Crown of the Stars, my coronet of the Moon elevates my life and illumine my mind to the foot stool of the Goddess. May it shine brightly as a beacon to all who are called to the Goddess and her Magick? May it show all my dedication as a Priestess of the Luna Mysteries".

You are all now readied for the Magick Circle, the only thing left to do is anoint yourself with your Consecrated Oil, but this is usually done within the Magick Circle.

THE WICCES RUNE

*"Darksome night and shining Moon, East
then south, then west then North.*

Harken to the Wicces Rune. Here I come to call you forth.
Earth and Water, Air and Fire, Harken ye to my desire.
Wand and Pentacle and Sword, Harken you to my desire.

Wand and Pentacle and sword, Harken you to my word,
Cords and Cense, Scourge and Knife,
the powers of the Wicces blade.
Waken all ye unto life, come ye as the charm is made.
Queen of heaven, Queen of Hel, with
Horned Hunter of the night,
Lend your power unto my Spell and
work my Will by Magick Rite.

By all the Power of land and sea, by all
the might of Moon and Sun,
As I do Will so mote it be, chant the Spell and be it done!

Eko, Eko Azarak, Eko Eko Zomelak,
Eko Eko Aradia, Eko Eko Cernunnos".

CONSECRATION OF WATER AND SALT

As I stated before all religions have Consecrated or Holy Water, they are basically all the same combining the salt and water to make it pure with a Blessing. Wicca is not different we too have out Consecrated Water. It is best to use Spring Water or water from a stream if not available then clean water from the tap are fine if it has been kept in the refrigerator as this makes it more receptive to the salt and the Blessing.

In our Magick Circle the Chalice of Water resides on either the Altar which is in the North, or on a small Altar positioned in the West of your Temple. The vessel that was once a Goblet is now through being consecrated ritually has now become a Ceremonial Chalice, which represents the sacred Womb of Life, which is metaphysically the Womb of the Great Mother Goddess. Your Chalice should be filled with pure water and ready to be blessed; in fact, it will be exorcised, as all waters are unclean on a deeper level. When exorcising your Water take up your Chalice and facing the West, place your power hand on top and your weaker hand on the bottom of the Chalice and say:

> *"O sacred Fount of the Great Mother Goddess,*
> *The Womb and tomb of Life, death and rebirth.*
> *Holder of the Living Waters, I exorcise you and cast out all impurities.*
> *I bless you with the radiance of pure divine Light.*
> *Be thou Consecrated Faithful Waters of Life, be pure in our service in the*
> *divine name of the First Mother and Father of the Old religion".*

Now place a few grains of rock salt or sea salt onto your Altar Pentacle, and facing North present it to the Gods, place your power hand on top and your weaker hand on the bottom. Visualise energy flowing through your hands into the salt and say:

> *"O Sacred Seal of the Goddess, Key to the Portals of other dimensions, sacred*
> *Knowledge holder of our Ancestors, we call upon your Magickal powers to awaken your*
> *servants – Azarak and Zomelak to bless this salt and make it pure on all levels.*

*Let it be the healing source of all life, thus are you Consecrated and truly blessed in
the names of the Goddess Aradia and the Horned God Cernunnos".*

Now mixing them around together, feel them mingle and become one within the Chalice and say:

*"As salt and water become one, so shall all things become one.
May we all be in balance each with the other?
Heaven and Earth be One, Night and day be One,
Man and Woman be One, Goddess and God be One".*

THE FOUR
QUARTERS OF
THE MAGICK
CIRCLE

The Magick Circle has four Cardinal Points, which are East, South, West and North. But in our reality, there are eight Power Points of the Magick Circle, so by adding the Cross-Quarters we have Northeast, Southeast, Southwest and Northwest. Plus, the two directions or polarities that tie them all together above and below.

The East: is the place of the Rising Sun, the dawn of new beginnings. The first stirrings of life as we know it. With the rising Sun all life awakens and sets out on their daily tasks. It is the Air Element where the sacred breath of the Goddess enters our lungs and all life, and keeps us connected by Her sacred breath. All vibrant youthful masculine energy enters in through the East; it is a masculine realm and is of the Mind. It is the Mental Plane - The Intellectual Realm where all thoughts are created and so eventually directed to the other realms to make them a reality on all levels. It is the place of Change and is also the Creative realm. The colours are blues, greys and whites.

When we use the Ancient Tarot Cards, we find that it relates to the Wands, which are grown from branches of trees and held high in the air. The Wands are for focus and direction, for Will power and for Innocence and starting anew. It is about Listening and learning especially during the Season of Spring, which also is associated with the East. It is here that we are ruled by the Astral World, this is the world of Magickal Creations assisted by its Element Air and their ruling Elementals - Sylphides. The Shining One associated with communication is Raphael Archangel of the East.

The East wind is called Euras, and we invoke his energies to assist our Elemental Magick from the East. The Divine teachers of this realm are Thoth, Osiris, Khepera, Aurora, Freya, Apollo, Orpheus, Mercury, Prometheus, Quetzalcoatl and Iduna. The Enlightened Magicians or Sages of Old are Merlin, Nerada, Serapis, Jesus, Imhotep, Khamua, Set and Buddha.

Women bring Power to the Magick Circle; in truth she is the strongest on the Inner Levels and in deeper touch with the fluid worlds of the Astral Plane. A male Wicce is best at directing that power once it has been passed onto to him. He is at his strongest on the Physical Plane.

Of course, in the Arts of Magick this alternates through the Planes, as there are and have been good female Magi, but in general it is best for a male to be the Keeper of the East.

In the Magick Circle it is the High Priest who holds all Magick together, dignity of bearing and calmness of the mind are attributes for every Wiccan to activate. Traditionally the High Priest is also responsible for all behaviour within the Magick Circle, but in our Circles, it is the Man in Black who takes on this responsibility. We call him affectionately "The Coven Cop".

The Astral Plane is called Yetzirah.

South: is the Realm of the Element of Fire, and the Powers of the Noon Day Sun. The Season is summer especially at its highest and hottest times. The colours associated with this Realm are reds, gold's, yellows and pinks. It is the sacred space of the Heart and connects to your Heart Chakra; it is the power of man and represents action. Its Power is of the mature wise man as a warrior. With flaming hair and robes matching. When using the Tarot cards, it is where you would place the suit of Swords or Athame's. The Elementals are Salamanders or Dragons who are Guardians of the South and Protector of Mother Earth. The South is a place of love, honour, vigour, courage and strength.

The other symbols associated with this Realm are the Ceremonial Sword, Athame, Ritual dagger, Shield, Bow and Arrow, the Chariot, the Flaming Torch, the Hammer and the Anvil, the Double Headed Axe, the Winged Disc, the Eye of the God Ra and the Lyre. The Shining One (Angel) as Keeper of this Realm is Michael, and the South Wind is called Notas. The Gods associated with the South include Mars, Helios as the Sun God, Ra, Athena, Brigid, Bran, Vulcan, and Hephaestus. The Enlighteners and divine teachers to the world are Arthur, Hercules, Llew, Gawain, Aesculapius and Chiron. Our Keeper and Warden of the South must be loyal and courageous, he should not be easily scared or upset, he is responsible for the safety of those within the Magick Circle second to the Man in Black.

The Kabbalistic God name for this Realm is Adonai and it is called the realm of Binah, which is the Creative World.

West: the Element of Water. It is the direction of Life Eternal. All feminine and psychic energy comes in through the West. The colours associated with this Realm are greens, silvers, whites, greys, mauves and purples. It is the Realm of the Womb, the sacred Cauldron of Cerridwen, and the Holy Grail of Immortality. It is the Realm of Fertility of Life and Love. When using the Tarot cards, you would place the Cups/Chalices in this direction as they represent the Womb and the Tomb the Realm of Life, Death and Rebirth. The Season is autumn, and the lessons to learn are about letting go of unimportant things or things that keep you tied to your past. The time associated with rituals in the West is at Sunset/Dusk. When all Magick kisses the Earth and the invisible within the visible awakens.

The Shining One known as Gabriel governs it, it is the Spiritual Realm known as the Divine World or in the Kabbalah is called Atziluth, the realm of Magick and Psychic energies. The Elementals are Undines, Water Sprites, Mermaids and the like. This Realm is the point of contact between all levels on the Inner. The Keeper or Warden of the West should be a woman with some psychic power; her task in the Magick Circle is to mediate the influence of the Inner levels, to become a point of communication using the Polarity of the West and East to achieve this balance and harmony.

The Symbols associated with this realm are the Chalice, Cauldron, Shells, Caves, Oceans, Ponds, and lakes, the Moon, the Womb and the Tomb. The Gods of this realm are Isis, Nephthys, Sin, Artemis, Selene, Hecate, Cerridwen, Diana, Ishtar, Aphrodite, Neptune and Poseidon. The Enlighteners and teachers are Oannes, Dagon, Ea., Hypatia the Virgin and Inanna. The Keeper or Warden of the West should be a woman who is a Seer, the Oracle of the Magick Circle; she must be honest, perceptive and truthful with herself and with all her sisters and brothers of the Craft on all levels. Of all the other Quarters and Portals or gateways of the Magick Circle this is the one through which all the Power of the Magick Circle will enter. The Kabbalistic God of this Realm is Eh-he-heh, and the West wind is called Zephyrus.

North: The Element of Earth. This is the most important direction of your Magick Circle as it is the direction of our Ancestors, of the Ancient Ones, and more importantly the Throne Realm of the Great Earth Mother and the Horned God, and where we place the Altar of the Mysteries. It is where all balanced energy enters the Magick Circle. The colours associated with this realm are russets, browns, blacks and greens. It is the World of Physicality, Solidarity and Intrigue. Being the Element of Earth, it is about all things physical, and its Elementals are Gnomes, Elves, Gremlins, Wood Sprites, and Unicorns.

The Season associated with this realm is winter and the most powerful time for your rituals are to be at midnight. It is the Material World and is also called by Kabbalistic Assiah. The Keeper or Warden of the North should be a woman with an affinity with the Earth and Nature, growing things, an herbalist. As the emphasis here is on growth both actual and spiritual, on benevolence and understanding of the needs of all life whether it is human, animal, fish, bird, tree or rock. They should be deeply attuned to nature in all her forms.

The symbols associated with the North are the Cornucopia, the basket, sickle, flail, scourge, plough, horn, seed, furrow, spindle, corn dolly, corn, wheat sheaf, scythe, the Altar and the Altar Pentacle with its sacred Sigils engraved or etched onto it. The Gods of this realm are Pluto, Ge, Gaia, Rhiannon, Cerridwen, Morrigan, Hathor, Demeter, Kore, Persephone, Ceres, Flora, Virgo and Changing Woman.

HIGHER
MEDITATION

"Meditation is the act of quieting the mind to "listen", and I mean truly to the inner communications that come from the Higher Self." It is about letting the mortal self-fade and the higher you come into being.

"Meditation techniques are discovered naturally by infants and little children: Holding their breath, staring unblinking, standing on their heads, imitating animals, turning in circles, sitting unmoving and repeating phrases over and over until all else ceases to exist. Look at the world around you as if you have just arrived on Earth. Observe the elements, air, water and fire in relation to our Earth. Rocks in their natural formations, the trees rooted in the ground, their branches reaching to the sky, the plants, animals and the inter-relationships of each to the other. See a flower through its essence, a mountain through its massiveness. When the mind allows its objects to remain unmolested, there may be No mind and no object – just breath unity."

Surya Singer

High Meditation is a technique of mind control that produces a feeling of tranquility and peacefulness that can lead to Transcendental Awareness and eventually what we term as spiritual Bliss. True deep meditation has thousands of differing techniques and styles depending on the culture of where it stems from. For the Wicce it is an excellent tool for absolute self-development and genuine spiritual ascension. Relaxation and empowerment are the basis for all forms of meditation, but the higher and deeper side of meditation is for strengthening Magickal and all psychic powers.

In deep transcendental meditation we take a long deep look at our Inner and Higher world, and hopefully find the answers and a deeper understanding of ourselves and of the Higher Truth that we have been seeking on our journey of the Spirit. To have this there must be a genuine shift of our mental and emotional conditioning that has been with us from childhood. We must become more open and sincere with our Natural environment, to the real beauty and immense living colours that Mother Nature reveals, but we need to take the time to stop and really look at the world around us, instead of just fleeting glances. If we connect our Higher Self with the higher frequency of every living thing, then we will be also in a higher frequency and able to communicate and learn at a deeper level of understanding.

Deep meditation is called "Samadhi", this is where the mind is completely merged with all that is, physically, mentally, Astrally, psychically and spiritually. This is the true world of perfect harmony, bliss and perfect spirit. By being at One with the outer world, it will help us to increase our sensitivity not only to the self but also to all forces on a higher level or vibration. Meditation usually precedes every Wiccan Esbat or Sabbat and is included in many of our rituals. Wiccans should meditate daily to be in touch with Deity and our inner Spirituality. I usually "close down" with a Self-Blessing.

Truth: You have seen through my writings that I mention Truth a lot, by this I do not mean telling fibs or truths, but by the ultimate realization that we are not just of one Realm, that we are a part of several levels of awareness; the physical, mental, astral, psychic and spiritual. What we are searching for spiritually is the Truth of our inner being within all these levels of awareness. In Wicca it is about acknowledging our "Shadow" and learning not to be afraid of confronting it as a Higher Being.

True Self: This is the awakening, meeting and knowing of three very powerful archetypes.

The Shadow: Is the dark side of our nature that we do not want to confront, the part of us we dislike, and do not want others to know or see. We try so hard to reject this side of our nature, but it can never be ignored, as it is part of our makeup. It is the part that we try to push deep down within us, so it cannot show its ugly head. But as a Wicce we need to confront our Shadow, see the true face of our darkness, forgive it and trust in your Higher Self to ascend beyond this Shadow.

The Anima/ Animus: Our sex is determined by the predominance of the corresponding genes, as each human derives from masculine and feminine genes. But sometimes-even Mother Nature screws up and we are born with a genetic variance. In man the conscious mind of man has the masculine sign, whilst the unconscious is feminine in nature and the opposite for women.

The Sage: is the old man or old woman that resides in our very unconsciousness. We are aware of her or him in our dreams and in our Higher Magickal Rituals. This Wise Crone or Magi is our true Higher Self. This Self has the combination of past, present and future personalities and collective of experiences that connects with the Goddess on all levels.

MEDITATING OF SOME GODS AND GODDESSES

I have been to Egypt several times and sat by the sacred Nile River and meditated on the Gods and Goddess of the ancient world. I have visualized the Goddess Isis, Hathor, Nut, Maat, and many more and found that the most sacred sound for invoking them is the ancient vibrations of their names. I have entered the Holy of Holies at the Temples of the Goddess Isis and Hathor, the Temples of Ra, Osiris, Horus, and more and meditated upon their names and personage. I found that that with each echoing and vibrating God name is the equal calling of power and spirit, an ancient power and spirit that still lives in this world of the 21st century. Sounds symbolize at the auditory level what geometrical designs do at the visual. Their repetition provides keys to the unconscious in a way denied to other sounds.

Horus: (Ha-ru)   Son of Asar and Aset the falcon-headed God of the skies and the Underworld and symbol of the link between matter and spirit; Horus represents the elevating of the divine spirit soaring into the heavens. Vibrate the name (Hor-uuus - Haaa-ru).

Thoth: (Toth) The arch Mage of Saiss High Priest of both Upper and Lower Egypt, the Ibis-headed Moon God of knowledge, writing, mathematics, and Magick; he is the true Enlightener of wisdom to the world that awaits us on the spiritual journey of the Tarot and its deeper meanings and understandings.

Isis: (The Greek Name) more correctly by Her Egyptian name Aset: **(Or-seta)** the Goddess of Magickal power and the symbolic mother of Horus, the Goddess of love, Magick and compassion. Aset is depicted as a woman with a solar disk between the cow horns on her head (likened unto the Goddess Hathor) or crowned with a throne, but also with the child Horus sitting on her lap. A vulture was sometimes pictured and incorporated into her crown. Also, she was sometimes depicted as a kite above the mummified body of Osiris. Aset's popularity lasted far into the Roman era. She had her own priests and hundreds of temples were erected in her honor all over the known world.

Osiris: (The Greek Name) more correctly by His Egyptian name Asar (Ay-sah) Husband and brother of Aset and Nephthys; he was God of the afterlife. He who resurrected all into a new life in the new world once this existence was finalized.

Nephthys: Aset's sister and protector of the Pharaohs, the protector and nurturing strength that cares for mankind.

Anubis: the jackal-headed God of the sacred land of Amenti, guide and protector of the soul in death, he rids us of the destruction of fear, and then provides of a safe passage through the hallways of death.

Meditating on any Goddesses and Gods involve much correct visualisation and the repetition of their sacred and true names. Learn about these Goddesses and Gods prior to Meditating or invoking them blindly. When you can truly contact your deity, they may assist in taking you with them on a journey into their world and Temple to learn more of their Mysteries. Look at the beginning of this book to get a bigger picture of how to do this by using the Trance State Portals.

THE WICCANING
OF AN ADULT

The Crafting:

The Rite of Crafting was designed to:

- Bless, Consecrate and awaken the Inner Wicce into their new Path with the names of the Ancient Ones and the Great Mother Goddess and Horned God.
- It was also enacted to make an oath of secrecy from a prospective Wicce to our ceremonies, rituals and festivals and to the secrets and knowledge of the Old Religion.
- It was also to introduce a Prospective Wicce to the ancient Mysteries of the Great Mother Goddess and the Horned God.

Requirements Are:

- The Seeker of the Inner Mysteries of Wicca must be interested in studying and learning more of the Wicca, and may commence on the journey of Metaphysics and Magick.
- The Seeker must have expressed to learn more of the Wicca and honour and worship the Great Mother Goddess and the Horned God.
- That they are also seeking likeminded Fellowship with the Wiccans of our Community.

The Abjuration

"I abjure you - Child of the Earth, Silence your
thoughts and fix your whole attention on the Great
Mother Goddess, to whom you do not see yet,
and feel within your heart and soul.
Merge into one sense, all senses of love and truth if you would
be secure against your foe. As it is by that sense alone which lies
concealed within the depths of your own ancient brain that the
steep and hard path will lead you to your Goddess will be revealed
before your dim eyes. Long and weary is the way of the Wiccan,
but know that a single thought of doubt and
of your past will drag you down,
and you will have to start your climb anew.

Kill in yourself all memories of past experiences of trouble and doubt,
as you are on a rainbow pathway to the Divine.
Look not behind you or you will be lost, as
your path leads you into your future.
Unless you truly hear, you cannot see, And
unless you truly see, you cannot hear.
Be always humble if you wish to attain to higher wisdom,
be humbler still when wisdom you have mastered. Be like
the ocean, which receives all rivers and streams. The oceans
mighty calm remains unmoved it feels them not
but is aware of their merging.

And know full well that before entering the Magic Circle that
many are called Gods and likewise with the names of the
Goddess are as grains of sand in number, but there is only one
source of Baptism in the Dominion of the Earth. Your Goddess
commands you TO KNOW-TO WILL-TODARE. The Goddess
councils you to keep your silence, experiences the desires of the
Goddess and then you will know the ecstasy of the Gods.

The Rite of Crafting

LBRP is performed first.

Casting of the Magick Circle is then performed.

Singing and dancing the Wicces Rune raise the Power. Then a doorway is cut in the Northeast to allow the Seeker entrance into the Magick Circle, after which it is then closed so as to not lose any power that has been raised. The Seeker is then brought forth robed and blindfolded. At the entrance they are challenged by the High Priestess (HPs) with her hand on their heart saying:

> *"Blessed Be and welcome to this Magick Circle the Temple of Wicca, although you are welcomed are you truly willing to be of this Fellowship, to accept its disciplines and observe its laws, and accept with an open heart all that you will see and be taught"?*

Answer: is given by the Seeker.

> *"Do you still with a true heart seek entrance into this Magick Circle with trust and love and a yearning to be closer to the Goddess"?*

Answer: is given by the Seeker. If answered yes, then they are escorted and led into the Magick Circle by the Maiden and Man in Black who takes them to the respective Watchtowers facing outwards saying:

> *"Mighty Ladies and Lords of the East (south, west and north respectively) Behold N: _____ who is presented in our Magick Circle and desires to be Crafted into the Mysteries of the Old Religion of Wicca, and in the names of the Mother Goddess Aradia and Father God Cernunnos".*

Then proceed to south, west and north respectively with the same. After presentation at the Watchtowers the Seeker is facing the Northern Altar of the Mysteries and asked:

"N: _____ do you openly and willingly deny any previous rites of dedication or baptisms that you may have entered into, and now before the presence of this Coven and the Goddess and God, re-affirm your decision to be Wiccan as a true Child of the Earth"?

Seeker: answers.

The Seeker is then asked and assisted to lie in prone position, head in the North, arms outstretched and legs together. The HPs then standing over the Seeker Invokes:

"Earth and Water, Air and Fire, Harken you to my desire.
Work my Will by Magick Rite and lend your powers to me this night".

After a slight pause HPs continues saying:

"Gracious Mother Goddess whose name is legion, Great Goddess of the Mysteries of Wicca, Mother of us all. Be here with us this night and bless this Child of the Stars and of the Living Earth. Bestow on N: _____ your true Blessing and make him of the Wicca in your divine name. Mighty Mother takes from him the impurities and torments that bind him to the world of mortals?

HPs then kneels and consecrates the Seeker by the laying on of hands saying:

Laying hands over eyes saying:

"I take from you your true sight for it is dimmed and sees only ugliness and dark shadows".

Laying hands over mouth saying:

"I take from you your ancient breath from which is manifested
only untruths and words of darkness".

Laying hands over heart saying:

"Take from you the beat of your heart for it beats without true divine love".

Laying hands above genitalia saying:

"I take from you your seeds of life from which only grows lust".

Laying hands on both feet saying:

"And from your feet I take the Living earth, for your feet have lead you on a path to nowhere".

After a short pause HPs continues saying:

"Great Shining Ones of this Magick Circle, Great Mother and Father of the Mysteries. This mortal lives no more, her/his body lies still, and she/he is no longer tormented by the evil of this world. She/he has given her/his life in the true Quest of the Mysteries of the Living Earth and the Universe. I pray you mighty Mother and Father lend your divine powers of life that she/he may be reborn into a life of love and beauty".

After a short pause the HPs kneels and anoints with oil saying:

Anointing feet first with an Earth Invoking Pentagram saying:

"Blessed Be your feet that shall walk upon the Living Earth and ascend to the Stars on the ancient path of Wicca".

Anointing the knee's saying:

"Blessed Be your knees that shall kneel in humility to all of life especially the sacred Altars of the Goddess and God".

Anointing the genitalia region saying:

"Blessed Be your Womb/Phallus without which we would not be, to you do I give the sacred Seeds of Life that you will know your immortality".

Anointing breasts/chest saying:

"Blessed be your breasts/chest shield of your heart of strength and love. To you I give and awaken your true heartbeat that you may love all life and in all life, you will know the Goddess".

Anointing the lips saying:

"Blessed be your lips that shall speak the Magickal names of the Goddess and God of our Mysteries. To you I awaken and give your true breath of life of the Goddess which breathes life into all life".

Removing the blindfold and asking that they keep their eyes closed, anointing and saying:

> *"Blessed be your eyes, to you I give and open your true Inner Sight that you may
> see true beauty in all Life and in all Life, see the face of the Goddess".*

The Wiccan is now asked to open their eyes and as they do they are looking deep into the eyes of their HPs, this lasts for a minute sharing that oneness and connection of rebirth into a new a beautiful path, as She is now her/his new Spiritual Mother. HPs then kisses them on the forehead and says:

> *"Blessed Be N: _____ you have been reborn into a new life of Love and Beauty and
> I anoint you and give you the Name of N: _____ Blessed Be consecrated child of the
> Living Earth, arise and meet your fellow sisters and brothers of your new Spiritual family".*

MiB and Maiden assist them to rise, and they are taken to the Watchtowers and presented again but this time under their new name as a Wiccan, saying:

> *"Mighty Ladies and Lords of the Watchtowers of the East (South, West and North
> Respectively) and the Elementals of Air (Fire, Water, and Earth respectively) Behold
> N: _____ who has been reborn into the Tradition of Elphane and of the
> Temple of Wicca. Give them your blessing and welcome them always".*

Continue around the Magick Circle respectively to the other Quarters ending in the North. They are then presented to all the other members of the Circle with the Elder of the Temple being last, they hug, and the Elder says:

> *"N: _____ are you willing to know and learn the Mysteries of your own true Being?"*

Answer is given:

> *"To learn is to suffer, and to suffer is to learn. You must ever give of yourself freely and without
> hesitation. For your love will be shared by all. So, give freely and without hesitation. For as
> you give, so shall you be given. For here lies a Mystery. It is a hard road walk it with pride".*

HP: steps forward and take up the Sword and it is handed to the Wiccan saying:

> *"Repeat after me".*

I am here a simple servant, holding my Goddess in honour. Long have I searched,
and far have I journeyed seeking that which I desire above all other things.
I know that if I find not the spark of light within me, I will never find it without. For Love is
the law and Love is our Bond. All this I do swear and do honour above all else so mote it be!

HPs /HP now kneels before the new Wiccan and holds the Chalice of Wine as they place their hands over the Chalice and Bless it with their own words of Blessing. They do the same with the Sabbat Cakes. Both are placed back on the Altar as HPs /HP presents them with their Singulum (Green Magick Cord). Which has been Consecrated and is now tied around the waist of the Wiccan, and now with the HPs /Hp take the Wine and Cakes around the Circle Deosil presenting them to all to partake in, and again share and congratulate the new Wiccan into their fold.

A Toast is then done to the Goddess and God.

The Magick Circle is then closed, and Cleared as Agape is prepared.

Merry meet, Merry Part and Merry Meet Again!

THE SINGULUM
LADDER TO THE GODDESS

The Wicces Singulum, or "Girdle of the Goddess", or "Ladder to the Goddess", is not only a symbol of Sacred Space, but it is a ladder to the lessons of a Wicce marked by several knots geometrically and mathematically placed at set intervals on the Singulum. It is nine feet in length, and aids in measuring out the correct measurement of the Wicces Magick Circle, the Temple of the Old Religion.

Traditionally it is nine feet long, which is 108 inches, 1 and 8 also equals 9, which is the Magickal number of the Moon and the Magick Circle, the Microcosm and the Macrocosm. (As Above, So Below). The Moon is 2160 miles round, so on a scale of 1 inch to every 10 miles, the Wicce is tracing out the Moons measurements as our Magick Circle with their Magick Singulum which is in truth the microcosm (The Magick Circle) of the macrocosm The Moon).

Using the Magick Sword or Wicces Athame as the central pivot, the Magick Circle has now proportionately the same diameter as the Moon, which represents our Astral Temple to the Goddess and God. The micro-macrocosmic worlds - our Astral Plane. The Sword therefore is a symbol of Infinity and stands erect in the centre of the Magick Circle, the point within the living Earth. The point has no magnitude of Space, but from it, with the Singulum creates our Sacred Space, our Magick Circle.

Singulum Magic
Cord Magic

This Spell is used when you have lost something or someone. It is a "Finding Spell". Visualise in your mind what has been lost, see it clearly and then do your Spell using your Consecrated Singulum, preferably within a Magick Circle.

> "CORD TWINE AND CORD CREEP,
> CORD SEARCH AND CORD SEEK.
> CORD SPELLED, AND CORD BLESSED.
> AIR SPIRIT, GUIDE ME IN MY QUEST.
>
> CORD MOVE, AND CORD SEARCH,
> CORD LOOK AND CORD LURCH.
> CORD TURN AND CORD TWIST AND CORD RUN,
> HOOP AND TWINE MY SPELLS BEGUN.
>
> CORD SEEK AND SEARCH AND SEARCH TO FIND,
> BLESSED BE SACRED CORD ENTWINED."

Allow visions to come, show you where the lost item is, focus on the surrounds and find with your mind what has been lost. It may take time, it may even come in dreams or when unexpected.

SHAMANISM

Shamanism another form of Wiccecraft is the most ancient primordial way in which humanity searched for a connection with all life on the planet, and in the search for the Creator of all that was. The origins of shamanism go back at least 50,000 – 60,000 years, back to the primitive Stone Age man. The difference between the true Shaman and normal man is that Shamans and Wicces see patterns in everything, they see the life-force as swirling patterns of energy, they see the auras of each living thing. They say that man has evolved from Shamanic cultures, maybe they have on an industrial and scientific level, but they will never reach the advancement and true ascended evolution of the spiritual Shaman, the rest of mankind has digressed.

Shamanism has absolute universal applications and is found in every land and culture on our planet. Shamanism is the basis of every spiritual path, wherever we live and whatever we believe. It has been the very path of all knowledge thanks to our ancestors and their very ceremonies, insight, rituals and deep meditations that through trial and tests and given us the knowledge that we now have for the benefit of all humanity. Whether it is science, medicine, food, building, sculpting, or understanding Nature.

The Shaman like the Wicce are "same, same but different". Both have drastically changed through the eons; the sad thing is that we have lost so much through ignorance and pride. The old saying is that the Shaman walks with one foot in the everyday world and one foot in the Spirit world! Shamanism is about true dedication and a lot of very timely study, meditation, visualization and research, but it is also about the courage to go where most fear to tread. It is about closing your physical eyes long enough to allow your inner sight to see the Truth behind everything, and learning to understand its vibration and MEANING. The Shaman knows that there is a special relationship between man and everything else, it's just that many of us have disassociated ourselves with the rest of the world due to lack of interest or brainwashing techniques that it is all fantasy and make believe.

In our Magick Circles we fill it with ancient Shamanic practices such as ritual singing, chanting, dancing, humming, and anything else that has a rhythm. We use the Didgeridoo, which is used by our HP and Bard, Asherah. Instead of cutting out our Magick Circle with a Sword we use the Didgeridoo to awaken the ancestral energies of the Australian land. We also use the Drum on certain occasions to welcome everyone into our Magick Circle by drumming them and awakening their Chakra's and connecting them to the heartbeat of the Magick Circle and the Goddess. We also use the Rattle as uplift spiritually to help s ascend the spiritual ladder. The use of any of these Tools or instruments if used constantly with repetition influences our energy patterns and elevates our brain waves to a more primordial and Earthy connection to the Earth, whereas others help us to go to Higher states of Consciousness.

POINTS ABOUT THE SHAMANIC DRUM:

- The drum is the Shaman's 'horse'.
- Awakening the Chakra's
- Soul Retrieval Ceremonies
- Calling to the Inner Child, Inner Adult, Inner Old One.
- Power Animal Retrieval
- Transferring Magickal Power to the Earth
- Finding your Animal Totem
- Elevating ones Soul
- Trance Dancing
- Calling to the Ancestors

The Shaman uses the rhythmical sounds to enter an altered state of consciousness, traditionally from drumming as it can slow or elevate the heart rate which keeps in unison with the drum. I have found that certain vibrational sounds help us to connect specific aspects of nature and the spirit world. Certain tones or sounds such as AH, AY, EE, EYE, OH OO, AR, I, each have the energy to take us to different places, whether the physical, mental, astral, psychic or spiritual.

If the Shaman constantly uses the Rattle or Drum, it can take you into a very deep meditational state, and even into a trance state that takes us to the altered state of consciousness. Brain research reveals that drumming above 205 beats per minute has an incredible effect on the brains electrical impulses that includes both alpha and the theta rhythms. As a Shaman you have to divide your life into three Otherworld's: The Lower World, The Middle World and the Upper World.

- **The Lower World**   this is where our ancient primordial animal-like powers dwell, it is the place of instinctual knowing. This appears like the Middle World but is not physical, but here you can find Earthy assistance and guidance.
- **The Middle World**   Although it is the Physical Realm it is also the paralleled Astral World, this is where all Physical phenomena occur, such as hunches, vibrations, feelings, telepathy, intuition, ESP, Astral thought forms, and all, weird and Magickal things

occur. The Middle World is where disease and sickness manifest before the Physical body has the effects. This is where the Shaman starts his healing process by clearing and working on the Astral or Magickal Realm first, thus alleviating the possibility of it occurring in the Physical. The Shaman has many great tricks to be rid of disease, pain, sickness and suffering by using his "Psychic darts" which are Magickly shot into the area afflicted.

- **The Upper World**   is the World of Spirit. Here you will find the Shining Ones, Spirit Guides, Totem Animals, Cosmic beings, Deity, The Enlighteners, and the Ancestors who will come to you in human form. These great entities are Higher Vibrations and usually revealed as translucent and radiating an auric field of light. In ascending to the Spirit world, you have to go through a membrane, which breaks as you go through. No World is better or superior to any of the others, as they are all complimentary to each other and equal in their levels. All of these worlds need the other, for without one of these worlds the others will also cease to exist. Remember Thoth's maxim: (As Above, so below, as within so without).

SHAMANIC CALENDAR

For the Shaman or Wicce of the 21st century you should be working on or near an ancient site that is near you, if you are allowed. Sometimes you need to get permission to enter these sacred places. These places still retain a lot of the original power and energy from the Shamans of the past.

In Perth, Western Australia, my home is a sacred site known as 'Boulder Rock', it is about 40 kilometres from the city, and has incredible energy, and Wicces of Perth for over 40 years for major festival gatherings, and certain Initiations have used this energy. Together with the ancient site powers and new Wiccan powers this site has become very special to modern day Wiccans and Wicces.

If there is no such sacred site near you or available to you, then the next best thing is to create your own sacred site, your own Magick Circle of stones somewhere in the forest or bush away from gazing eyes and people that may just cross your path and stress out by calling the police. It does not matter where your Magick Circle is, what matters the most is that you reawaken the Earths energies within and around it, as all places on the Earth are sacred. Whenever we think of Shamans we picture in our minds the Shamans and medicine men of Native America and of South America. But the first Shamans were of Europe, Africa and The Blessed Isles.

The ancient Samethoi, the first peoples of the Blessed Isles were Shamans and Shamanka's and from them and their ancient lineage we get our present Magickal Shamans and Wicces of today and with them the Magickal Calendars. Some of the oldest Calendars were found as artefacts at Coligney, etched on sheets of bronze and bone, which gives an astounding accuracy to the seasonal changes and into the very changes in nature herself, and the celestial changes of the Sun, Moon and Planets.

If we look at the days of the week they are named after the Seven Known planets of our solar system.

Monday	Moons day	ruled over by Luna and Diana and all Moon Goddesses.
Tuesday	Tiwsday	ruled over by Mars and Aries.
Wednesday	Wodensday	ruled over by Woden, Odin and Mercury.
Thursday	Thorsday	ruled over by Thor and Jupiter.
Friday	Freyasday	ruled over by Freya and Venus.
Saturday	Saturnaliaday	ruled over by Saturn.
Sunday	Sunsday	ruled over by Apollo and the Sun.

Even our months are named after Gods and Goddess:

January	Janus
February	Februa
March	Mars
April	Aphrodite
May	Maia
June	Juno
July	Julius Caesar
August	Augustus
September	Eostre the 7th month
October	the 8th month
November	the 9th month
December	the 10th month.

If we look at the ancient Calendar of the Wicces we see the same rhythms and changes of the four Seasons, and then when we add the cross quarter times to these they don't correspond to the modern months, but represent the agricultural and hunting cycles of the ancients in their search for food sources, and when the best time was to seek them out. Below are the original Gaelic names and approximate times as shown by the ancient Coligney Calender they are Southern Hemisphere times:

Gaelic Name	English	Times
Samionos	Seed time/ Autumn	April/ May
Dumannios	Dark Depths	May/June
Riuros	Coldest Time	June/July
Anagantios	Stay Home Time	July/August
Ogronios	Time of Ice	August/September
Celtios	Times of Winds	September/October
Giamonos	Growing Shoots	October/November
Samivisionos	Time of Brightness	November/December
Equos	Horse Time	December/January
Elembiuos	Claim Time	January/February
Edrionos	Arbitration Time	February/March
Cantlos	Song Time	March/April

These dates are for the Southern Hemisphere, for the Northern Hemisphere just adjusts accordingly (opposite). Knowing these you can also see where each Full moon resides and what power they too have over the Seasons. They align with our Festivals of today:

Samhain	Halloween	30th April	Wicces New Year's Eve.
Winter Solstice	Yule	21st June	Life triumphs over death.
Imbolg	Candlemas	1st August	Purification and Initiation.
Spring Equinox	Ostara	21st September	Conception, new birth.
Beltane	Bale Fires	31st October	Passion and fertility
Midsummer	Litha	21st December	Day of Power
Lughnasadh	Lammas	2nd February	Harvest
Autumn Equinox	Fall	21st March	End of Harvest

These dates are almost Universal, and knowing these you can even add your totem animals for the land you live on, and add them also herbs, crystals, trees, birds, etc to your Wicces calendar. It can also be a tree calendar or whatever you feel is the balance and harmony of that time of the Seasonal Wheel.

THE ANCIENT
DRAGON DANCE

Wicces believe that the Goddess and God gift all our power to us. That we also have within us an innate latent power that needs to be awakened and then released using the Wicces Tools and the Eightfold Paths of Enlightenment, this is known as Etheric or Akashic Power, or Light of the Spirit force.

That is why we believe that clothing dilutes or absorbs that power which is raised by our bodies, which is why many Wicces prefer to be Skyclad (naked), this way the energy is not absorbed into our clothing and then taken out of the Circle into our everyday life to run willy-nilly. For these reasons many also wear ceremonial robes that are only used within the Magick Circle. But I feel when we have a specific and higher ritual to be done, we need all the power that can be raised, so being Skyclad helps us in raising the ancient and Mystical Wicces "Cone of Power". We in our Temples usually wear Robes and are only skyclad on Initiations and with serious Magickal Ceremonies, which is rare. The ease with which the power can be released is in part a matter of practise. It takes time, but all things of learning and importance take dedication and time. It is also a matter of the Moon and quite possibly a matter of strengths of certain celestial influences that are invoked.

Many Wiccans are aware that the Moon affects the emotions and moods of us; it has a massive effect especially on those who are either Spirituality advanced or scientifically unstable and mentally ill. The Moon affects the ebb and flow of the Earth and the oceans, as well as the human bodies especially the female bodies with her monthly bleeding. Also, if you research our history many outbreaks of epidemics and certain diseases have affected mankind. The electro-magnetic push and pull of the Moon and its effects are what Wicces tune into and work with in our Magick.

This is the ritual dance that raises power from outside the Circle drawing it into our Circle and then drawing it into our bodies and magnifying it out into the centre of the Circle creating the Mystical Magickal Cone of Power. The HPs stands in the North of the circle of dancers facing South as the HP stands in the South facing north. All Coveners are linked with joined hands male to female alternating, with their right hands facing down and their left hands facing up this creates the Magical Link. The power that will be brought into and magnified enters and moves around the Circle in a Deosil movement, throughout the bodies in a systematic manner.

If a Wiccan is in true balance within them and can provide both polarities they can take the role of either male or female, then the energy can be repolarised then this is usually acceptable.

All standing still and deep in meditation after doing the Wicces Rune to help raise energy and Power, the HPs starts by drawing in the outer power into her base of the spine at her Root Chakra, she draws it in through her back and out through her front, feeling it raising in vibrational energy like the power of an ancient Dragon. As she sends it now out into the next Wicce on her left it now comes in through her spine and out through her front into their back of the spine at their base Chakra, and doing the same in a snake like pattern, moves throughout all the Wicces around the circle moving in through their back-base Chakra and out through their front into the next Wicce on the their left. This Dragon moving in and out of their bodies is an Earth Dragon raising everyone's energies, as all visualise this energy as a russet brown Earth dragon moving around the circle as one pure light energy.

When the HPs is ready she now raises that energy up her body to the next letting everyone know, the energy now raises up to the Root Chakra coming in through her back through her genitalia and out through the front of her body, awakening the Fire Dragon within and sending it forth around to the left to each Wicce moving in and out as before but now at the Root Chakra of the genitalia, allowing the Fire Dragon to be awakened and raising their power. All visualise the Fire Dragon in reds and gold's moving throughout the Wicces bodies vibrant and strong.

When ready again the HPs raises the energy of the Dragon to the Sacral Chakra where the Fire Dragon now glows a brilliant orange as it moves up and through the Sacral Chakra, moving around the circle as before. All visualise the Orange Dragon of the Fire and Fertility. Then the next stage again is raising the energy of the Dragon up to the Solar Plexus Chakra to a Yellow Golden Dragon of the Sun, repeating the same as before. Next raising the Dragon energy up to the Heart Chakra and seeing the Dragon as a Green Dragon of Water twisting throughout the bodies of the Wicces. Then the next level is at the Throat Chakra with the Light Blue Air Dragon, then up to the Third Eye Chakra as the Dark Azure Blue Magickal Dragon of Merlin, then when getting the Crown Chakra at the top of the head the Dragon changes colour to a purple and silver white radiating spirit Dragon and is released into the centre of the Circle creating a Spiralling vortex of Dragon energy forming a upside down Cone with the peak at the top radiating and glowing brightly.

When the HPs and or HP feel the time is right in releasing that Dragon Energy, they start the Chant to release the energy, as this is said all Wicces take a deep breath and then at the same time release their breath slowly as the HP directs the Power to where it is needed. When everyone has expelled all their air in their lungs they then each drop to the ground and gently just focus on the intended goal of the Cone of Power.

THE EIGHT PATHS
AND THE TOOLS

In dealing with the sacred Mysteries of Wicca and of the Goddess it is said that no secrets can ever be given away, as they each belong specifically to the individual and their own Truth, as we are each awakened to our own Inner Truths, which can never be fully explained to those that did not see within your journey. One, who has been initiated into the Wicca, has gained this by their readiness to receive and perceive the Mysteries of the Goddess and the Path of the Old Religion. The word 'Initiate' means a neophyte, someone who is willing to begin or start anew through the act of total dedication. The Wiccan Mysteries are certainly not the private possession of any one person or group, as they are universal knowledge and belong to all. The true meaning of Initiation into Wicca means nothing except to those who have already initiated into a traditional coven.

All the Wicces Tools are either masculine or feminine, and each has its microcosmic or macrocosmic analogies of unifying them in harmony and balance with what they are intended. In researching and examining the 'Tools of the Wicce' you will notice that I have grouped the Tools, corresponding them not only to the Three Degrees of Wicca, as part of the composite formulae, but also to the Eight Spiritual Paths of Wiccecraft and Enlightenment I will be concentrating a good deal on their Magickal uses, rather than the more usual Elemental associations, although I will refer to these as well.

The macrocosmic Stellar Three Degrees have much to do with the Mysteries of the Magick Circle, they are all important and no Magick Circle can be truly complete without them. The Wicces Tools also have their correspondence with the Eight Paths to Magick and Enlightenment; they are the powers with which the Wicce develops the skills necessary to build their Temple of Love, which shall be our Temple of the body, mind and soul. This is sort of restoring ourselves as whole Magickal beings so that we can stand with Nature in beauty and with strength.

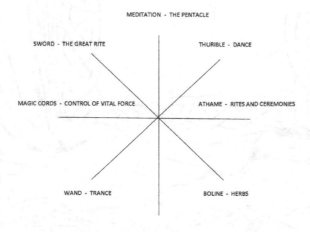

MEDITATION - THE PENTACLE

SWORD - THE GREAT RITE   THURIBLE - DANCE

MAGIC CORDS - CONTROL OF VITAL FORCE   ATHAME - RITES AND CEREMONIES

WAND - TRANCE   BOLINE - HERBS

CHALICE/CAULDRON - HIGH MAGIC

THE EIGHTFOLD PATHS

1. **Meditation or Concentration:** this in practise means forming a mental image of what is desired, and Willing yourself on a Higher level that it is fulfilled, with the fierce unwavering belief and knowledge that it can and will be fulfilled. This is called for short 'Intent'.

2. **Dance:** is about the methods used through ritualised dance and movements, like the flowing of the breeze through the trees and all kindred practises.

3. **Rites, Chants, Spells, Runes, Charms:** It is important that all these should be done in rhyme, with faith that it will work, and with absolute belief in Magick and the Goddesses energies, and with Will Power.

4. **Incense, Drugs, and Wine etc.!** Whatever you use to release the Spirit (note) be careful of this, as you need to always be in control and the use of these items usually means that they are in control and not you. Incense is normally harmless, but sometimes it has dangerous ingredients such as Hemp etc.! If you find only bad after effects, reduce the amount used for the duration of the time inhaled. Drugs are very dangerous if taken in excess, but it must be remembered that there are many drugs, which are harmless, though people abuse them and talk of them with gated breath. Drugs unlock the Inner Eye so fast that it has a spiralling affect, yes it may feel great and feel as though it is working, but it is the drug taking you there and not your hard work and effort. I prefer the way of hard work and study to reach our ascension not the lazy way.

5. **High Magick, Ceremonial Magick:** This level of Magick takes many years to master and only after working with Sympathetic Magick, and being trained slowly up to this level can you truly succeed to meet this level with a true heart and mind.

6. **Trance:** Trance State is for the priesthood where certain training is taught to take you through the Astral Projection stage and eventual Astral Travel to different times and places in safety. During the Trance State anything is Magickly possible.

7. **Warlocking:** Blood control, breath control and the use of the Magick Cords as used in the deprivation of blood flow and kindred practises.

8. **The Scourge:** For Purification and Enlightenment, is only used gently and in a set method for gradual elevation through the Mysteries into Enlightenment.

9. **The Great Rite:** This is the act of the Highest Wiccan Magick, where you become the Goddess and God through ceremony and Divine Love.

These are the Eight Ways of Magick within Wiccecraft. You may combine many of them into one Ritual, the More the better. But remember that Intent" is one of the most important parts of all ritual. Absolute belief in what you are doing with NO doubt. "KNOW THYSELF AND BELIEVE IN THYSELF".

- Remember Properly Prepared You Must Always Be according to the Rede of the Wicca. Otherwise you will never succeed.

- The Magick Circle must be Properly Purified several times if necessary. LBRP performed. Casting of the Magick Circle in preparation for any Spell or ritual. All tools and items must be clean.

- You must have Properly Prepared and Consecrated Tools.

THE SPELL

"May we Wiccans work and Will together,
May we reap the Magickal fruits of Fellowship?
How rough and course our garden can become
If we let the weeds of contempt and pride divide us.

There is always danger that the Weeds will grow back,
We may give up the struggle for hopeless.
Work energetically then in this time for the Earth and for us,
And blossoms of a new spring will flourish with opportunity and love.

Nurture the seeds of Love with the warmth of our heart for one another
And blossoms of Perfect love and Perfect Trust will grow.
Let us share the Joys and Mysteries of Magick in harmony,
And uproot the weeds of contempt and fear.
Let our love be undaunted and free as the Wild Flowers of Spring.

So, mote it Be!"

REQUIREMENTS
OF THE
PRIEST/ESS

The Rite of Ordination into the Second degree is the acceptance of the fitness and emotional strengths of the Wicce by the High Gods, as a member of the Priesthood of Wicca, to become an official Elder of our Path.

The Second Degree is the Level of Knowledge

1. The Wicce must have been a member of the Wiccan community for at least a year and a day, unless special circumstances exist which allow this to vary.

2. She/he must a good experience of meditation, healing or Clairvoyance.

3. She/he must have a good understanding knowledge of all the aspects of the Eight Paths of Enlightenment.

4. She/he must be able to carry out the Rites of Wiccaning and Initiation to the lesser Degree.

5. She/he must be able to Perform and cast the complete Magick Circle.

6. She/he must have a good knowledge of Ritual Construction.

7. She/he must be capable of running under supervision a new Coven, Circle or Church.

8. She/he must understand the symbolism and deeper meanings of the Second-Degree Ordination into the Priesthood.

9. She/he must have a devout desire to worship within the Wiccan Priesthood, through commitment and dedication in the Ministering to the Outer Community.

10. She/ He must have completed at least one act of Ceremonial Magick successfully.

11. She/he must have shown that they can offer more time in service to the Priesthood as a Teacher and Mentor to all Seekers and Wiccans.

12. She/he must have written a Full Moon ceremony, A Lesser festival of their choosing, a lecture for the Outer Court, and a Charge of the Goddess and God.

- Once Ordained a Priest or Priestess they must realise that they are then accepted and acknowledged as part of the Wiccan Community and the Priesthood of Wicca. At this stage they should commit themselves for a period of at least 3 more years.
- The newly Ordained Priest or Priestess now commences in the deeper training of the Priesthood and the ancient Mysteries of the Old Religion.
- They should have copied and written out their Book of Shadows from their HPs. And understand its writings and know it basically by heart.

Before advancing to the Priesthood they should have also learnt how to Cast the Magick Circle completely, and understand its symbolism. They should have also chosen or selected an area to specialise in. It is good that our Priesthood take on outer assistance in the outer community as Chaplains, Celebrants, healers, Psychics, etc. They should offer some time to assist with the basic running of the Wiccan community and its administration.

As a Priest or Priestess, they are taught how to direct Power, which is raised by the Wicces Cone of Power. They should also select one of the Eight Paths to specialise and train in. The mastery of Trance State is the main objective of the Priesthood and Community assistance. At this level they focus more on the spiritual and religious side of the deeper Mysteries of Wicca and the Goddess and God. From here you may always be a Wicce, but you have elevated past this and am now a Priest or Priestess. "Properly Prepared you must Always be"!

THE SCARAB RITUAL

This ritual is to gain knowledge of medicine, inventions, writing, or healing. Take a sculptured Egyptian Scarab Beetle and place it on a paper covered Altar, and under the Altar there should be pure white virgin linen altar clothe. Under it, place a piece of olive wood, and set in the middle of the Altar a small Thurible of Myrrh and Kyphi incense, which shall be offered. Have at hand a small vessel of Chrysolite into which Consecrated Oil of Lilies, or Myrrh or Cinnamon, shall be placed. Take the Scarab Beetle and lay it in a safe place. On a side Altar there should be some pure freshly made loaves of bread as buns, and fruit that are in season, and also some stick incense, all these are for offerings or sacrifices for the ritual.

During the offering take the Scarab out of the Consecrated Oil, and anoint yourself at sunrise, and turning towards the North East, speak the words written here below; bore it and press a gold wire through it and beneath the beetle and carve the symbol of the Holy Mother Isis, and having Consecrated it, the Spell is recited thus several times saying:

"Great Thoth, Magi of all Magick, Inventor of Mysteries
Founder of Great Medicines and Healer of the Gods
High Priest of letters and numbers.
Come now to me, for you are of the Earth,
Rise up to me Great Spirit of Life and Light"!

The appropriate days for this to be held in any month are; 7.9.10.12.14.16.21.24.25.

FIF-FATH FOR LOVERS

Collect some fresh clay and make two dolls, one of yourself and one of your love. In your doll add your blood urine, nails, hair and more, and in the other, do the same with their parts, then write a Spell in rhyme and continue:

Take a clump of clay, wet it and pat it, and shape it. Make it a statue of me and a statue of you. Then shatter them, and then batter them. Add some Consecrated Water. Then again shape them and mould into a statue of you and a statue of me. Then in you is me, and in me is you, and we shall become one, as nothing can keep us apart.

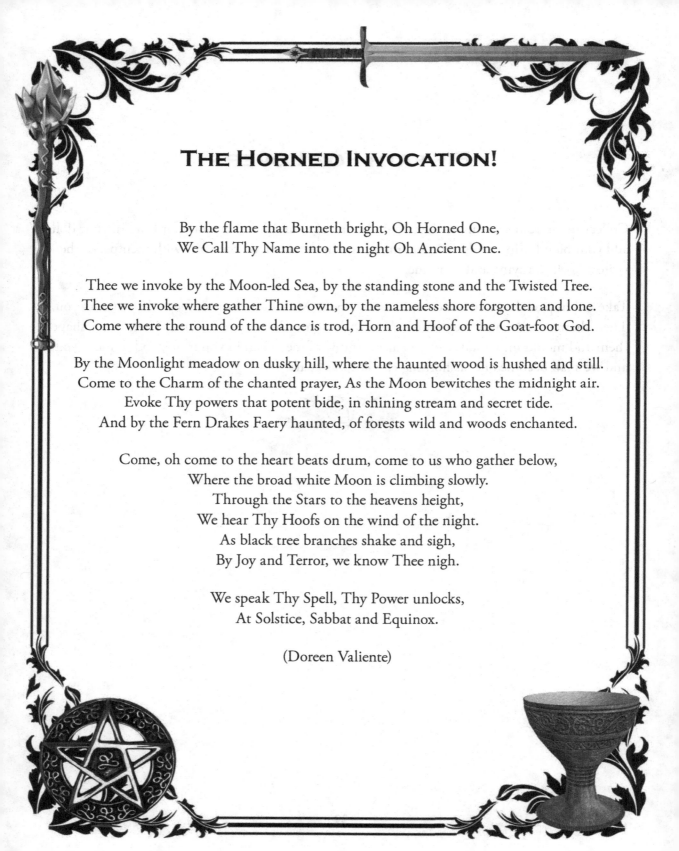

THE HORNED INVOCATION!

By the flame that Burneth bright, Oh Horned One,
We Call Thy Name into the night Oh Ancient One.

Thee we invoke by the Moon-led Sea, by the standing stone and the Twisted Tree.
Thee we invoke where gather Thine own, by the nameless shore forgotten and lone.
Come where the round of the dance is trod, Horn and Hoof of the Goat-foot God.

By the Moonlight meadow on dusky hill, where the haunted wood is hushed and still.
Come to the Charm of the chanted prayer, As the Moon bewitches the midnight air.
Evoke Thy powers that potent bide, in shining stream and secret tide.
And by the Fern Drakes Faery haunted, of forests wild and woods enchanted.

Come, oh come to the heart beats drum, come to us who gather below,
Where the broad white Moon is climbing slowly.
Through the Stars to the heavens height,
We hear Thy Hoofs on the wind of the night.
As black tree branches shake and sigh,
By Joy and Terror, we know Thee nigh.

We speak Thy Spell, Thy Power unlocks,
At Solstice, Sabbat and Equinox.

(Doreen Valiente)

NATURES
SECRETS THE
FESTIVALS

NATURES SECRETS

The cycle of the Seasons, Nature's way be wise,
Presented is our learning before our very eyes.
She is the greatest teacher of the cycle of rebirth,
She shows the way so timelessly in the seasons of the Earth.

The Waning of the autumn, the endless winter sleep,
And the joyous birth of springtime in
the promise that She keeps.
Summer is the highest climb when all that is made new,
Flaunts its Natural Magic in the shades of brilliant hue.

O that we could but understand, O that we could but see,
The Blessed gift of nature in Her Deepest Mystery.
She is a patient teacher for mortals learn but slow,
Eternity She does parade before our gaze to know.

Profusion of the springtime and the brilliant summer hews,
The gentle breath of autumn and the silent winter mews.
O mortal man could yeou but see this glorious parade,
Then would you ken the glory of all
this the Goddess has made

In winters silence there is much that we do not see,
Hidden beneath its covers are the likes of you and me.
And in the buds of springtime lies to the glory of all life,
Hidden and undetected from the drought of mortal strife.
In summer do we show ourselves before the eyes of man?
But mortal man beware - beware for you do not understand.
For we are Natures children and of us you know naught,
Elusive as the Shadows that forever is not caught.

But can't you see of mortal man the ever-changing tide,
For when it be you understand we will no longer hide.
You have no wisdom mortal man, you be the cause of grief,
For Nature is our Mother and mortal man be thief.

Destruction rendered by your hand, O man you do not know,
Your ignorance and your splendour and grandly does it show.
For we yet be the Faeries Folk, we be beyond your ken,
But to learn our Magical wisdom, you
must first walk the world of men!

THE APPLE -
FRUIT OF THE
WICCES

Since the beginning of time Apples have been associated with Wicces, and rightly so. It is our sacred fruit and so is Pomegranate. It has always been sacred to ancient peoples especially Wicces for many reasons. The Sacred Apple tree flourished in ancient times wild and free in all the lands of the Celts, Egyptians, Teutonic races and the Scandinavians. It was in many of these countries illegal to cut down an Apple tree, as in some places the person who did such a sacrilegious act was put to death. The reason being that many believed it was Magickal and the very tree contained certain Magickal forces and an ancient Spirit that healed and protected man and the ancient forests. Our sacred Paradise called Avalon (Apple-land) the tree was used traditionally and ceremonially by the Priestesses. Even the Christian faith stole this idea from us, changing the Garden of Eden's Fruit of the Tree of Knowledge that Eve picked and gave to Adam from a Pomegranate to an Apple. Which helped to connect this act against the word of God to the downfall of evil in Wiccecraft.

Look even at the Disney film of Snow White and the Seven Dwarfs; again, it was an evil Witch that gave over a poisonous Apple to Snow White, gee thanks again. There's a saying I like in the 21st century: "An Apple a day keeps the doctor away". This is so true as the Apple has so many medical and health benefits produced in the Spring and Summer months alongside the Orange and lemon for our health in the Winter months, Mother Nature knew exactly what She was doing.

The Magick of the Apple is infinitesimal, and the greatest secret of the Apple is that within its very core is our sacred symbol, embedded there by the Goddess as a reminder of the Five Planes of existence - the Pentagram. If you cut the Apple exactly in half sideways and open it up it reveals to the world our sacred Symbol, the Pentagram of the Wicces. This sacred fruit was used as our first Seal and Pentacle to invoke the energies of the Magick Circle and by awakening the power of the Apple and its very seeds and using its Magick for awakening and calling to the Elements in Nature. It also awakens the ancient Spirit of the tree to act as our aid in learning the mysteries of Nature itself.

THE WICCES FESTIVALS

Over the past 50 odd years in the Craft I have seen many variations of the Festivals from the most Traditional, basic and very advanced and some very far-fetched. I have always believed in allowing the Wicces of my Circles to write and perform their Ceremonies in full Coven as this is a great form of training and empowerment even though a little stressful when first performed. But our Festivals are not performed by just one individual Wicce but by the Coven, as we do not believe in spectators. In all my years I have never seen nor performed the same ritual, (except for Initiations) as there are many variations of everyone's own Truth of how they see the Festival at the time, and also on the night we go by what Mother Nature and the Spirits show and guide to us, this make it always a surprise when it is real and heartfelt.

The series of Festivals and ceremonies that follow are the very best of these celebrations written not only by myself but also by members of our Coven. I have also added a few extra little tantalising titbits, which I feel is beneficial for the everyday Wicce or Wiccan.

As you will also see by the following Celebrations they are very eclectic as we believe in freedom of religious choices and the myriad paths of the Gods and Goddess and their Festivals over thousands of years, are drawn by each one of us in different ways and feelings. Some of our brethren follow the ways of the Samethoi and Celtic traditions of the Blessed Isles, some Greek, Roman, Egyptian, Nordic, Germanic, Teutonic, Australian Aboriginal, Pacific Islander, Native American Indian and much more to be divinely drawn to. Even though these many cultures and beliefs are thousands of miles apart and have never had contact with each other, they all have a similar story to tell, and are in all essence, part of the same Divine Drama or Truth. All the new religions tell the same borrowed stories as the Old Religions.

When I started Wiccecraft I stood alone, and slowly through the year have seen the Craft grow into a formidable asset to the world Religions of the 21st century, seeing the Wiccan movement grow with millions of devout followers this very day, is awe inspiring, and reveals a Truth that is needed in this time of uncertainty of the 21st Century.

There are 21 accepted Celebrations of the year, 13 Full Moons, which are called Esbats dedicated to the Goddess (each Esbat we celebrate and honour a different Goddess from different Pantheons), and 8 Festivals or Sabbats dedicated to the Horned God.

BLESSING OF THE ANIMALS
4TH JANUARY

"Strong and noble, willing beast,
Welcome to our blessing feast.
Gratefully we give love and thanks to thee,
With blessings of good health and fertility."

The ancient Egyptians and their predecessors, along with the ancient Samethoi peoples of the Blessed Isles were the first peoples of the Western World to become aware of the existence of Spirits. They knew that some spirits were hostile towards man, whilst others assisted man, and some Spirits were wholly occupied in carrying out the various functions of Nature.

These spirits were commonly visible to man in the form of animal, bird, fish, reptile etc. During this early period many ancient cultures adoration of animals was almost Universal in not only the land of the Nile, but throughout Europe, The America's, Scandinavia, Germany, Britain and Australia, in fact most of the ancient lands and peoples honoured and respected all life within Nature, and treated the animal kingdom as their brethren. The ancient peoples considered animals and inanimate objects such as trees, plants and rocks to have intelligence like their own just a different vibration than mans. Ancient man knew that inanimate objects and animals communicated, reasoned and had feelings. Religious writings of many ancient cultures contain numerous proofs of this well accepted knowledge.

There are many examples even in Hebrew and Judaic teachings, the bible contains many accounts of the understanding of man's fundamental motive for worshipping animals was probably fear. He saw in animals, skilled warriors and survivors, because they possessed strength, power and cunning. Man, also knew that animals were endowed with some ability that enabled them to injure or cause death to man.

This later developed into reverence of the various forms, and the Gods and Goddesses were given characteristics, traits and virtues of various animals of power with their abilities. This form of worship continued down to more recent times when we find man becoming more independent on animals for his survival, like the water buffalo in Asian cultures, the Elephant for moving large objects in the jungles, cats for clearing out mice from their grain silo's, dogs to protect against unwanted visitors etc. Although man still followed the animal's symbols for the Gods, a different attitude and respect to animals began to emerge.

With this changed attitude they became a gesture of gratitude to the animals that worked side by side with man. In appreciation, the animals were accorded a special Blessing by the Elder, Wicce or the HPs of the village. Animals were brought together from near an afar to be blessed with health and fertility. Christianity also later adopted this festival celebration of animals into the day that St. Francis patron saint of animals would offer a Blessing, it is now performed yearly at the Vatican by the Pope.

This ritual is still done in many cultures, especially within the Wicca around the world, as we praise all things in life especially our little sisters and brothers.

BETROTHAL DAY
14TH FEBRUARY

"Love is as sweet as red the rose,
I will only love the one I chose.
For if another calls to thee,
Remember by love-bound thou art to me."

In ancient times this special date was set-aside for the young men and maidens to announce their betrothal. The couples presented themselves to the Elder HPs who wore a crown of red and white roses and carried long stem red roses, the couples would line up to receive a blessing from the HPs. One by one she Blessed them for a year and a day, at which time they returned if still in love to be wed, as each received her blessing she gave to each Maiden a red rose to remember this commitment for a year and a day. This eventually became the Handfasting Ceremony, which is now used as a Wedding in present days

Later the village Wicce performed this ritual, and with an introduction of Christianity this ritual was gradually changed to St Valentine's Day. But in the Mystery Schools of the Wicca, the deeper significance is taught:

"It is the Marriage of minds of the Conscious to the Subconscious!
The Human nature of female and male, the very Yin and Yang.
The summoning and focus of equally balanced Will,
In complete harmony and equilibrium of learning and understanding.
That within all men is found the feminine within,
And that within all females that they have the male within them.
When we bring these two into balance and harmony,
Through divine Love and Magick it is called the "Beloved Oneness".

LUGHNASADH
FEBRUARY 1-2ND SOUTHERN HEMISPHERE

This is the time of Thanksgiving, as we are celebrating the beginning of harvest and all that our crops have released to us. We mourn the soul of the Horned God, who dies at harvest for our good, only to be reborn again by our devotion in the spring. This Festival is also known as Lammas (a later name), which comes from the Saxon word, 'Feast of the Bread' (Half-mass). It was and still is a major harvest festival all over Europe and the Western World. The Goddess Ceres, Demeter and Juno Augusta were all names presiding over the new harvest. To us, Lammas is still the Lady's Rite, when the first loaf of bread is made from the first sheaf of the year's harvest; it is fashioned into a person surrounded by other offerings from harvest time, that we call a Corn-dolly.

Lughnasadh, February Eve, is the Festival of the ancient God Lugh, the Samethoi (later Celtic) God who gave his name to London - originally Lughnum. This Festival celebrated the death and resurrection of Lugh as Grain God. At this Festival we commemorate his death and the sacrifice of the harvest for the good of his children. There are three rituals presented on Lammas Eve, the first is by the men folk. The male Elders tell stories of old of the growth and decay of the Lord of the Sun, who having given his strength, is now cut down. This is a solemn ritual, for everyone thinks of the sadness, which comes with ultimate growth, for all that is given life also at the end of their demise has it taken away from them. We know that now, harvest is inevitable.

Lughnasadh Sabbat:
February Eve to February 1st

Lughnasadh is known as the ladies Festival as it is performed in the Magick Circle as a Thanksgiving for the Harvest and a Blessing upon our Great Mother Earth for Her bounty. We have made the first sacrificial loaf of bread from the first harvested grains along with freshly brewed beer usually from last year's Hops. We will now start to reflect on everything achieved and done during the Summer Months, as the cold months are the time to learn and connect.

Materials Needed: Red and orange candles, a Cauldron, Methylated Spirits, Corn Dolly, Loaf-man, 2 Sickles, Fennel Storks, 2 masks and Coronets. The Altar and Circle are decorated with harvested grains and flowers such as wheat, barley, fruit, corn and Poppies.

All are Properly Prepared, and all Wiccans are led to the Circle by the Man in Black, saying the Chain Dance; all acting out their roles as various animals, this is a fun journey of laughter). HPs tolls the bell with her Athame, around the Circle 40 times in all, that is 10 to each Watchtower. Then all meditate for 5-10 minutes. The Magick Circle is cast in the usual manner, but on a lesser level. All are then brought in to the Magick Circle and challenged by both sickles at the throat asking what do they bring to the Magick Circle. They are then anointed and welcomed. All go into God Position as the Watchtowers are invoked, and then all form a ring and do the Wicces Rune.

HPs breaks from dancers to the centre and chants; 'Bagabi Lacha Bachabi,' holding Phallic Wand and Chalice going Widdershins around the Circle whilst all go Deosil chanting the chant of Bacchus "I.O. Evo HE (ee-o-arvo hay). Blessed Be." Softly chanting and building it up, then slowing to a stop, all stand still as HP says:

"We are gathered here this night to celebrate the Festival of Lughnasadh, the Games of Light. The Festival of the God Lugh is the Samethoi God of light, the Sun-King who is born at Yule. The Saxons' Lammas or Loafmas' also calls this Festival, where the first grains are made into sacrificial bread as a sacrificial offering to the Harvest. Today we celebrate and acknowledge

the part played by the great Lord in his three aspects. We also remember our younger brothers in life, as they too are beginning to collect their stores for the winter months that are fast approaching, and the migrant birds that are leaving us for a warmer environment. The summer has been cool/wet/hot/sunny. Yet our Lay mother, the Earth has given us abundance.

The days are getting shorter and colder, and we know that after harvest is completed, Autumn will be well on its way, and with it the last of the fruits and berries of the Summer Season."

HP then says:

"Traditionally this was a week-long celebration for the first harvest and all its bounty, which ended with the sacrifice of the God-King to ensure the fertility of the land for the coming year. The corn is now ripe, and the grass is lush and green. We the Children of the Goddess and God look forward to the Harvest.

The Great Seasonal Wheel is turning towards the Mists of Autumn and we gather in our bountiful fruit and grain of the Mother Earth. As we begin to gather within ourselves. We pray for good weather to gather the remainder of the harvest from the fields, we pray for soft gentle winds to dry the grains.

Let us give Love and praises to the Goddess and God who have shown their love for us by this gifted great bounty.

Maiden then says:

"The meaning behind this is that the God-King and the Land are deeply connected. When the God is young, virile and healthy so is our land. But if he becomes sick, frail and old, so also will the land be sick or barren. So, whilst the God-King is still in his prime, before he gets too old or sick, he has to be sacrificed so that his divine blood, his divine life-force will go into the land, nourishing it until the God-King is reborn again to resume his place as the sacred eternal ever turning link with the land."

Elder then says:

"This night we celebrated the ways of the Old Religion. A long time ago, when all were of the Pagan traditions, we openly honoured the land in open fields and large gatherings

at sacred sites. Our echoing chants were carried on the winds afar and our prayers were heard and received upon the rising incense smoke from our Magick Circle to the Gods.

But sadly, in times of the past, we were enslaved and tortured by the followers of a jealous new god of a new religion. Our villages and homes were given over to cruel Lords and priests. Eventually our ways, the ways of the Goddess were forbidden under threat of death, and we were forced to accept the ways of our oppressors.

But this is a new time, a time of facing the Shadows. We no longer suffer persecution by the law for our gentle natural ways and beliefs. We have been lucky to be reborn in a new age among our own spiritual family again as we were in the past, and now governmental charter and the rights of the freedom of religion protect us.

Always has it been that the cycles of life must pass and return. These terrible things of the past we must remember but not dwell on. For all things are restored by the grace of the Goddess with balance and harmony. I am one of the Hidden Children of the Goddess. From generation to generation have the Wicces knowledge of old been passed down so that the ancient ways are never forgotten.
We who kindle the ancient flame shall always remember, and in this remembrance, we shall come together beneath the stars to honour the past, bless the present and secure our place in the future. By doing this we shall receive the Light of the Goddess and God, as it was in the beginning, so it is now, and so shall it always be".

HPs:

"We shall now choose two of our brethren to be as the young God and the Old God, for they shall dual as in the days of old. The winner will receive a kiss from all the maidens and be crowned our King for the night".

(Half cheer for the young God, the other half cheer for the Old God) They both do battle and the young God defeats the Old God who lies down and becomes one with the Earth.

Wicce:

"The Gods have their representative in this young strong N:
_____ for now he will receive his prize".

(Winner is crowned and gets a kiss from all the Maidens) Everyone now joins hands and forms a ring of dancers around the Young God, and all send energy as he invokes the God into himself.

Young God says:

"I am the Lord of the Corn, I am the Greenman on Earth and the Dread Lord of Shadows. I am the One that upon death shall lead you into the awaiting arms and bosom of the Goddess. The dance, which is my sacred life, shows you that life in never ending. Moving ever forward. All life returns, and all things are remembered, nothing is ever lost".

The Old God Says:

"I am the Old God, and in the past if the God-King wanted to extend his rule, he would elect a substitute to take his place as the sacrifice, he was called "The man in Black". A portion of his life-force would then be transferred to the substitute so that the Earth would continue to be fertile and thrive".

Wicce:

"As this is the 21st century, we do not sacrifice either people or animals, and never have done so. But we have substitute (in token) in the form of grain and a loaf of bread. The young God has invoked energy into himself and will now infuse and bless this substitute with his blessing".

All stand in a semi-circle as HP says:

(Raising left hand open)
　　　""Blessed Be the hand put forth with MEANING". (All repeat)
(Raising right hand closed in fist shape)
　　　"Blessed be the hand put forth with MIGHT". (All repeat)
(Rubbing both hands together vigorously)
　　　"Blessed be what we must do with MIGHT and MEANING that our HANDS may hold the HARVEST of our HIGHEST hopes". (All repeat)
HP then says:

"This is the time when the Divine Priest-King was scattered in the fields but today we scatter the grain made into bread to represent his body. The God must die to be reborn".

HPs stabs the loaf of bread and scatters it around the Circle saying:

*"As the Sun disappears in the dust of the night, as the old Moon dies to be reborn,
as the flower gives way to the fruit, so the seed can be implanted into the soil.
So the God must die and descend into Annwyn, that the earth may be fertilised to bring new fruit
and grain. Although the God has gone from the face of the Earth, we of the Wicca know that he
lives on within us, for there is no part of us that is not of the Gods. May everyone now partake and
eat of the body sacrifice as God, so that he never dies but lives on within us and shall be reborn".*

THE CLOSING RITE

HP leads all seven times around the Circle. He concentrates on drawing strength into them and into himself. We all share the wine saying:

"We make a toast and drink to the Harvest and to the abundance of the Earth".

We then pass around the first loaf, and the Barley Cake, saying:

*"We share the first fruits of the Harvest and give thanks to the Great Mother. Let us dwell on the
bounty of the Goddess, let us think on the strength of the Great Lord God who gave his life for us".*

Finally, all walk Widdershins three times around the Magick Circle and we banish the Watchtowers. The rite is ended. So, Mote it Be!

All salute God in usual manner

Cakes and Wine and Games.

Banishing.

THE AUTUMNAL EQUINOX
MARCH 21-22

"Gifts of fruit and grain for the poor,
Food and gifts, we leave outside your door.
This welcome treat we leave for you,
With blessings and love and not a clue.
Never ever will you see?
That these gifts were left by me".

The Autumn Equinox is when the daylight and night-time are equal, it is when all the trees are letting go of their past so that new life grows and creates a stronger and healthier future. It is also analogous to the mystical fall of man. At this time the human Spirit descends into the Realms of Annwyn, by being immersed in the illusion of the physical existence. In ancient Egypt, the Autumnal Festival re-enacted the grief and joy at rediscovering the Goddess Isis' husband, Osiris, and son Horus. The Autumn Equinox is also celebrated in the name of Diana who is the Italian Goddess early identified with the Greek Goddess Artemis. She was the Goddess of the Moon, of the country, the forest, and the hunt, of springs and brooks, chastity and of childbirth.

Her powers were over women who prayed to Her for offspring. She was thought of as the Protectress and Mother to all especially women. Later, Christianity in the form of the Virgin Mary adopted and changed the worship of Diana into Mary. The Autumn Equinox is also the time when the Elders gathered food and grain, and at night left it at the door of the poor. This was to ensure that they would have food for the coming winter, and again emphasises the role of Provider and Protector. Today we of the Wicca carry over this tradition and have a collection from our community of canned goods, food and whatever else can be needed for the coming months.

The Autumnal Equinox is a time of balance or equality and harmony. We give thanks for the Harvest, which has been safely gathered, and we say farewell to the strength of the Sun. At this point of the year, the Sun loses his power and the dark of the night begins to gain dominion over the days. The Autumnal Equinox is also a time of looking forward.

As the leaves change colour, we think about the final gathering of grain, berries and fruit; as these will be used to make potions and wine for the Winter months; crab apples for jelly, flavoured with mint and sage; Rowan jelly to eat with beef; quince for the rare occasions when we attain venison or pheasant. Elderberries are gathered to make Elder Rob, and as soon as the first heavy rains soften the Earth, we pick our citruses, to fight against the winter colds and flu's. The birds are not forgotten either. We pick the dried sunflowers to see when their seeds will be ready for harvesting. In this way we can feed the birds when everything is sleeping. In some countries due to heavy snow there may be few flowers blooming in winter, so we look out for teasels, dried kex, and the stalks of hedge parsley to make decorations for the house later on, especially with Mistletoe and Pine.

THE AUTUMNAL RITE

Everyone is asked to bring a candle, fixed securely in a jar of sand, or soil, they are also requested to hunt out some sprigs from an Oak Tree, Pine-cones, Autumn Flowers, Ears of Wheat, Oats, or Barley and a piece of fruit. We have an Altar, where a bowl of fresh flowers in clear spring water has been placed. This symbolises the Mother, and is surrounded by berries and fruit and dried leaves and items of autumn. A Bale Fire is lit outside the Circle in the South, representing the Sun, which is leaving us.

In Celtic Mythology, the great tree of Munga was a combination of Oak, Apple and Hazel. This Magick tree produced oak apples, acorns, hazel nuts and apples, all at the same time. It was also a tree of Sanctuary where the white hind, a form sometimes taken by the Goddess, could lie protected and sheltered. The fabled Unicorn also rested beneath this sacred apple tree, symbolising immortality through wisdom.

A virgin could only tame this beautiful mythical creature. Nowadays we think of a virgin as a girl with an intact hymen, but in the old legends it meant a woman with spiritual integrity, or attributes of the Goddess - who was not a virgin in the physical sense, but free to make her own decisions.

The Isle of Avalon, a Celtic name for the Otherworld, also means "Apple Isle". These trees bore both fruit and flower at the same time, and probably gave rise to the old saying:

> *"A bloom in the tree when the apple is ripe,*
> *Is a sure termination of somebody's life"?*

The Goddess Diana, Lady of wild and free creatures, was for centuries Goddess of the Sacred Grove. The two main ones were at Ephesus and Nemi; an apple tree and a deer, are two symbols associated with Diana, or later as Artemis as she was known to the Greeks; called Newhain by the Celts, also presided over Holy Groves, and is often portrayed with an apple branch in her hand. Later the Christians destroyed as many of these groves as they could to remove the aspect of the old Goddesses, and their followers.

The Autumnal Equinox Rite

Everyone are asked to bring a candle, fixed securely on a jar of sand or soil, and they are requested to hunt out some sprigs from an Oak, Pine-cones, (something of a special Magickal tree grown in Australia) Autumn flowers, and ears of wheat, oats or barley, and a piece of fruit. This gathering should be done with care, for it represents each Wiccans token offering to the Goddess and God. All are asked to bring a parchment written of what we wish to discard within their life and be rid of and also what we need for the coming year. The Altar is decorated with symbols of autumn that all have brought for the Festival. The Magick Circle boundary is scattered with wheat and autumn leaves and the Altar is in the centre of the Circle. HP forms the Magick Circle, then brings the HPs into the Circle, followed by all Fellow Wiccans by being anointed on the brow and entering with the Shepherds Dance. All form two circles, women on the inner and men on the outer, women going widdershins and men going Deosil. After the dance all stand still then slowly walk around in the same direction and chant:

> *"The Seasonal Wheel has turned to autumn time,*
> *The God is strong and in his prime.*
> *We share our love and feelings anew.*
> *Giving praises Great Goddess and God to you.*
> *Let our power bring the balance in,*
> *That the Wheel retains its sacred spin."*

East Warden:

"The Autumn Equinox is symbolic to the mythical fall of man. At this time the human spirit descended into the realms of Annwyn (The Underworld) by being immersed in the illusion of Physical existence.

In ancient Egypt the autumn festival re-enacted the grief and joy at rediscovering the Goddess Isis' husband Osiris and Her son Horus. This festival is also celebrated in the name of the Wicces Goddess Diana; She is the Goddess of the Moon, of the country, forest, of the hunt and of wild and free things. She was the hunter of men's souls to guide them into Annwyn. She was protector of springs and brooks, chastity and of childbirth. Women loved her and prayed her for her powers and gifts, especially for offspring. She was the protectress over pregnant woman and new mothers. Later adopted as the Virgin Mary, the Vatican took over "Diana's Temple", and changed it into their Mother Temple now called the Hill of the Mother behind the Vatican. But this was consecrated to our Goddess, Diana".

Maiden:

"On behalf of our Coven we wish to welcome you into our Magick Circle, our halloed Temple to the Goddess of love, to celebrate the Mysteries of Autumn. Now is the time of universal balance where day and night are the same, it is the balance of worlds, where the Goddess and God are one, male and female are one, fire and ice are one, light and dark are one, labour and rest are one.

We bring with us the harvest of autumn, the last offerings from the Earth Mother for this time of the year. We thank the Goddess and God for all that they have given us, and all that they have guided and aided us as their children."

North Warden:

"Autumn is the season for our rewards, for our labours of the past year. Now is the time that we celebrate for all that we have been given. Know that the reward is not only for the physical labours, but also for the labour of our spirit. Our bright Sun Lord is still strong, and since the spring he has been passing his strength to us. Giving us his warmth, his light and his fertility to the Earth. We must now return his favours back to him by giving back some of the fruits of his gifts."

South Warden: Takes a round a basket of which each person places their offering of fruit that they have brought with them. When all have been collected the Warden does a Blessing over them. Warden then says:

"Now as the bright Lord begins his journey into the darkness of Annwyn and into the awaiting arms of the Crone. We too must pass on those things of our lives that we no longer need, things that are dragging us down, let them be taken into Annwyn. We can recognise the lessons that we have learnt and know also what we still have to learn".

MiB: Lights the Cauldron and says:

"Now is the time to let go of the past, as the darkness and winter gain strength, we must let go of that which we do not need. Please focus on that which you wish to release from yourself, and take hold of your parchments that you have prepared. It is time now to release and be freed from your past pains, negativity, ignorance, laziness, guilt, weakness and whatever else we know to be holding us back. Now as we each throw our parchment into the flames we chant:
Grief, negativity and sorrow,
For none serve you or me.
I pass them into these flames,
And from them I am free".

South Warden:

"Everything has its Season, has its time of birth, life, death and ultimately its time for rebirth. Death is the time when we must rest and recoup ready for our next busier life. The wheel of Life returns with the spirit of love driving it ever onward eternally. Now is the time to give thanks for what we have been given over the past year, and it is time to remember what it is that we have done or deserve".

We all now spend a couple of moments remembering the things in our lives that we have been given over the past year and what do we wish to bring into our lives over the next year?

Maiden:

"Bright Lord we know that your unconditional love has given us that which we truly deserve, not necessarily what we want. As we know that you will ever return to us

*in the Spring to again gift to us with the Spring breezes, the beautiful budding new
life that smile in splendour on the Earth, and to the newborn cries of Nature.
Each year we gather the best seed of the harvest to plant for the next year's
season. So, we must plant the seeds of our labour, as our hopes for the next
year. We must plant each seed in its correct season, guide us Great Mother in
the planting of the seed, which shall bring forth new life and growth".*

Wicce: Carries around a large Pentacle of Harvest seed for each to select, all then bless their seed.

Wicce:

*"The earth is our Mother and she freely gives of Herself to all. Let us now take time to charge
and Consecrate our Crystals that we have each brought as an offering to the Goddess with
our thankyou energy. Let us infuse our energy to help heal all Her wounds. Send all our
love and devotion into the crystal and send thanks for all that She freely gives to us".*

All: Then one by one plant their crystal in the Earth in the Cauldron with the Seed, as we all sing:

*"Love is all we need, Truth is all we seek,
Light is all around".*

Couple then consecrate the Wine.

Couple then consecrate the Sabbat cakes.

Followed by the autumn leaf game.

Close the Magick Circle.

Samhain: All Hallows Eve
May Eve:

Samhain is the end of the Wiccan year, and also, it's beginning. It is the Wicces New Year. We begin with an ending because we are working with the continuous tides of Nature, and one thing always leads to another, the never-ending circle. When the leaves begin to fall, we get ready for the start of the Wicces Year. We play the game 'Catch the Leaf', which is not so easy as you may think. Just as you clutch one, it rises and floats away; through the heat of the hand as it creates a little thermal. When the leaves have let go of the trees and nature puts on a display of colour this is the time of Samhain.

Another name for this Festival is the West Wind Sabbat, for at this season we celebrate the end of autumn and the Western Quarter of the Circle, it is also the time when the winds pick up and come in through the West. Samhain is a Cross Quarter and Nature Festival, one of the four most ancient Major Bale Fire Festivals situated between the Seasonal Festivals. The other Major Festivals being Imbolg or Oimelc, Beltane and Lughnasadh or Lammas. The Solar Rites fall upon the Equinoxes (equal times) and Solstices (Sun standing Still), were a later imposition upon the original Old Religion.

The times between these festivals are almost equal; there are six weeks from a solar to a Nature Rite, and seven weeks from a nature to a solar festival, making four equal divisions of 13 weeks in the year. These form the structure of the Wicces Calendar. In the days before there was a written calendar, Samhain would have come on the first hoar frost, or when the Oak Trees lost their leaves; Lughnasadh, now February 2nd, with the first rains; Beltane, when the Hawthorn Blossomed, and Imbolg with the cutting of the first sheaf of corn at Harvest.

The origins of the word Samhain are a bit obscure. But the original peoples of the Blessed Isles were known as the Samethoi, so it could be a short debasement to the Festival of the Samethoi named Samhain. Another possible explanation is in ancient writings of a sacred place of the Fae called Emhain (the Faerie Realm of Elphane), or that it stems from a Gaelic word, pronounced something like 'Raven'. This was the time when surplus was killed, both to provide meat for the winter months, where the blood being mixed with the grain to make a kind of haggis, and to conserve dwindling supplies of fodder for the nucleus of the stock. Traditionally, the scent of such a copious amount of blood was thought to attract the Spirits of the Dead.

At Samhain the veil between our world and the otherworld is thinnest, and it is thought to be the best time to attract those who have passed before. I must emphasise that to Wicces, these are the Spirits of the long dead - the old masters and elders, the archetypes, the great Sages who have served the land and Mother Earth. We are not spiritualists and do not try to contact family members who have been deceased. We understand that there is someone, or something, far greater than ourselves who can help us in our quest for knowledge, light and truth.

I prefer the second explanation of Samhain, which follows on from this. The Ancient Greeks spoke very highly of the Priesthood of the Hyperboreans, whom they called Samethoi, followers of an ancient God of the Underworld whose name closely resembled Sam ethos. These Priests were Shamans, and their role was to enter the realms of the dead at the time of the first frosts to conduct the souls of those departed from this life during the year of their place of rest, and to bring back knowledge and enlightenment. Their training was long and arduous because the one thing you must not do in the Land of Mists is lose your nerve, it is the place of courage and absolute faith. The Samethoi were the Priesthood of the inhabitants of Britain before the Celts arrived and should not be confused with Druids, who were Celtic Priests.

SAMHAIN: ALL HALLOWS RITE.

The place of worship is duly Consecrated and prepared, with 2 black candles on the Altar and red candles in carved pumpkins at the four Watchtowers. The Altar and Magick Circle are decorated with Autumn Flowers and whatever Magickal tools are in required. The tools used for recalling messages from beyond are also in the Magick Circle ready for using. Red tapers (enough for everyone). The Cauldron is also prepared with a small Balefire atop of the large Balefire, which is unlit. Wicces and guests wait silently away from the Magick Circle. The Meeting dance is led by the maiden to the Magick Circle with the MiB who comes up the rear, with the Scourge, after the bell is tolled 40 times, the Maiden leads the way to the Magick Circle, and all chant:

"Come, come, come to the Sabbat,
Come to the Sabbat with Love and join us there".
(This is repeated as many times as it takes to arrive at the Circle)

HP: forms the Magick Circle assisted by the HPs, all are then brought in for the Conjuration and the Wardens invoke the Watchtowers. Being drummed into the Magick Circle then purifies all. Everyone then does the Wicces Rune with the dance of the Grapevine, which slows, to a stop. HP then breaks out of the ring of dancers, in the South facing North and says:

"O Great Gods of the Wicca, Beloved by us all,
Bless this our Rite of Samhain, our sacred Sabbat.
Where your humble servants meet in Love, Joy and Bliss.
Bless this our Samhain Rite with the presence of our departed kin."

Wiccans standing in semi-circle in the South facing North as HP returns to join the rest, as HPs then stands in the North facing all and the Heavens with her arms upraised and Staff held aloft. HPs. then invokes with the Horned Invocation and all Wicces Will their energy into the centre. HPs then joins the slow dance and it builds up all chanting:

"Fire flame and fire burn, make the mill of Magick turn,
Work the Will for which we pray, Eko Eko He ha Yay". (Hay he Yay)

This is chanted 7 times, building energy more and more. Dancing stops and Wicces form a semi-circle in the North holding hands and everyone's heads are bowed and eyes closed, opening all their psychic senses, as HPs goes and invokes with Earth Invoking Pentagram on HP saying:

"Great Shining Ones of the Shadows,
Goddess and God of Life and received of Death.
We seek your divine Knowledge if Life and Death,
We seek the Mysteries of you.
Open wide the Veil of Annwyn, through which all must pass.
You, who have received our loved Ones, please let them return this night,
To make merry with us and join in the celebrations of death and rebirth.
O Great Horned God of the Shadows, the Comforter, the Consoler,
And the Bringer in of peace and rest.
We know that when our time comes, as it must,
We will enter with devotion, and unafraid,

That you will wait with open arms and an open heart in our acceptance
When we enter your dark realm of Shadows,
To rest, amongst our dear ones who have gone before.
We will again be awakened to the Divine Light
And be reborn into a world of love and beauty.
By your Grace and the Grace of the Great Mother,
Please let it be at the same time and place as our loved ones,
That we may meet, and know, and remember, and love them again".
(A slight pause is here)
"Gathered neath a Wicces Moon bold galleon of the night,
Blessed lady and Lord conjoined in sacred rite.
Gods of Light and darkness and all you held within,
Come forth now from the Shadows, as the Holy Rite begins.

Hail you Lord of the Shadows, the Mighty Ones come forth,
Archangels and Elementals, of East, South, West and North.
The Elements of Fire we summon you this night,
To witness this our Magick and the greatest of the Rites.

We of the Luna Children stand skyclad as decreed,
In Blessed salutation of the Holy Wiccan Rede.
Before you stand the Maiden, radiant in full bloom,
The Virgin and the Ancient One, the aspects in Triune.

We celebrate the ancient way, the powers of the Sun,
To herald your return again, when winters night is done.
We call upon the Ancient Ones and those who've gone before,
That you may stand among us as you did in days of Yore.

We stir, we call, and we summon thee, to stand with us this night,
Before the burning Cauldron to witness this our Rite.
We dance the Wicces Rune as the Holy Rite begins,
We Summon, Stir and Call thee up to enter now herein.

Within the Magick Circle united do we stand?
Joined in love and harmony as Children of the land".

Invocation:

> *"O Great Horned One descend now into the centre of this Magick Circle,*
> *We pray you to enter thy ambient flames of our High Priest with love, strength and*
> *Faith. Come thou forth I say, come thou forth so that all spirits be subject unto me,*
> *So that every Spirit of the firmament and of the Ether and of the Earth and under the*
> *Earth and on dry land. And in the water, and of whirling air, and of rushing fire, and*
> *Every Spell and Scourge of the Shining Ones. Be present here in this Magick Circle,*
> *to be of assistance in this Holy Rite. So, Mote it Be".*

HPs. then invokes with fire in the air, then on the wreath. The Wreath is then taken to the centre, and given to the HP. Maiden then approaches the Altar and gets a handful of incense and throws it onto the Bale Fire, lights her taper and joins the rest in the South as all start to form a ring, as Man in Black blows the Ceremonial Summoning Horn, once to each Quarter, and the HPs rings the Bell with her Athame saying:

> *"By the Grace of the Horned God we ignite this Bale Fire today, in the presence of*
> *The Ancient Ones, without jealousy, without fear, without envy, without doubt.*
> *We invoke the High Gods of Light and Life.*
> *Be you a bright flame before us, be you always a guiding star above us.*
> *Ignite within our hearts a flame of love to our friends, our foes, to our kindred all.*
> *To all man on this wide Earth. From the lowliest to the name which highest of all,*
> *Welcome we the Spirits of our departed Kin".*

All then say:

> *"Welcome we the Spirits of our departed kin".*

All walk slowly around chanting the chant of Bacchus. As many times whilst the HPs rings the Bell 40 times. HP places the wreath on the fire, as all gaze into the flames whilst chanting slowly and quietly. HP says:

> *"Listen well to the ancient call of our souls, hear us*
> *You who wander the land of Shadows.*
> *We call upon all who have passed from this world back through*
> *the ancestral generations of time to our first parents.*
> *We have lit and illumine our Magick Circle that it be a beacon to guide you here.*

We call upon you by the Power of Magick and Love, listen to the voice of our Souls
all those of the past. Come to us now as the time is short with the veil opened for you
to enter herein. The gulf between our worlds is narrow, see the light of our beacon
and come to us. Approach all of you with only joy, love and light in your hearts.
Come and share our joy this night. Let the Chalice be filled in the name of the sacred Triune.
For we will speak once more to those who have passed, and we will see those who are yet
to be. Come and rejoice in the names of the Great Mother and the Lord of Shadows".

Dancers slow and stop as MiB breaks from the ring and fills the Chalice who presents it to God and says:

"O Ancient and Mystical Lord of the Shadows,
Bless this wine in this sacred Chalice in token of thy Mothers Cauldron,
Which contained three drops of wisdom for all in the world.
Elementals of Air and Elementals of Water, friends in life and friends in death.
To all those who have gathered in the dark Lords name,
Through this divine act bestow blessings to all your children who will hide
no more but shall shine as the stars in the dark of the night".

God Consecrates the wine then says:

"I bid you all my children drink of my Blessing".

HPs drinks and then says:

"In humility as the Ancient One asks, I bid you all my children to drink of his Blessing".

All then pass the Chalice around the Circle saying, 'Blessed Be May you never thirst'. All then sit around the fire and meditate for 5 minutes. If any wish to call up a particular Spirit, the member will dance slowly around the fire and all helping to visualise the Spirit. This is the night to call the Dead forth either by Ouija, Séance, crystals, invocation, Trance etc.

"All is ready save the cakes, may we bless then with Light".

HPs and HP then Bless cakes.

Agape.

Also, a Dumb Supper is prepared outside the Circle for the Spirit Realm.

Celebrations of song and dance.

Finally, the Banishing of the Magick Circle

THE MAYPOLE RITUAL
MAYDAY MAY 1ST

"We dance around the Pole and play,
To welcome in the dawn of May.
Young innocent children without a care,
With flowers and ribbons and laughter everywhere."

As we have seen the Beltane Festival begins on May Eve for all the adults and carries over to the next day, the 1st May as a family day of celebration. In the Southern Hemisphere it is a bit hard to celebrate May Day as to us it would be November Day, as October 31st is our Beltane. So, should we call it November pole Day, (doesn't quite roll off the tongue).

In Wiccecraft the Sun and the Moon are the two great hands of our Cosmic Clock. The hour hand (The Sun) governs the Seasons of the Year, and the minute hand (The Moon) governs the Lunation's and the tides of the great oceans along with the hidden knowledge and thoughts of the human mind.

The Moon rather than the Sun is a Wiccans main concern, as the Moon Goddess religion predates all solar and patriarchal religions. The Festival of Beltane is traditionally celebrated by the community as a great day for a family picnic, we here is Perth call it "Pagans in the Park Picnic" with the erection of the Great Maypole and its myriad of coloured ribbons for the children. The ages of the children who perform this symbolic dance are between the ages of 6 to 14 years of age, and it is part of the Rite of Passage, from the stage of a child to a young adult into puberty. It also signifies the bonds being tied one to another as a joyous occasion for the whole family.

The Maypole Ritual is also used as a Fertility Dance, where the Maypole represents the Phallus of God who penetrates the Earth, and the ribbons are the impregnating of the Living Earth, The Goddess, to bring forth new life to all. A very old Maypole song goes like this:

"In the centre of the Circle there grew a tree,
And a fine, strong tree was he.
And from that tree there grew a branch,
And on that branch there grew some leaves,
And in these leaves, there was a nest,
And in that nest, there was a bird.
And from that bird a feather came,
And from that feather a bed was made.

And on that bed, there was a woman
And on that woman, there was a man.
And from that man there came a seed,
And from that seed there grew a tree.
And a fine strong tree was he".

(Thus, conveying the circle of life and fertility)

THE STORY OF YULE

"Once upon a time, long, long ago before the time of the Industrial Revolution that changed the living Earth. Their lived a beautiful Maiden who lived on a Magickal Island of blue and green. She had many friends on this sacred island, Faeries, rabbits, deer, wolves, birds and even flowers and trees. But she was the only one of her kind, different from all the rest.

She so loved where she lived and especially all her friends whom she wanted to share with others like her, but there was none. So alone she felt, that her body started to change and, so she began to give birth to herself! Every month when the Moon was hiding in the Shadows, she gave birth. The first of these six Moons she gave birth all to daughters with dark brown skin and deep brown eyes, and for the last six Moons of her year she gave birth to fair skinned daughters with fair hair.

But on the seventh Moon of every year the First Mother, the
original Goddess gave birth to a Magickal Oak Tree.

As the years passed by, she gave birth to many daughters, and a great deal of Oak trees where they created a sacred Grove. The daughters were always happy and played many games, they sang and danced with all the animals. This was a very happy time. They shared their laughter as they climbed the great Oak Tree brothers and they gathered flowers whilst singing and dancing with the Fae, the faeries of the land.

One day in spring the firstborn daughter of the First Mother gave birth to herself. The First Mother was so very proud and content and her favourite friend Oak Tree (who was very wise) gave her a silver crown to wear and told her that she was now a Grandmother! It came to pass that many of her daughters gave birth unto themselves, and as the Grandmother, The First Mother became happier than she could ever dream, as her Island was full of babies, big girls and lots of mummies, all who played and laughed together with the Fae, the animals and the trees in a world of absolute happiness and bliss.

One dark winter night when the Moon was hiding, one of the daughters gave birth to a baby that was very different from anything that they had even known, it was not a daughter, it was not an Oak tree, it was a baby boy, the First baby Boy! This night was the darkest and coldest night they had ever known, it was the longest night of the year.

All the daughters and all the Fae and the animals were all snuggled up together to keep warm and cosy.

They had never felt a cold like this before, and they did not know what else to do, they just could not get warm. The wise old Oak Tree then suggested that they take from him some of his limbs that they cut him down as a sacrifice for the first-born son. They took his Oak Tree body in pieces to their home, which they did. The Elder Fae used a Magick Stone that she had and struck it on another stone and a Magickal spark appeared, and thus the first fires appeared which frightened everyone at first. But after a while they realised that it gave out radiance and warmth that kept them all alive, especially the baby boy that would have surely died if the Old oak did not sacrifice himself.

The mother brought the baby boy close to the edge of the fire, closer than anyone else, as they were still a little scared of this new Magick thing that the Fae called Fire The baby boy opened his eyes, and began to wiggle his fingers, then he smiled and he Moved close to his mother's breasts and drank of her milk. Soon everyone was certain That the baby boy was going to survive. They were all so happy they danced and sang Around the fire singing their praise to their old friend the First oak. They kept giving Gifts of the old Oak to the fire.

The baby boy grew up strong and happy because of the sacrifice that the Old Oak gave. He had many sons of his own, and taught them all how to plant Acorns on the Seventh Dark Moon of the year so that there would always be many, many Oak trees. The Fae and the Oak trees made a shining necklace of Acorns (40 in number, the number of human gestation in weeks) and presented to the First Mother as a sign of Life and Rebirth.

Every winter on the longest, darkest and coldest of nights the people of this sacred Island built a fire, to honour the tradition of sacrifice and rebirth. They brought in a special tree and honoured it with placing on it shiny ornaments and glittery Faery dust to help bring back the light of the Sun. They picked one special Magickal log and decorated it as a gift of appreciation to the fire, and all the children would hear the story of the first Oak Tree.

So, on the longest night of the year whenever you light a candle, build a fire or decorate a special Yule Tree remember the story of the First Grandmother and the Fae who told her their secret of fire. No matter how cold or dark the world seems, the Sun and Light will always be reborn and bring us warmth with hope and light with love.

Blessed Be the First Grandmother and the First Oak!"

THE MIDWINTER SOLSTICE
JUNE 21 - 22

"The Mistletoe and Holly are all in full bloom,
Showing courage and have strength and removes darkness and gloom.
It is a Magickal time for decorating the Yule Tree,
Filled with tinsel and baubles for all to see.
The light of our Lord shall return when winters night is done,
This is a symbol that shows our faith and Magick to bring back the Sun".

Everyone loves the Winter Solstice and very loves Yule, not only because of the idea of giving gifts, but we decorate our homes in a cold and bleak time to celebrate with our family and friends a grand feast. Since the beginning of religious Truths there has always been a divine child born at the Winter Solstice, Jesus was only one of them. There was Dionysis, Attis, Mithras, Baal and Osiris, and have course the first-born baby boy, the symbol of Light. They have all been honoured throughout time as the bringer in of hope and light, in a time of its greatest fears and darkness.

Norsemen also celebrated the birth of Freya and Thor as this time of the year. Wiccans do the same that Christians do, but we did it first with the original son of Light.

THE RITE

The HPs is alone in the Magick Circle contemplating this day. She lights a very large, red candle, which stands in her Cauldron surrounded by the beautiful Holly, Ivy and Mistletoe. When she feels that the atmosphere has stilled, she takes up a Temple singing bowl and runs a piece of mahogany rod around the edge. A strange belling noise reverberates through the Magick Circle; other Bards come to the HPs and play their Mandarin, Flute, Drum and Lyre.

On hearing the music, the Wiccans approach the Portal to the Magick Circle, where the MiB, holding a bowl of Hyssop and Lavender fused water and a clean towel, is awaiting. Each person rinses his or her hands before entering the Magick Circle. Once all are inside, they circle three times Deosil around the glade to the music of the Bards, and then stand in an inward facing ring.

The Four Circle Wardens take their places. Beginning in the East, and with all facing that way, they call up the Guardians, the Archetypes and the Totems of each quarter in turn. We are all expected to visualise these images giving them a sense or reality. In the East we imagine an early morning in spring, Merlin the Archetype and the Totem Cernunnos, Stag of the Seven Tines. We should watch them approach through a misty woodland glade, alive with birdsong. Once the Warden of the East has this firmly in his mind, he lights a blue candle and turns to the South. This is the signal for all to turn that way.

Here Arthur, King of Logres and holder of the Magickal Sword of Albion, approaches the Magick Circle on a hot midday in high summer. Sometimes he is riding the totem Epona, White Mare of the Sacred Hills. At other times she simply accompanies him. Epona lifts her beautiful white head, snuffles the air, and gallops toward the Magick Circle. A red candle is lit, and we turn to the West. West is the place of water, here Morgan, the Priestess of the Holy Grail, as its Archetype. The Totem is Mona the Sacred Cow of the Western Isles who brings with her the sweet smell of hay. All imagines a glowing autumn sunset over the sea, a green candle is lit, and we turn to the North.

In the North we visualise Guinevere, Queen of the Round Table, and Artos, great Bear of the North. These mythological figures are seen approaching through a frosty midnight landscape. A dark green candle is lit, and the Magick Circle is open. When all is still once more the HPs walks Deosil around the Magick Circle, holding a sword waist high, straight out in front of her. She states her intent. Our Bards begins playing a merry tune, while the drum beats our one, two, three rhythms for the vine dance. We pass alternate shoulders, touch hands and make eye contact. The dance winds down, and we sit thinking about the woods and what it has to offer.

When the Circle reforms, we do another weaving dance and sing a very ancient chant, all stand holding hands, chanting the Wicces Rune continuing the chant of Bacchus. All directing power to the HP, he then speaks for the returning Sun. Elder then answers the returned Sun. Sun God then leads traditional dance of the return. All repeat and sing along:

East Warden East Says:

> *"Day by day, for half of our year, the Earth has grown darker,*
> *Night-by-Night for half of this year the darkness has become longer.*
> *Week-by-Week for half this year, the darkness grows much colder,*
> *Tonight, that ends, for the Sacred Wheel of Arianhrod has turned,*
> *And lands heads back to the Sun, for the light calls again".*

South Warden Says:

> *"The darkness is never complete, as a sacred Spark is always waiting to return,*
> *And as the Wheel is turned over and over again, the light will*
> *return and grow stronger, brighter and greater.*
> *Behold the Light is coming, and the cold in the Shadows fades away.*
> *The Wheel is turning again, let us each turn our own Wheel until the Sun returns, and*
> *With it the Light and warmth to awaken the Living Earth. All life is in a Circle.*
> *We as devoted Children shall follow the laws of Nature.*
> (He lights A Bale Fire)
> *Behold the Light, it has been rekindled and through Magick is Reborn".*

All chant:

> *"The Wheel turns onward, ever turning, to make the Light return.*
> *Feel the warmth of the Sun, Fire Flame and Fire Burn.*
> *Feel the Magick of the Wheel return.*
> *We work our Will, and with Magick we pray,*
> *And herald in the Light of the Sun this day.*
> *Eko, Eko Ha He Yay".*

West Warden says:

> *"Let the Elements awaken that reside both within and without,*
> *Feel the warmth and light throughout and about,*
> *May our divine light within shine forth without,*
> *May our light bring a little more warmth and love into our world?*
> *Within and without.*

North Warden: Speaks from the heart saying something about exchanging energies and how to honour each other with a special exchange gift. HPs and HP are the last to receive gifts. All then play 'Pass the Parcel' as a fun start to the night.

All then stand and do a traditional yet ancient dance of the Spiral to make everyone warm and happy. Bards start to play as all join in.

> *"Dance, Dance, wherever you may be,*
> *For I am the Lord of the Dance said He.*
> *I will lead you all wherever you may be,*
> *And I will lead you all in the Dance said He".*

All stand facing the East, in receiving position imagining and absorbing the Sun-God energy of the rising Sun, with open mind, heart and a sense of welcome. Whilst this is being done the HP circles around all reverberating the Fire Elemental Didgeridoo, aiding all to open their Solar Plexus Chakra. HP then bids all to be seated and in turn each share their experiences on the rite. HPs and HP then consecrate the wine, all share. HP says:

> *"Hail to the Light of the returning Sun,*
> *We drink to the Old Gods, to the Horned One,*
> *To Cernunnos, to the Mighty Oak Tree and to the First Grandmother.*
> *A Merry Yule to all, Happy Yule everyone and Blessed Be".*

Sabbat Cakes are now consecrated. The Circle is Banished and closed, and Agape is set up for the merry feasting.

THE WINTER SOLSTICE MIDNIGHT RITE

Form the Magick Circle in the usual manner. Invoke the Mighty Ones of the Watchtowers. The Cauldron of Cerridwen is placed in the Temple at the South. It is wreathed with Holy Ivy and Mistletoe, with a Red Bale candle within. There should be none other light except this and the two Altar candles. All are purified, after which the Drawing Down of the Moon is performed onto the HPs. Then the HP stands behind the Cauldron symbolising the rebirth of the Sun. All Wiccans stand around the Magick Circle in appropriate places. HP faces the HPs with a bundle of torches or tapers, and the Book of Shadows. MiB stands beside him with a lighted taper, so that he may read by. All Wicces begin to slowly move around the Magick Circle Deosil, as each one passes between the HPs and HP, he hands them a taper already alight, until all have a lighted taper. Wiccans still dancing slowly around the Magick Circle chanting as HP says the Invocation (Cauldron is now lit) he invokes:

"Queen of the midnight Sun, Queen of the Celestial Moon,
Queens of the Stars, and Queen of the Fertile Fields and Waters.
Queen of the Living Earth, bring us the Divine Child of Promise!
He is the Lord of Light and Life, who shall be reborn again,
By the Grace of the Great Mother who gives birth to all life.

The new Sun shall arise early banishing all tears and darkness from the world,
Illumine our land golden Sun of the morning sky, illumine us with your Light.
Awaken and illumine the whole Earth, the waters and the seas,
Awakening and giving light to all life, bringing joy and love to the world.

Blessed always is our Great Mother, without beginning without end,
Everlasting to all Eternity".

HP joins the ring spiral dance, and carries the Cauldron to the centre of the Magick Circle and also joins in as all do the Chant of Bacchus. HP signals for the Sun dance to commence by calling aloud 'Bacchus'. The Sun dance continues until the last taper goes out naturally. All leap the Cauldron in pairs and in turn, the ring reforms and all stand holding hands as God speaks: Then the dance slows with 'The Horned Invocation'. Build up the Cone of Power, then change to the Wicces Rune and call drop. The energy and Magick is now sent back into the Earth to heal and awaken.

All are then purified three times each. Last candle has to pay an amusing forfeit as the HPs so Ordains. Sometimes the Cauldron is relighted several times for this purpose.

Banishing and Agape.

Yule Songs

Hark the Neo-Pagans Sing

"Hark the Neo-Pagans sing, glory to the newborn king.
Peace on earth and mercy mild, Goddess and God reconciled.
Hear us now as we proclaim, as we have risen from the flames,
Our ancient Craft we now reclaim, in the Goddess and God' loving names.
Hark the Neo-Pagans sing, glory to the newborn king.

Herne of Nature by love adored, Herne the ever-born Sun lord.
Always behold him here to come, offspring of the Ancient One.
Veiled in flesh our God shall see, hail incarnated Deity.
Our ancient Craft do we reclaim, in the Goddess and Gods loving names.
Hark the neo-Pagans sing, glory to the newborn king".

Dancing in a Wiccan Wonderland

"Wiccans sing, are you listening, Altars set, candles glistening.
It's a Magickal night we are having tonight,
Dancing in a Wiccan wonderland.

Blades held high, censer smoking,
Goddess and God, we are invoking.
Through Elements five we celebrate life.
Dancing in a Wiccan wonderland.

Queen of heaven throughout all space,
The triple Goddess all a beautiful face.
Above and below the Goddess we all know,
Dancing in a Wiccan wonderland.

Now God is the provider, supplying game for our fire,
Above and below it's the Horned One we know.
Dancing in a Wiccan wonderland.

In our Circle there is a Yule Fire, with desire await the rising of the Sun,
It's the Great Wheel turning for the New Year,
Turned with abundance and great fun.
Later on by the Fire, Cone of Power, getting higher,
It's a Magickal night we are having tonight,
Dancing in a Wiccan wonderland".

SHARE THE LIGHT

(The First Noel)

"Share the Light, share the Light, share the Light, and share the Light.
All paths are one on this holy night.
On this winter holiday, let us stop and recall,
That this season is holy to one and to all.

Unto some a Son is born, unto us comes a Sun.
And we know if they don't, that all paths are one.
Be it Chanukah or Yule, Christmas time or Solstice night,
All celebrated the eternal Light, lighted tree or burning log.
Or eight candle flames; all Gods are One God,
Whatever their name."

YE CHILDREN ALL OF MOTHER EARTH

(It Came Upon a Midnight Clear)

"Ye Children all of Mother earth, join hands and circle round,
To celebrate this Solstice night, when our lost Lord is found.
Rejoice, the year has begun again; the Sun blesses the skies up above,
So, share the season together now, in everlasting love."

OH, COME ALL YE FAITHFUL

"O come all ye faithful, gathered round the Yule fire,
O come ye, O come ye, to call the Sun.
Fires within us call the Fire above us
O come let is invoke him, o come let us invoke him,
O come let us invoke him, our Lord the Sun.

Yea, the Lord we greet thee, born again at Yuletide,
Yule fires and candle flames, are lighted for you,
Come to thy children calling for thy blessing.
O come let us invoke him, O come let us invoke him,
O come let us invoke him, our Lord the Sun".

MOON OF SILVER

(We Three Kings)

"O Moon of silver, Sun of gold, Lady and Lord so bold.
Guide us ever, failing never, lead us in the ways of old.
Maiden, Mother Ancient crone, Queen of Heaven on your throne.

Praises we sing thee, love we bring thee, for all that you have shown.
Lord of darkness, Lord of Night, gentle brother, King of might.
Praises we sing thee, love we bring thee, on this our Solstice night."

JOY TO THE WORLD

"Joy to the world, the Lord is come, let Earth receive Her King,
Let every heart prepare him room,
And heaven and nature sing, and heaven and nature sing.

Welcome our King who brings us life, our Lady gives him birth,
His living light returneth to warm the seeds within us,

And wake the sleeping Earth,
And heaven and nature sing, and heaven and nature sing.

Light, we the fires to greet our Lord, out light, our life, our King.
:et every voice be lifted to sing his holy praises
As heaven and nature sing, as heaven and nature sing".

SILENT NIGHT

"Silent Night, Solstice Night, all is calm, all is bright.
Nature slumbers in forest and glen, till in springtime she wakens again.
Sleeping Spirits grow strong, sleeping spirits grow strong.
Silent night, Solstice night, silver Moon shining bright.

Snowfall blankets the slumbering Earth,
Yule Fires welcome the Suns rebirth.
Hail the light is reborn, Hail the Light is reborn.
Silent night, Solstice night, quiet rest till the light.
Turning ever the rolling Wheel,
Brings the winter to comfort and heal,
Rest your spirit in peace, rest your spirit in peace".

Snowfall blankets the slumbering Earth,
Yule fires welcome the Suns rebirth.
Hail the Light is reborn hail the Light is reborn.
Silent Night, Solstice Night, quiet rest till the Light,
Turning ever the rolling wheel,
Brings the winter to comfort and heal.
Rest your spirit in peace; rest your spirit in peace.

GLORY TO THE NEWBORN KING

"Brothers, sisters come to sing, glory to the newborn King.
Gardens peaceful, forests wild, celebrate the winter Child.
Now the time of glowing starts, joyful hands and joyful hearts.

Cheer the Yule Log as it burns, for once again the Sun returns.

Brothers, sister are come and sing, glory to the newborn King.
Brothers, sisters singing come, glory to the newborn Sun.
Through the wind and dark of night, celebrate the coming Light.

Suns glad rays through fears cold burns,
Life through death the wheel now turns.
Gather round the Yule log and tree celebrates life's Mystery.
Brothers, sisters singing come, glory to the newborn Sun."

GOD REST YE MERRY PAGANFOLK

"God rest ye merry Paganfolk let nothing you dismay.
Remember that the Sun returns upon this Solstice day.
The growing dark is ending now, and spring is on its way,

O tidings of comfort and joy, comfort and joy,
O tidings of comfort and joy.

The Goddess rests ye merry too, and keeps you safe from harm.
Remember that we live within the circle of her arms.
And may hr love give years to come, a very special charm,
O tidings of comfort and joy, comfort and joy,
O tidings of comfort and joy".

THE GODDESS BLESS THEE COVENFOLK

"The Goddess bless ye Covenfolk, let nothing you dismay,
For lo the Sun is born again upon this Yuletide day.
Delivering us from the dark, and leading to the day.
The power of the Pentagram is old, yet ever new.
The Goddess doth three faces have, the Lords is three-faced too.
And three faces are the Holy Fool, a Mystery waits for you.

The dancers of the Holy year are eight, both great and small,
The Circles three, the Quarters four, Watchtowers standing very tall.
Be joyful for the secret is the Goddess who rules them all.
Within the blessed Apple lies the message of our Queen,
For from this Pentacle shall raise the orchards fresh and green.
The Earth shall blossom once again, the Air be clear and clean.

Ye sisters of the sacred Moon, ye Sun Lords of the day,
Remember when the blessing comes, it alters every way.
Encircling then the world of men, and leading to the May.
So Merry meet, ye Covenfolk in forest, field or hall,
And hold your freedom close at hand, no more to be enthralled.
The Goddess and God love ye every single one and all,
The time is past when we need to bow to words laid down by men.
Tear down the walls that bar our way, and once more seek the Glen.
The tree they turned into a cross is growing green again".

Imbolg
August Eve

Riding Poles and Besoms.

Imbolg or Oimelc (mothers milk). Proceed to site, with dance step and chant waving Besoms and Torches. HPs. carries a Phallic Wand or Besom (erect). The Volta Dance.

> *"Come, come, come to the Sabbat,*
> *Come to the Sabbat with love and join us there".*

When the procession enters the Magick Circle the chant changes to:

> *"Black Spirits and white, red spirits and grey,*
> *Come ye and come ye, and come ye that may.*
> *Around and around, throughout and about,*
> *The power coming in and the Love going out".*

The Magick Circle is formed in the usual manner; HP enters with Sword in right hand, Phallus in left hand erect. All then drink of the Chalice of milk and honey, it is passed around the Circle, this represents the Goddess within them. They are all presented with a small white candle lighted.

HPS says:

"Blessed Be and welcome to our Sacred Temple of Elphane, One of the Old religion, and the Realm of the Living Goddess and God. Know that this is a time when the Goddess returns from the Annwyn (The Underworld), and the ancient Mother Earth rejoices. The Earth is about to be reawakened after a long winter sleep. It is about the Earth and new beginnings. The ritual itself celebrates the Quickening, the defeat of winter and the growing Light of Spring. New things are starting to happen, flowers are renewing their birthing smiles to the world, lambs are being born, trees are showing off

their new display of colour in their leaves. And if we listen carefully we will hear the birds singing more and more, for they are already preparing their last years nest, or making a new one for their offspring.

A child may stir in the womb for she who waits, and may the love and light of the Quickening become stronger. Each face of the Goddess has her own colour and tonight we use white candles and white flowers to symbolise the Maiden Goddess.

Know that the maiden Goddess lies within your own being. Within our sacred Temple are the Pathways to many chambers and within these chambers are stored many Magickal treasures to which you can attain. As they are unfolded unto you, let them be unfolded by you for the Magickal tree of Life thrives upon the leaf that it casts unto the Earth".

HP: Asks the Wiccans what it is in their lives that they wish to quicken in their life, focusing on their candles and telling all. After all, have said their piece, we all call upon the Goddess. The HPs stirs the Cauldron of water as they are saying their parts. They then place their lit candle near the Cauldron as it is swirling. HP says:

> *"On this night the Goddess awakens and comes unto us,*
> *Let us open our hearts and call unto her.*
> *Candle flames lightly burn by the Cauldron in a churn,*
> *Making this Wheel of Magick turn.*
> *Candle flame and candles burn.*
> *May North and South, and East and West this night bless us all!*
> *By the One, the One in Three, consecrate our wishes, so mote it be".*

Elder says:

"Everyone now turn your attention to our Mother Earth and ask Her to awaken once more from the winters months. After Her long-deserved rest. We also ask that all those who dwell on and within the Earth to awaken as well".

Wicce Lights a candle from the Bale fire and presents it to the Maiden.

Wicce light a candle from the Bale Fire and presents to the HPs.

Wicce PRESENTS UNLIT candle from the Bale Fire and presents to the Crone.

Then says:

> *"Behold the three formed Goddess in Triune.*
> *She who is ever three, the Maiden, Mother and Crone.*
> *Yet without spring there can be no summer,*
> *And without summer there can be no winter,*
> *And without winter there can be no spring".*

He then lights the Crones candle.

Maiden lays aside posy and candle, and takes up the Besom and sweeps the Magick Circle. She then takes up the posy and the candle. Goes to the Altar and extinguishes the flame saying:

> *"The quenching of the flame in this Magickal Realm is the sign of the awakening of*
> *The flame of Divine Spirit, within the Womb of the Great Mother Goddess.*
> *I now declare this Rite ended. Let we Her children go forth bearing the sacred Light of*
> *The eternal Three Faced Goddess. So, mote it be!"*

Initiations if any, then cakes and wine.

Candle Games.

G/R if possible.

Agape and Dances.

THE SPRING EQUINOX
21-22 SEPTEMBER

Ostara marks the first day of spring, which is the 1st of September, this is the Awakening of the Earth. The actual Equinox is between the 21st – 23rd, at this time the world is Quickening, young animals race through the fields playing and frolicking just as humans are doing for the Sun has returned. Humans are starting to busy themselves again for summer. Tea-trees, She Oaks, Golden Wattles and Eucalypts are putting on new leaves, Crocuses, Spring Bulbs such as Daffodils, Primroses, Iris's and Violets are with us once again. We can now see the corn growing in the fields, and the wheat reaching high for the Sun, as the grass is beginning to grow. Soon it will be time for the Blackthorn to blossom, whilst apple orchards make a lovely display of flowering colours. It is time to celebrate the equality of Light and dark in all life. The exact time of the Equinox is almost invariably early in the morning just before sunrise. We have to coincide our time of the festival, for on the Vernal Equinox both day and night are equal. At Samhain, we said goodbye to the old year before midnight, and sent up rockets and fireworks to greet the new at midnight. Now we bid the dark farewell, and greet the light the following morning.

All in attendance bring their own hand decorated Eostre Eggs (boiled eggs) and place them around the perimeter of the Magick Circle. Everyone is robed and readied for the Rite of Spring. All Wiccans wearing dark robes and capes, all Wicces wearing strong vibrant colours, and Priesthood wearing Spring colours. Ladies bring a plate of food and the males bring drinks. The Maidens bring flowers to the Magick Circle. The circle is covered with spring flowers and leaves of spring. On the Altar are seeds, unleavened bread and a mixture of apples and nuts, and whatever fruit is ripe at this time.

All dance to the Magick Circle following the Bards saying:

"Come, come, come to the Sabbat,
Come to the Sabbat with Love and join us there".

(All repeat until arrival at the Circle) All assemble on the outer of the Magick Circle, then they are brought in with The Shepherds Dance, Priesthood first who form a central circle and the others form an outer circle and the Magick Circle is then cast. The symbol of the Wheel should be placed on the Altar; flanked with burning candles. The Wicces Rune and appropriate chants are then done.

Everyone is then asked to be seated around the Circle and meditate and visualise a happy experience in the Lands of Hearts desire - Ildathac, having read these ancient words spoken to Bran by a Faerie woman:

> *"Take this branch from the sacred Apple Tree of Emhain, like those that are familiar, twigs of white-silver are on it, and crystal buds with flowers. There is an Island far, far away, around which the sea horses glisten, flowing of their white course against the glistening shore. Four magnificent Pillars support it, shining through aeons of beauty, a lovely land through the ages of the world on which many flowers rain down.*
>
> *There is a huge Magickal Tree there with blossoms on which the birds call at the hour. Colours of every hue gleam throughout soft familiar fields without sorrow, without grief, without death, without any sickness at all.*
>
> *That is the character of the many coloured rainbow land – Ildathac.*
>
> *Let the God Bran listen to wisdom expounded to Him. Do not sink upon a bed of sloth; do not let your bewilderment overwhelm you.*
>
> *Begin a voyage across the clear sea to find if you may reach the Land of Woman".*

All now stand as the Magick Circle is cast, followed by the Wicces Rune. The Goddess of the night is Dana and the God is Bran.

HPs:

> *"Let us now welcome spring as a symbol of life, of growth and of rebirth, a symbol of the Light of the Eternal Spirit. Today we celebrate the unification of our Great Mother with Her Consort the Honed One. Together they are the radiant Light, the Eternal Spirit of all that is, for today the almighty father, Her son is born, dies and is reborn anew, but know that our Great Mother is forever".*

HP:

> *"To day we have kindled the flame this day in the presence of the Ancient Ones,*
> *Without jealousy, without envy, without malice,*
> *Without fear of anything beneath the Sun.*
> *We Invoke the Great God of the solar powers and who is the Light of all life.*
> *May he be a bright Light before us, and a bright Light behind us, and a bright Light?*
> *Within us, and a bright Light above us as a Guiding Star.*

> *Ignite within our hearts a Light of Love unconditionally for everyone and for everything,*
> *to all of life on our beautiful large Earth. We call upon the Sacred Light which is the*
> *great merciful son of the Great Goddess come thou forth and be with us on all levels".*

Maiden:

> *"All winter long did our Great mother nurture Her Divine Son that he may*
> *grow strong into His manhood as a good a loving Man and God.*
> *As the Sun has entered the first degree of the vernal Equinox, so did the Great Father*
> *become One with the Eternal Spirit, where they dance eternally together as One. Now*
> *the Great Mother and Father, Her son, speak to us once more saying: 'Each Spring let our*
> *sacred Union be celebrated by all who through us are United in the Eternal Spirit".*

All:

> *"Glory is to the Great Mother and to the Great Father Her Divine*
> *Son and to the Eternal Spirit which is the Light of Man".*

Elder:

> *"And so were the Great Mother and father united, that all life flourish on Earth, and then*
> *in their Union in all humanity is made whole. So, we need to listen carefully for the Great*
> *Mother speaks to us through Her Nature and her daughters say: 'Through our Union are all*
> *redeemed from the concept of original sin. For just as my son was born from me, so has all of*
> *humanity issued forth from me pure and without sin, and all who join in me are sanctified*
> *by me. For the power of life and of Love are Holy, so let bondage be replaced by freedom, and*
> *sadness by singing and rejoicing, and as our Divine Father planted the Sacred Seed of Life,*
> *so let us plant seeds that life must continue to flourish in their divine names on Earth".*

MiB:

> *"But before we share of the seed let us here of the Creation from the First of the Mothers and Father of time and space. 'The Megaliths of the Old Religion Wicca'".*

Elders: All Elders standing within the centre of the Magick Circle, each steps out of the circle and speaks as they walk around the circle Deosil.

- Crone Elder:

"I am the First of the Ancient Ones. I have been here and seen the Dawn of Time from the Sun beyond our Earth. Men call me 'The Stone Goddess', ancient, steadfast and very wise".

(She moved around to all the Elders and faces each and looks into their eyes)

- Magi Elder:

  "I am the Second of the Ancient Ones. I opened my arms to the Stone Goddess and cooled Her Fire with my breath. I am the Primordial Movement, the First stirring of the Winds of Time and Space. Men call me the 'Father of Chaos'."

- Crone Elder:

  "I am the Third of the Ancient Ones. I was the Water upon the face of these Two. From my depths, all life was formed. The breath of the Father of Chaos softened my face. Men call me 'Mara, the bitter One, the Primordial Sea".

- Magi Elder:

  "I am the Fourth of the Ancient Ones, I gave my warmth to the Three. From my brilliance, Mara was given beauty. Men call me Sol, I am the Sun".

- HPs:

"I am the Fifth of the Ancient Ones. I gave my Light the Darkness. Mine are the tides to rule. Though my brother the Sun shows greater brilliance. I too have My Bounty. Men call me the Virgin, I am also named Luna, and I am the Moon".

- HP:

"I am the Sixth of the Ancient Ones. I ride the earth on cloven feet, or on wings of Air. I am the Hunter and the Hunted, the Stag and the Horse, Bud and beast are mine, and with the aid of the Sun, whose call I must answer. I reproduce my kind. Men kill in lust for me, for I am named Herne, Pan, Cernunnos, I am the Horned One".

- HPs:

"I am the Seventh of the Ancient Ones, I am the Floral One. All laughter and joy are mine. With Cernunnos I call all living things to join our sacred dance. I am the eternal She who knows not destruction. The silvery fish are mine, as are also the spinners of webs, the weavers of dreams. Men know me as the Great Mother".

- Priest: MiB:

"I am the Eighth of the Ancient Ones, I am a Mystery, for I am my own Twin. My two faces are Life and Light. Sol and the winds that cool him are both of my essence. Men know me as the Mover and fertilizer, and call me Air and Fire".

- Priestess: Maiden:

"I am the Ninth of the Ancient Ones. With Life and Light, I am wholeness, for I am Love and law. The Father of Chaos and the Bitter Sea are my parents. Men know me as the Nourisher and shape-giver, and call me Water and earth. My brother Air and Fire and I are the Quartered Circle of Creation".

- Priest:

"I am the Tenth of the Ancient Ones. I am the Pupil of all the others. I began with Sol, and then entered into Chaos, and ended with the dark Waters of the ocean. From the belly I came unto the womb I go. I am nothing, and yet I am Lord of all. I shall cease and yet return. I am good, and I am more terrible than those who have been before me, for I am Man".

- Priestess:

"I am the Eleventh of the Ancient Ones. I too am the Pupil with Man. I seek the Truth. Mine is the Great Cauldron of Cerridwen of Creation, yet I am ever Virgin. I am more terrible than man, for logic and reason are not mine when my little ones are destroyed by any of the others. I am warm yet cold, gentle yet destructive. I mirror the Stone One and the Floral One, I am Woman".

- Priest:

"I am the twelfth of the Ancient Ones. Hide from my face if you will, but know that I am the most powerful of all. The Man and Woman dance within me, and even the Floral One weeps summers tears at my command. For I am an ever-turning Wheel. I am the Spinner and the Weaver and cut the silver cords of time. Men know me as Fate, and I am the Hermaphrodite".

- Priestess:

"I am the Thirteenth of the Ancient Ones. I am the Shadow of the Sanctuary and the Silver Wheel of Arianhrod. I am feared, yet loved. Often yearned for. I ride my white Mare over the battlefields and in my arms the sick and retired find rest. We shall be together many times, for though I am the victor, yet am I also the loneliest of all the Thirteen. To seek the Hermaphrodite is to know that I am but an illusion. Woe is to me, the Thirteenth One, and yet all Joy is mine also. For from my embrace is renewed life, and to know Me is to meet, and know and remember and love again. Men know me as Death, yet I am the Comforter and Renewer, the corrective principle in creation. The Scythe and the Victors crown are mine; for of all the Thirteen, I am the only one who is not Eternal".

All Elders now link hands in the centre of the Magick Circle and slowly dance and move around the Circle as HPs says:

"We are the Henge of all Creation, we are the Megaliths of Old, the
Ancient Ones, the Guardians of the Path of true Knowledge, and we are the
Thirteen Keepers of the Inner gates of the Magick Circle - HOLD".

All Elders in turn then acknowledge who they are by saying again, *"I AM"*.

HP places a Pentacle of mixed seed in the centre of the Magick Circle as all link and chant and dance starting slow and building gradually to a sudden stop chanting:

"EE-YAY-OHHH-HMMM."

MiB: Takes up the Pentacle of Seed and takes it around to each Wicce saying:

"Out of all that we have been, three seeds must be selected. Then out of the three, select only one
to the holy seed out of which will grow the souls and selves we shall become. For this is a constant
process. Let us now charge the one selected seed with strength, light, love and good health".

HPs: Goes to the Altar and takes up the Pentacle and raises it high and says:

"We call upon the Ancient Ones the wisest of all, along with our very
selves to bless these seeds with your eternal spark of Divine Life".

All then lead by the Bards as we sing and dance and plant our Seeds into the cauldron filled with Earth. After this is done. Crone HPs and Magi HP approach the Altar and take up the Chalice of Wine and the Sabbat cakes and hold them whilst Magi says:

"Man and Woman approach the Altar of the Mysteries, come forth and bless these gifts".

They approach and place their hands over the cakes and wine as Crone HPs says:

"O woman, O man, it is for you to fathom the Mysteries which have here been shown.
Thus, it has ever been since we first gave birth to you. Therefore, it is to you we give
this food and wine, which being of the Earth, is the fruit of us all, that you may bless
it for us all for as you have need of the Gods and Goddesses, so also do the Goddesses
and God have need for you. Here lies the Mystery of Truth. So, mote it be".

All now share as Man and Woman pass them around the Circle with the saying:

"May you never thirst, May you never Hunger".

Beltane:
November Eve

The Magick Circle is cast in the usual manner. Men supply the torches for the Meeting Dance; all supply their own Riding Poles and Besoms.

Fire - a small fire will be prepared in the centre of the Magick Circle, with a mini fire on top within a Cauldron. The Maiden supplies the red tapers. The Meeting Dance all rides their Besoms and Poles to the site with laughter and excitement. HP leading, the men who are carrying torches. Men go first as women chase. Man in Black brings up the rear with the Scourge, all mime and says the Chain Dance; this is repeated until they arrive at the Magick Circle.

HP and HPs enter Circle then cast it whilst others remain outside. After the Conjuration all are brought in and greeted clearly 'Blessed Be' with their craft name if they have one. HPs. closes the Circle and the Watchtowers are Invoked, then the Wicces Rune. HPs. says the Invocation to the Goddess, and then a ring dance, Maiden stands outside dancers with the chant. HPs. goes to the inside of dancers. Dance slows and quietens but continues except when the Coven are invoking.

Narrator:

"O Great Mother Goddess, O powerful Father God,
Here our call and answer to all the Mysteries especially the Mysteries that are yet
Unanswered. In this sacred Magick Circle of great power we open ourselves to your
Guide us that we may walk the sacred Ley lines Wicces long past.
We dedicate ourselves to you and all that you stand for mighty Mother and Father.
(Pause for a moment)
May we breathe in your sacred breath and absorb your radiant energy deep
into our bodies. Mingling, merging, blending yours with ours.
May we see with your eyes and know the divine to be in all life and that all is Divine.

We dance with your divinity within our very souls.
Make us One with you both and let us radiant your divine Light, make us divine, and
Make us truly blessed with your all-knowing Knowledge and with
that knowledge, the wisdom to use it wisely. Blessed be".

The Magick Circle is now cast in full.

Narrator continues:

"The Major Festival of Beltane is symbolised by Fertility and Fire,
The ever-burning flame of Divine love.
The holy Union of the Goddess and God, the Blessed fertility of the Great Rite.
The awakening of the Great Sun God, the birthing in summer.
He who seeks the ever-changing feminine Goddess.
Yet which is she The Virginal Maiden. Or the nurturing Mother or the wise old Crone?
Which strictness is to behold.
Arise black goat of the North so you may face that which you deserve.
We say farewell to the ancient God of Darkness; may you
slumber peacefully until your rebirth."

All say with Horned Salute:

"Hail and Farewell Great Lord of Darkness".

Narrator continues:

"At this time as with Samhain the veil between the worlds is at its thinnest. May we
Think of those of the past with blossoming love and deepest respect.
Know that they watch and smile down upon us, as we celebrated this Fertile Sabbat.
May the smoke from our Bale Fire spiral upwards towards them wrapping around
them with our love, blessings and best wishes. Let the Rite of Beltane begin".

All:

"Let the Rite of Beltane begin".

HPs. Steps forward and extinguishes the candle in the Cauldron and says:

"The Bale Fire is out, and the Light of our Lord is no more, the King of the dark is dead. For he loves of the Goddess has put him to rest, and along with him has gone the Stirrings of all life. Where are the birds? Where are the crops? Where are the Flowers? Where are the young? What shall we do to overcome this time of? Darkness"?

Narrator says: (Parts of this ritual are excerpts from Dion Fortunes book "The Goat-Foot God" which was published in 1938 and taken from its original text in a 15th century novel of the same name.)

"I heard the voice of destiny, calling out over the Ionian Sea,
The great God Pan is dead, is dead. Humbled is his Horned Head.
We shut the door that has no key, and waste the Vales of Arcady.

Shackled by the Iron Age, lost in woodland heritage.
Heavy goes the heart of man, parted from the Light-foot Pan.
Wearily he wears the chains until the Goat-God comes again".

Women invoke:

"Half a man and half a beast, Pan is greatest, Pan is least.
Pan is all, and all is Pan, look for him in every man.
Goat hoof swift and shaggy thigh, follow him to Arcady".

Men invoke:

"He shall wake the living dead, cloven hoof and horned head.
Human heart and human brain, pan the Goat-God comes again.
Half a beast and half a man, Pan is all, and all is Pan.
Come O goat-God come again".

All: Chant with gusto.

"Relight the Fire of Beltane, relight the Fire of Beltane,
"Relight the Fire of Beltane, relight the Fire of Beltane".

Elder:

> *"I ignite this Fire for Beltane and all that it symbolises.*
> *Come forth God of Light and take hold of that which you deserve.*
> *O Great God pan, return to Earth again, come at our call and show yourself to man.*
> *Shepherd of goats, upon the wild hills way, lead your flock from darkness unto day.*
> *Forgotten are the ways of sleep and night, men seek for them whose eyes have lost*
> *The Light.*
> *Open the doors of dreams, whereby men come unto thee,*
> *Shepherd of goats, answer unto me".*

HP: then invokes onto himself as coven invokes with the Horned Invocation. HP turns to the South in God Position with Wand and Scourge. HPs. covers him with a black veil and horns as she gives him the 5/s.

Women Invoke:

> *"Half a man and half a beast, Pan is greatest Pan is least. Etc".*

Men invoke:

> *"He shall wake the living dead, cloven hoof and horned head. Etc".*

Women invoke:

> *"I.O.Pan. I.O.Pan. Pan. Pan. I. O. Pan". (ee-oh-pan)*

Men invoke:

> *"I.O.Pan. I.O.Pan. Pan. Pan. I. O. Pan". (ee-oh-pan)*

Continue chanting alternatively until Power is raised and the HPs. raises her hands in invocation. At this signal slow the chant and stop. HPs. gives 5/S whilst removing the veil, and returns to her position. The females come forward and give 5/s, while the males give Horned Salute. All dance around chanting quietly, speed up then slow, and stop and face God in God position HP as God says:

> *"Half a man and Half a beast, Pan is greatest Pan is least.*
> *I am all and I am Pan, Look for me in every man.*
> *I bring life and I bring fear, by joy and terror knows me near.*
> *I shall wake the living dead, cloven hoof and horned head.*
> *Human heart and human brain, Pan the Goat-God comes again.*
>
> *Half a beast and half a man, I am all and I am Pan.*
> *Prepare the fertile soil for me, prepare the wine of ecstasy.*

Plant the vine and plant the grain, for Pan the Goat0God comes again.
O faint of heart prepare to flee, for I am Life, and Life is Me.
I am the Goat-God and I come again".

HPs. takes the Chalice and HP Consecrates and all drink.

Feast and Games.

SUMMER SOLSTICE
PAGANS IN THE PARK

DECEMBER 21 – 22

This is a day of family and celebration without so much ritual. It is about sharing with brothers and sisters and our families and enjoying the rebirth of the warm summer, and our beautiful beaches. Life awakens and revitalises all our energies into a new world of hope and strength, in readiness for the New Year ahead. We welcome La Bafana the Yule Wicce/Faery for the children, and we have a few dressed as bad Pixies who are constantly trying to steal the children's gifts to be presented later by La Bafana. So, we make sure that the children are on guard watching for the bad Pixies so they do not take their gifts before La Bafana presents them to the children. This keeps the children amused and at times chasing away the bad Pixies, who always seem to return.

It is a social day for Elders, Priesthood, Wicces, Wiccans and all are invited, as it is an open day of Celebration, out in the community mixing one with all. We usually have the Morrison Dancers invited to perform, we also have a Court Jester for the children as well.

There is Circle Dancing and singing with the Bards, followed by barbecues and feasting usually alongside the beach where we all swim and enjoy the day and the community. In this way without words we are honouring our returning God of Light who brings the warmth to the Earth for all to enjoy and thrive. It is our way of Thanksgiving.

La Bafana then one by one hands out the gifts from her (from the parents) to all the children, but if the child has been bad they receive a lump of coal, usually this goes to a chosen adult and definitely the Pixies.

THE CHAIN DANCE

(This is where the Goddess transforms through these
animals to escape being found by her chaser).

All:

"Cunning and art he did not lack, but aye Her whistle would fetch him back".

Male:

"Oh I shall go into a hare, with sorrow and signing and mickle care.
And I shall go in the Horned Ones name, aye till I be fetched hame".

Females:

"Hare take heed of a bitch Greyhound, will harry thee all these fells around.
For here I come in our Lady's name, all but for to fetch thee hame".

Male:

"Yet I shall go into a Trout, with sorrow and signing and mickle doubt.
And show thee many a merry game, ere that I be fetched hame".

Female:

"Trout take heed of an Otter Lank, will harry thee from bank to bank.
For here I come in our Lady's name, all but for to fetch thee hame".

Male:

"Yet I shall go into a bee, with mickle horror and dread of thee.
And flit to hive in the Horned Ones name, ere that I be fetched hame".

Female:

> *"Bee, take heed of a swallow hen, will harry thee close both butt and ben.*
> *For here I come in our Lady's name, all but for to fetch thee hame".*

Male:

> *"Yet I shall go into a Mouse, and haste me into a miller's house.*
> *There is his*

Female:

> *"Mouse takes heed of a white tab Cat, which never was baulked by Mouse or Rat.*
> *For I will crack thy bones in our Lady's name, thus shalt thou be fetched hame".*

THE CANDLE GAME

Men form a circle sitting on the floor or standing as arranged. They pass a lighted candle from hand to hand, Deosil. The women form a circle outside, standing on something of too short. They try to blow it our over their shoulders, whosoever hand it is in when it is blown out. Must give 5/S and penance to the lady in return.

This game may go on for as long as the Circle likes.

Other games and dances are at Will.

Cakes and Wine.

THE EIGHT
GATEKEEPERS
OF THE ANCIENT
TEMPLES

We call upon these archetypes as Gatekeepers and Guardians of the ancient Temple, the Magick Circle of Wicces. They were the keepers of the wisdom of man and our cultures and Magickal Arts. Create your sacred space, and no tools are required except a true and open heart, a focused will, and a devout belief.

Warden of the North East Invokes:

"Mighty Uranus God of change we call, charge us with freedom, one and all.
Breath to the east and the circle round, the ancient Truth we seek to be found.
Guardian of this Magick Sphere, come forth, we seek your Powers here.
Come Mighty Lord by hearts command in Light,
Great Uranus, your powers we call to this sacred Site".

Warden of the East Invokes:

"Great Winged Mercury, Gatekeeper of the East, I call your sacred Breath by Power
Of mind, new knowledge and truth I seek to find.
Clear our thoughts that we may share, with One and all the Powers of Air.
Gatekeeper of the Sphere of the East we seek your Powers here.
Come Mighty Winged Mercury, Messenger of light,
Be here with us this sacred Night".

Warden of the South East Invokes:

"Mighty Mars sacred hearts Ether and Spirits Power,
Send forth your Flames of faith from your great Watchtower.
Spiralling cones of illumined energy going higher and higher.
Enhance my Will with the Dragons Sacred Powers of Fire.
Gatekeeper of the South-east Sphere brings thy Power of Light here.
Come mighty Mars with all your might, send forth your Powers this sacred night".

Warden of the South Invokes:

"Jupiter of grandeur and Mars so bright, the flaming Sun so full of radiant Light
Flames of South bring passions heat, warm energy; awaken our hearts, merry meet.

Great Gatekeeper of the Sphere, we seek your Powers of Fire here.
Come Great Jupiter planet of Hidden Sight, be here with us this sacred night".

Warden of the South West Invokes:

"I call to the primordial soul of Neptune's Great Power,
Send forth your Magick tides from your Western Tower.
Bathe us in your love with feelings true, great power of Water we welcome you.
Gatekeeper of the South-western Sphere sends forth you Magick powers here.
Come great Neptune keeper of the laws of right, be here with us this sacred night".

Warden of the West Invokes:

"From the Primordial depth now rise, lift thy trident Great Neptune to the skies.
As Silver Moon dances on waves of night, sent forth to bathe us with your Light.
Gatekeeper of the Western Sphere, Secrets of Waters Powers be here.
Come mighty Pluto with your powers of Might, be here with us this sacred night".

Warden of the North West Invokes:

"I call unto the Earth and Venus too solidarity of great power,
Send forth your strength and courage in this needed hour.
Seasons come, and seasons go, Magick of Nature help us to grow.
Gatekeeper of the North-Western Sphere, we seek your Magick here.
Come bright Venus Goddess of love and Light, be here with us this sacred night".

Warden of the North Invokes:

"Powerful Saturn of all that's solid and firm, send forth your knowledge that we
may learn. Throughout our lands its change we seek, bring forth your Magick make
us strong not meek. We call for more strength and time to build anew, on all levels
guide us true. Gatekeeper of the Northern Sphere we seek your firm Powers here.
Come great Saturn with your power of flight, be here with us this sacred night".

Everyone now sits and meditates drawing in the energy that they require and visualising these Gods and Goddesses walking amongst us and bestowing their gifts upon us. At the end we share the Chalice and Cakes, then ask the Gods and Goddess to happily return to their own realms, thanking them for what they have given us, and they are also welcomed here.

SPELLS

SPELL OF GIVING THANKS

"As Wiccans we give thanks to the Ancient Ones,
To our Goddess Aradia and God Cernunnos.
For this richness and all the beauty in our life.
Bringing us positivity and removing strife.
As there must be rain with the Sun, to make all things grow,
Plant a seed in my mind so Truth I will know.
We must know pain and sorrow with our heartfelt happiness and love,
Water the garden of our mind with your light from above.
In this we learn to know all things, lift our hearts so that may sing.
Oh, Goddess and God our Love is ever with you,
Always guiding, and loving and knowledge so true.
Even though we know not your thoughts, we believe within our soul and heart,
We will always be together through love and never apart.
Aradia and Cernunnos bless your children now,
Keep us devout and true in your service, and the service of the Living Earth,
We thank you for your bounty and the harvest that we reaped.
We thank you for being tolerant of our ignorance, by giving us hope, love, laughter
and joy. We thank you for that sacred spark that illumines our souls and brings us
together as spiritual kin. We thank you great Goddess and God for everything".

To Banish Evil

"*Hekas, Hekas Este Bibeloi! Hekas, Hekas Este Bibeloi!*
Hekas, Hekas Este Bibeloi! Hekas, Hekas Este Bibeloi!
Hail Aradia Goddess of the East, hail Cernunnos of the East.
Hail Aradia Goddess of the South, hail Cernunnos of the South.
Hail Aradia Goddess of the West, hail Cernunnos of the West.
Hail Aradia Goddess of the North, hail Cernunnos of the North.

From the Amalthean Horn pour forth-great gift of Love,
I bend my knees before thee; I adore thee to the end.
When other Gods are Fallen and put to scorn,
Know that your foot is to my lip, my sighs upborne.
My prayers answered upon the rising incense smoke.

Rise Great Ones and curl about my heart,
Mighty Mother Goddess and Great Horned God.
Hekas, Hekas Este Bibeloi! Hekas, Hekas Este Bibeloi!
Hekas, Hekas Este Bibeloi! Hekas, Hekas Este Bibeloi!

O Ancient Ones place a shield, a barrier around me like a mirror,
To reflect all evil and harm that comes my way.
Defend me, protect me, and keep evil at bay be you far from me all that is profane.
Keep all darkness and evil away, for this is my Will make it as I say".

Ancient Invocation to Aradia and Cernunnos

(Invoked by Elders)

"Enos Arida Juvate, Enos Arida Juvate, Enos Arida Juvate.
Neve Luerve Cernunnos, Neve Luerve Cernunnos, Neve Luerve Cernunnos.
Sins incurrere in Pleores, Sins incurrere in Pleores, Sins incurrere in Pleores,
Satur Fu fere Dianus, Satur Fu fere Dianus, Satur Fu fere Dianus.
Linen salt sta Berber, Linen salt sta Berber, Linen salt sta Berber,
Triumphe, Triumphe, Triumphe.
Seminis alternate advocapito, conctos, conctos, conctos".

"Enter I the Circle old, with Love and Courage so bold.
Great Goddess and Horned God hear me call, Guardians of the Wicces all.
Take my token, take my love, given to you beneath and far above.
As the mill around I tread, guide me in my ways ahead.
Guide me and forge my spirit keen and bright,
Leading from darkness into the Light.
Spells and symbols, thoughts and deed,
Prompted by the Holy Wiccan Rede.

Green is the Goddess and green is the God,
I praise you both with Flaming Rod.
I.O. Evo. He the Ancient Ones I call to thee,
I.O. Evo. He send your blessings and powers to me".

SUMMONING THE ANCIENT WATCHTOWERS

"By Easterly Air I conjure your Wind, that malice will not enter herein.
Sacred Sylphides at play, bring your powers this sacred day.

By Southerly Fire I summon Blades of Will,
That I be safe at gate, and door and windowsill.
Sacred Salamanders with Dragons Breath,
keep me with life and at bay keep death.

By Westerly Water I conjure peace and calm,
That envy and pride do me no harm.
Sacred Undines flowing with tides of Life,
Protect my Magick Circle from all approaching strife.

By Northerly Earth I summon walls so strong,
That harming hand will do me no wrong.
Sacred Gnomes so strong and bold,
Protect my Magick Circle as in the days of old.

Air, Water, Earth and Fire combine,
To keep and Guard this Magick Circle of mine".

ANCIENT MAGICKAL RING SPELL

"By Air and Fire, Water and Earth, O graven ring that I gave birth.
Art, thou made of silver pure, from the gaze of Luna's bright allure?
Do my bidding every hour, for within are the Elements of Power.

Be now as Wand, Sword and Staff, to bind such foe that I may laugh.
To invoke, banish and to heal, by powers of the Goddess to whom I kneel.

All Powers do invoke unto this Ring, by Elemental powers make this Magick sing.
Powers above and below combine; awaken this Magick Ring of mine.
For this is my Magick ring, so mote it be!
No powers of darkness can ever touch me".

GRACE

"Maiden, Mother and Crone Divine, bless my food and bless my wine.
Give us health, wealth and wisdom, the divine three, for as I do will, so mote it be".

CALLING THE MATRIARCHS

"Humbly call forth through space and time,
Calling all the Matriarchs of the N: _____ family line.
For all who want the truth revealed, and all who wish the past be healed.
Open secrets and hearts unsealed bring forth your Magick as it is Willed.
From now until its now again, I call forth all Matriarchs of my kin.
Across time and space be welcomed here; aid us now so please be near.
Awaken great mothers from time first begun, come now great mothers as the Spell is
done. Come Matriarchs come mothers let the Spell be won".

Love Chant & Binding Spell

"I sew your Shadow with my hair, I bind your Shadow unto me,
By night and day, you will remain, before the Triune Goddess Three
I bind your Shadow unto me, Maiden, Mother and Hecate.
Dawn and noon and night black sea,
Free thou art but bound to me.
You are now mine eternally".

SEXUALITY ATTRACTION SPELL

"I dance the dance of dreaming, lonely by the crystal sea,
I spin the web of mist and Moonshine, lover come to loves demand and follow me.
I chant the chant of two souls entwining, around and through the sacred lustful fire,
Come drink the well of mist and Moonshine, loved one come beloved to loves desire.

Dream the dreams of solemn passion, through the star encrusted night,
I weave the web of mist and Moonshine, loved one know our Loves delight.
Hear the tides of heaving waters, sombre on the crystal sand,
Hear the chant of longing and waiting, come fulfil at my loves demand.

Seek and love my waiting body, that's is waiting by the sea,
Tread the path of mist and Moonshine, love, come Beloved to me".

EXORCISM

"Dark souls and demons who hide in space,
Who hide amidst the Shadows behind an innocent's face?
Know this Wicces Magick to be powerful and true,
Be gone evil forces dark entities too.
My Spell casts you out, so be gone and disappear,
For you are not welcomed anywhere near.
Darkness dissolves by Loves pure light,
You are Banished and exorcised by Magick this sacred night".

TO HEAR SECRET THOUGHTS

"As my Altar flame illumines and gives birth to new Shadows,
And true Light gives and removes darkness and fear.
Open your secret thoughts to my Magickal ear.
And from the rising of incense smoke,
Twist and turn and creep, whether you are awake or fast asleep.
Open your mind, and your thoughts open now unto mine,
Bring forth your secret thoughts to me, all your secret thoughts so I may see.
Bring your innermost thoughts and voices unto my mind,
To understand your secret speech.
Open your thoughts and let them be drawn to me like the drawing of a leech.
Come oh secrets, oh thoughts come unto me,
As I have willed so mote it be".

TO FIND A LOST SOUL

Place the following ingredients into a mortar and mix well:

- A pinch of fresh Rosemary
- A small sprig of Cypress
- Piece of Yarrow Root
- Pinch of Rock Salt.

Grind all these ingredients with your Pestle whilst constantly chanting.

"Spirits of all lost souls arise and come unto me,
Floating lost and unseen across the skies.
The one I seek I call out to you, I call to your soul whether near or afar.

Come to me now as this I do Will. Show me your spirit ever so bright.
Lost Soul, Lost One, Child of Earth come to me this night.
Show me your radiance and reveal where your Soul resides,
Show to me who and where you are, and where it is that your Soul abides.
Awaken your electric Soul side so that I may see, drawn by my Magnetic Spirit in me.
Come Lost Soul, come unto me, show me forth where you may be,
Come forth from the Shadows as I do Will, so mote it be".

Now add a drop of their family's blood into the Mortar and continue chanting:

"Light unto Light, Blood unto Blood, By Magick I call unto thee,
Soul calling soul, blood to blood, I call unto thee.
Visions clear, blood to blood, I call unto thee.
Your pathway is clear, blood-to-blood, I call unto thee,
My Magick is strong, blood-to-blood return now home unto me,
As I do Will so mote it be".

TO CREATE CONFUSION

Create and make yourself a Fif-fath (doll) in the likeness of the person you wish to confuse, chant and say:

"Confusion and uncertainty, you foolish one, and you will not come up.
For tangled mind with twist and turn, and tangled foot will follow.
You are confused, you are unsure, of all that you think, and much, much more.
Your mind breaks down and you stumble and fall, and you will not come up again.
So, tangle, tangle twist and turn and tangled foot will follow.
With Magick at my hand, for tangles webs are now woven".

To Create an Illusion

This ritual and Spell was done by the Wicces of Britain against the German attacks, that their ships would get lost and not find their way to the shores of the Blessed Isles of the Goddess. It can also be made to make a fleet of ships appear. Cast your Magick Circle and raise the Cone of Power, build a large fire in the centre of your Magick Circle with a boiling Cauldron of water and Magickal Oils.

"Wind and water, Moon and sea, make enemy ships disappear.
Whirling currents of tidal waves, compass not working no path is paved.
Moon pulling tides and storms on water be,
I invoke the Magickal Powers of the mighty sea.

Thick Mists, walls of Magickal fog surround them and make all unsafe,
Your compass is spinning, Moon and waters, wind and waves,
Carry the winds to the enemy ships let us be saved.
By winds, moonlight storms and the thrashing sea,
Turn them around, away from our Blessed land and from me.

Ghostly oceans riding the swell, putting fear in your hearts, Magick serves me well.
Moon and oceans dark and free, take these enemy ships away from me.

Take them from whence they came across the sea, and lead them far away,
Give up your quest, run away, run away, run away,
Or I will destroy your ships and all within, as this is my Will, so mote it be".

Venus Love Spell

This Spell is created to bring true love, not lustful love, but real deep down Unconditional Love. The Spell should commence on a Friday, the sacred day of the Goddess Venus, the Goddess of Love. This ritual should be repeated each day for seven days, as seven is the Magickal number of Venus. You should have collected all your requirements for this Spell, such as Anointing Love Oil of Ylang Ylang, A White Altar Clothe, a cut out red heart shape big enough to wrap what is to be wrapped, a blood red candle, a looking glass seven coloured pins of the rainbow, and Incense of Lavender and Rose.

On your first day, bathe in a warm bath of Lavender and Rose petals and milk. After which you anoint yourself with Ylang Ylang Oil. This Spell should be conducted Skyclad (naked). Prepare and cast your Magick Circle and lay out your Altar white cloth. Position yourself in front of the looking glass. Then ceremonially light your incense and red candle and focus all your desire and need for true love. Feeling very sensual and alive, then chant your spell saying:

"By love I open my heart and call unto you my Beloved one.
To love me more than anyone. Be true with your love unto me,
As I call to your body, heart and soul, for 7 times I shall pierce your heart,
For today the Magick of Venus truly starts.

I call to thy heart and soul to bind your love unto me,
Only if it is real and you truly see, who I really am and what I am to be,
Hopefully in your arms for all eternity.
I bind your heart and soul unto me, as this is my Will, so mote it Be".

Repeat this same ritual seven times, preferably at seven pm each day, placing the pins into the red heart after repeating: "SEVEN TIMES I PIERCE THY HEART."

Blow out the candle until next time, but do not close or banish the Magick Circle, letting the powers build more and more each day until finished. But do remember to keep the Magick Circle closed when not in use to not wreak havoc.

Creating Your Own Familiar

This ritual is very advanced, and better done by those who have been proficient in their Wiccan training, and mastered meditation, and how to use their Will Power. It comes with much practise and expertise. Remember never give up until you succeed. It is a beautiful ritual when done correctly and sincerely, always for the right reasons, remembers the Wiccan Rede.

- Set up your Magick Circle, and have it Properly Prepared.

- Do your LBRP.

- Cast your Magick Circle correctly and completely.

- Have all lights extinguished except your Altar candles and your favourite attracting incense.

- Sit and meditate in peace and quiet until you are completely relaxed and ready to proceed.

- Start to chant in your mind over and over exactly what it is you want to create, (remember a Spell in rhyme says itself, and empowers your Spell). Try to keep it a simple two or four-line phrase.

- Centre your thinking and your chanting down to just one line, over and over. Use it as a command when needed. Keep repeating this phrase in rhyming chant form.

- Now you are Properly Prepared to create and give birth to your Familiar. Start with holding your hands about six inches apart with your palms slightly cupped and facing each other. Feel the ebb and flow of the electro-magnetic pulse between your hands.

- Imagine an upright triangle of pulsating energy radiating from your Third Eye and your heart to a central point between your palms. You can also visualise it as an illumined pyramid of electro-magnetic Power. The sides of the Triangle are taking in all the head and chest area.

- When this is strong and holding steady, call upon your Goddess and Horned God to help you breathe life into this Familiar that is being birthed between your palms. Remember to constantly keep the vision of the Triangle of Power flowing from your forehead and your heart.

- Thank the Goddess and God for their help. As you can now feel the pulsation of life in your Familiar grow. As you breathe, let your palms move slightly and gently in and out, back and forth toward each other, creating a pulsating heart pumping sensation in rhythm with your own heart beat and with your breathing.

- Breathe in and out, as you breathe your hands move inwards, and as you breathe out your hands move out. Until your living Familiar becomes a swirling ball of living pulsating energy between your palms. Remember to continue your mental chant of your one-line phrase. Keep the vision of the Triangle strong flowing from your Third Eye and your Heart to the form between your palms.

- Now bend down and breathe gently but strongly tour vital breath into your Familiar from the very life of your Goddess and God within and without, giving more life to your Familiar, your Magickal child.

- At this stage you have been doing this for quite a while, you may feel a little trance like and in an altered state of consciousness.

- Now rise to your feet, gently and steadily still maintaining focus and visualisation.

- When steadied, command your Familiar to go forth and fulfil its mission in attracting more energies from the electro-magnetic universe, absorbing spiritual light and love to give it strength and sustenance. Before it departs into the outer world, surround it with a shield of Divine Light, a Magick Circle of Protection, also visualise an umbilicus cord coming from it to you, so it will always find its way home when called or needed. Now when ready throw it into the air as if releasing it to fly free in to the world of Magick.

- Spread your arms wide standing in the ancient Pentagram Position. Repeat your line phrase again ending with:

"What I have birthed has divinely begun,
So be it done, 3. 7. 9. 21"

MAGICKAL DIVINE FIRE OF DESTINY

"Divine Fire Above and Divine Fire Below,
Divine Fire without and Divine Fire within.
Created by Magick, ignite and appear, bring forth your light, welcome here.
By Archangel Michaels spirit come forth,
Bring In your fires from East, South, West and North.

Send Longinus, the Spear of Divine Fire, come forth-great Angel and appear.
Divine Fire Above, and Divine Fire below, Divine Fire within, and Divine Fire without,
May all Elementals Fire mingle and become One,
Divine Light of this Magick Circle and power of the Hidden Sun.

Illumine my future, and let me see, through the flickering flames to see my destiny.
As this is my Will, so mote it be".

REQUEST A SIGN

Perform on or just after a New Moon, with a dance and chant around your Magick Circle saying:

> *"My Goddess Diana, Uranus and Mercury,*
> *Is Magick true? Can Magick really be?*
> *A Magickal sign I ask from thee,*
> *Shaddai El Chai (shoddoy el hoy) and Ea. Binah Ge.*
> *A Magickal sign send forth now to me".*

The sign should appear before the next Full moon. After the sign appears, as a thanksgiving and offering throw white petals and flowers into a pond, or lake even a dam. Must be still water and say:

> *"My Goddess Diana, Uranus and Mercury, a Magick sign I asked from thee,*
> *And a Magickal sign you sent to me.*
> *Shaddai El Chai and Ea Binah Ge.*
> *My grateful thanks but thrice you are blessed,*
> *Blessed Be".*

SACRED
SYMBOLS
AND SIGILS OF
WICCECRAFT

We have lived by symbols and signs in every way possible since the dawn of man. Symbols are the first forms of communication, a system of meanings that must be interpreted and understood, no matter what the symbol is it has to be charged with a thought from the primordial person who is using it. These ancient symbols are universal keys and they are timeless, some are transient, and parochial. Signs, symbols, Sigils, shapes and designs used by Wicces are by no means inclusive; they are symbols that will aid you in your studies of the Ancient Craft. Also know that in the using of any Magickal symbol for Magickal purposes and ritual without truly understanding or knowing its hidden meanings as well as its basic knowledge is highly dangerous, so be careful when using Sigils of the Art without their full knowledge.

Please research and learn more of these symbols, as they will help bring you closer to a deeper understanding of the Mysteries of the Universe, and then the ascension to the Goddess.

- THE POINT - The innermost point of the Universe, but the essence of all things. The ancient sign of the Phallus, the ancient God Force that descends from heaven, within the Magick Circle or the yearning of mankind for higher things.

- THE WOMB Goddesses Sacred Power descending from heaven, or the deep yearning of man for higher things.

- THE GODDESS ON EARTH - Although it is the sign for NEGATIVE, its true meaning is a life flowing evenly along the same path or Plane.

- THE GODDESS AND GOD - Although a sign for POSITIVE, it's true meaning is Perfect Harmony.

- THE GODS OF ETERNITY - Ever flowing, ever alive and always changing; yet staying the same.

- THE ACTIVE MALE ELEMENT - The fertile symbol of the Phallus, arrow of Power.

- THE SACRED ALTAR OF THE MYSTERIES - The male God force penetrates the female Goddess force within the Magick Circle, so Creation takes effect on all Planes, (the human Altar).

- THE WORLD OF NATURE - The Sacred Number of the Goddess of Four, Four Directions, Four Elements, Four Planes, Four Elementals, (1 is the God and 3 is the Triple Goddess, together in balance = 4).

- THE SIGN OF MAN - With outstretched arms in praise, he is the expectant and awaiting Soul.

- THE SIGN OF MERCY - This symbol represents the love of the Gods towards Mankind.

- THE COMBINATION OF MAN AND MERCY - Representing man and the Gods in perfect Harmony and Equilibrium, which illuminates strength and light on all Planes from a central point.

- THE SYMBOL OF MAN - as opposed to God, representing the male element.

- THE SYMBOL OF WOMAN - as opposed to the Goddess representing the female element.

- SIGIL FOR A PREGNANT WOMAN.

- SYMBOL FOR MALE AND FEMALE IN SEXUAL UNION - Also the sign of the Wiccan Handfasting.

- SIGIL FOR A WOMAN GIVING BIRTH.

- SYMBOL FOR THE FAMILY - Man, Woman and Children, also represents a Covenstead.

- WICCE IN STRIFE - When you see a broom outside a Wicces home, warning that there are hostile people inside, do not enter.

- WICCES SANCTUARY - Represent a safe house for Wicces and their families.

- DEATH WITHIN - Either someone has just died or is terminally ill and dying.

- SYMBOL OF A WICCAN WHO HAS BEEN CRAFTED - letting all know of their rank within the Wiccan community.

- SYMBOL OF THE INITIATED WICCE - This symbol is bestowed upon the Initiate at their Initiation. It is the rank of the 1st degree Wicce.

- SYMBOL OF AN ORDAINED PRIEST OR PRIESTESS OF THE WICCA - With their spirit descended into the Earth, this is the Rank of 2nd Degree.

- SYMBOL AND SEAL OF THE HIGH PRIEST OR HIGH PRIESTESS -

- THE SACRED GREAT RITE - Between HPs and HP within the Magick Circle for High Magick.

- THE CRONE, ELDER OF THE CIRCLE - Retired HP or HPs.

- THE MAGIC CIRCLE - This is the mystical symbol for the Wicces Magick Circle, the Temple of the Old Religion and of the Goddess and God.

- MICROCOSM AND MACROCOSM - As Above so Below, As Within So Without. The Hermetic Law.

- THE MAGIC CORDS - These three Magickal Cords being white, red and blue not only represent the Triple aspect of the Goddess, also the ranks within the Wicca, but also are for Healing within the Magick Circle.

- THE CEREMONIAL SCOURGE - The true symbol for Purification and Enlightenment.

- THE KISS - Representing the kiss of chastisement and of love and respect, used in the Five-Fold Salute. As awakening the Goddess within.

- ALEXANDRIAN OR GARDNARIAN WICCECRAFT.

- SYMBOL FOR WICCECRAFT - The True Seal for Wiccecraft and the Magickal Pentacle as the Key to the Magick Circle.

- THE SPIRAL - Representing Blood Wicces or Hereditary Wicces.

- THE CEREMONIAL BELL - The bell represents Attunement, the tuning into Nature and the Awakening of certain Etheric energies. It is used in the Magick Circle.

- THE CEREMONIAL CHALICE - This is used for Consecrated water or for Wine in ceremonies.

- THE ANKH - The Sacred key to the afterlife and the next world, the Seal of Eternity.

- THE SACRED TAU - The Holy Crossroads of the Goddess, where all Paths lead to the centre. Also, the Cross of the HPs.

- THE BOLINE - The Holy Sickle, traditionally silver, used for the ceremonial cutting of herbs and for etching in Candle Magick, only to be used within the Magick Circle.

- BREASTS OF THE GODDESS - The Luna phases of the Triple Goddess.

- SIGNATURE OF THE HORNED GOD - The sacred seal of the Horned God Cernunnos.

- SIGIL OF THE HORNED GOD - Sacred symbol for the Horned God, also used as the sign for Taurus.

- SIGIL FOR THE WATCHTOWERS - This symbol represents the four Quarters of the Magick Circle, the four worlds, planes, elements, elementals and the Guardian of the Magick Circle.

- SIGIL OF SPIRIT - The Divine Source, even the centre of the Magick Circle. Also, the symbol for the invisible Sun within the visible Sun.

- KNEELING MAN - With bended knee always in humility and prayer.

- KNEELING WOMAN - With bended knee always in humility and prayer.

- THE ARROW OF POWER - Sigil of the Athame of the Wicce, also the direction of Willed intention.

- DEOSIL - The Way of the Sun and the direction of movement or energy within the Magick Circle, going Deosil in the Magick Circle is for Invoking and welcoming.

- WIDDERSHINS - The Way of the Moon and the direction of releasing or banishing energy within the Magick Circle.

- THE EIGHTFOLD PATHS OF ENLIGHTENMENT - Also the corresponding Wicces Tools, and the Eight Sabbats.

- THE HEXAGRAM - Sacred Sigil of Unity, the intertwining of Heaven and Earth, Male and Female, Light and Dark, above and below, and Gods and man.

- THE HEPTAGRAM - Sacred Seal of the Goddess, especially Isis and Ishtar. Also, the Seven levels of the rainbow, the Chakra's etc.

- THE TRIANGLE OF LIGHT - Symbol of the Element of Fire,

- TRIANGLE OF DARKNESS - Symbol of the Earth Element.

- TRIANGLE OF LIFE - Symbol of the Water Element.

- TRIANGLE OF LOVE - Symbol of the Air Element.

- TRIQUETRA - Symbol of the Three Phases of the Moon, the Triune of the Goddess.

- THE MOON OF HOPE - Sigil to attract what you are hoping for.

- THE MOON OF THE EARTH - Used to attract Luna energies to the Earth.

- THE MOON OF BALANCE - Sigil to attract balance into your life.

- THE MOON OF ENERGY - Sigil to draw down energy.

- THE MOON OF POWER - used to invoke Luna Power.

- THE MOON OF FIRE - To attract Luna Fire of the hidden Sun.

- THE MOON OF WATER - To create ebb and flow of the waters of life.

- THE MOON OF AIR - To draw in the vital force of Air.

- THE MOON OF LIGHT - To attract and illumine Luna Light into your being.

- THE MOON OF FEAR - To banish fear.

- THE MOON OF TIME - To make a shift in time to your advantage.

- THE MOON OF BLOOD - To find a family member who has been lost.

- THE MOON OF WILL - Sigil to empower your Will.

- THE MOON OF DEATH - Use this symbol to help those who have passed move on.

- THE NEW MOON - POWERS OF THE NEW MOON.

- THE WAXING MOON

- THE FIRST QUARTER

- THE FULL MOON

- THE WANING GIBBOUS

- THE LAST QUARTER

- THE WANING CRESCENT

- THE CAULDRON OF THE MYSTERIES

- THE BESOM - THE WICCES BROOMSTICK.

- MOTHERS BLESSING

- YIN YANG - balanced energy.

- BALE FIRE - For ceremony awakening of the Sun energy.

- PURIFICATION BY WATER - Ritual cleansing.

- SIGIL OF THE MAIDEN

- SIGIL OF THE MOTHER

- SIGIL OF THE CRONE

- THE OLD MOON - July

- THE STORM MOON - August

- THE SUGAR MOON - September

- THE GROWING MOON - October

- THE FLOWER MOON - November

- THE HONEY MOON - December

- THE MEAD MOON - January

- THE LIGHTNING MOON - February

- THE HARVEST MOON - March

- THE TRAVEL MOON - April

- THE FROST MOON - May

- THE WINTER MOON - June

- THE HEXAGON -

- THE HEXAGRAM - two interlaced Triangles of Tiphareth, 7 Planets

- THE HEPTAGRAM - Netzach, the 7 Planets, continuous reflected at every 3rd point.

- HEPTAGRAM - THE STAR OF VENUS - Continuous, reflected at every 4th point.

- OCTOGRAM - HOD the 8-lettered name. Two squares reflected at every 3rd point.

- OCTOGRAM - STAR OF MERCURY - Continuous reflected at every 4th point.

- ENNEAGRAM - Triple ternary of 7 Planets with Lunar nodes. Continuous reflected at every 3rd point.

- ENNEAGRAM - Triple ternary - Three triangles reflected at every 4th point.

- ENNEAGRAM - THE STAR OF LUNA - Continuous reflected at every 5th point.

- DEKAGRAM - Malkuth - Two Interlaced Pentagons reflected at every 3rd point.

- DEKAGRAM - THE TEN SEPHIROTH - Continuous reflected at every 4th point.

- DEKAGRAM - DUPLICATED LETTER HEH - Two Pentagrams reflected at every 5th point.

- ENDEKAGRAM - EVIL TRIAD DUKES OF EDOM - Continuous reflected at every 3rd point.

- ENDEKAGRAM - RESTRICTION OF EVIL - Continuous reflected at every 4th point.

- ENDEKAGRAM - THE QLIPPOTH - Continuous reflected at every 5ᵗʰ point.

- ENDEKAGRAM - QLIPPHOTIC PRINCES - Continuous reflected at every 6ᵗʰ point.

- DODEKAGRAM - MASCULINE AND FEMININE SIGNS OF THE ZODIAC - Two hexagons reflected at every 3ʳᵈ point.

- DODEKAGRAM - THE THREE QUADRUPLICITIES - Three squares reflected at every 4ᵗʰ point.

- DODEKAGRAM - THE 4 TRIPLICITIES - Four Triangles reflected at every 5ᵗʰ point.

- DODEKAGRAM - Continuous reflected at every 6ᵗʰ point.

- PROTECT YOUR NEW HOME

- PROTECT YOUR HOME FROM ALL WATER DAMAGE - floods, storms, cyclones, broken pipes.

- PROTECTION FROM DISEASE AND ILLNESS

- PROTECTION FROM EVIL ATTACKS

- GUARD AGAINST EVIL SPIRITS

- BANISH NEGATIVE ENERGY AND PEOPLE

- PROTECTION FROM ACCIDENTS

- BANISH POSSESSIVE OR DANGEROUS PEOPLE

- GUARD AGAINST BAD LUCK

WICCES HOME
BLESSING

The Rite of the Goddess Hertha

This beautiful and happy Home Blessing Ritual is also a kind of exorcism and home-warming ritual with friends, family, laughter and much love. It focus's your concentration on putting in positive feelings and love rather than banishing or removing negative energies. If celebrated with like-minded happy-go-lucky people in high spirits, then it can be positive where nothing negative or evil will want to stay. I have always believed that nothing evil can survive in an atmosphere of pure love and light. These House Blessings can be for many reasons if your main purpose is concentrated upon. The one that I did for my home was to protect the home from harm and unwanted visitors such as burglars and prowlers. It is where we buried at the Four Quarters of the property four waxen Pentacles to seal and protect from all directions, we also incorporated four small Mars Pentacles as well.

It is also excellent when moving into a new home, to do the House Blessing to remove past negative vibrations and energies to make the home clear and clean ready for the new family. This is usually where the House Blessing starts as a type of Spring Cleaning, with everything being washed, dusted, cleansed and made pure and clean in readiness for the Blessing. You ask your family and friends to bring some Flowers, herbs, and symbols of the Season for the house to be placed in vases. The owner of the home should either make or acquire a small box (like a tarot card box) this is called the Hertha Box (pronounced HER-TA).

To start you firstly take a raw fresh egg (I prefer a duck egg as they are a bit bigger and stronger) and pierce a small hole in each end of the shell, then blow the inner egg out of the shell so the egg is empty. Rinse and wash carefully the shell in water infused Hyssop, then seal one end with pure beeswax. You then carefully, after grinding finely the Nine Magical Love Herbs in through the small opening hole of the egg. The Love Herbs are: Bay Laurel, Cinnamon, Jasmine, Lavender, Lovage, Mother of Thyme, Orris Root, Rosemary, Rose Petals, Rue, Sandalwood, and Yarrow.

Protection Herbs are: Benzoin, Dill, Gums resins from Frankincense and Myrrh, Garlic, Rowan (mountain Ash), Mistletoe, St. Johns Wort, Dragons Blood, and vervain.

You may wish to also include some personal items of your or your families such as hair, fur from your cat or dog, some blood, whatever you heart desires.

When all are placed within your eggshell, seal it with wax and then place it in your small Hertha Box padded with cotton wool and then sealed and tied closed with red cotton or red wool.

You also need a Home Blessing candle traditionally made of pure beeswax and it should be at least 24 inches tall with a 2 1/2-inch girth, onto which your either carve, etch or paint the appropriate symbols that will run down its length. Carefully carved or painted in the centre are the names of the home dwellers, or an appropriate saying. At the very top and bottom should be placed a Pentagram, for protection and faith. Then next to them at either end place the Noonday Sun. Followed by the Setting Sun; this then symbolises time, day and night, and the Sigils of the four seasons. So now your Blessing candle can be burnt throughout the appropriate times of the year. You should also acquire as many candles as you have separate rooms in your home, and place them safely in the centre of each room.

The colours of the Candles are whatever you feel are appropriate, check the colour chart in the Candle Magick Section.

THE RITUAL

Start with the LBRP Ritual then casting a full Magick Circle around the whole perimeter of your property. Consecrate your Hertha Box, Blessing Candle and room Candles. These are done only by the home owners/dwellers in the centre of their Circle whilst all others dance around them chanting in a low gentle and loving voice:

> *"Come, come, throughout and about, the good coming in and the bad keeping out.*
> *Bless this house and all within.*
> *Come, come throughout and about,*

HPs or Lead Wicce leads the dance and chants out loud saying:

> *"Great Mother Hertha be present here with gladness and joy in your heart.*
> *Grant all that we have asked this day and protect our home,*
> *And all who dwell within.*
> *Protection, honour, riches, marriage blessings, good health, and many happy times.*

Hourly joy and laughter will fill this house with love and light,
We ask for Notas and his Elemental Salamanders to send forth their Blessings".

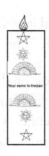

"Firm power of the earth, Bureaus, and your Elemental Gnomes,
Increase and give solidarity to all good things.
Fill this house with the Magickal Horn of Plenty.

Magickal ebb and flow of Water of the West, we ask you Zephyrus and your
Elementals the Undines to send forth your flow of Love and laughter,
And the constant movement of all Positive energies.

Great Winds and Power of the East, and your Elementals of Air, sacred Lord Euras
Send you're sacred winds to bless this house and keep all-safe within.
Great Mother Hertha send forth your constant Maternal Blessings keeping
our home and family under your protective wings from harm".

Continue building the Wicces Runes and raising the Cone of Power with the chant:

"Come, come, throughout and about, the good coming in and the bad keeping out".

HPs signals to atop as all hold tightly their hands and send forth the energies into the home and land, and all say:

"By the Power of the Elements and the Elementals and by the Grace
of the Great Mother Hertha, this house is blessed".

The Hertha Box and the Home Blessing Candle are both held aloft by the owner and the Incantation is said:

*"O sacred Stars above and below, within and without, may the troubles with
which you are charged have exhausted their burden. May no illness remain, no
danger threatens, no malice disturbs, and no harm comes to this place.
By the Power of the Rising Stars may they always shine in peace over this our loving home".*

The Home Blessing Candle is now carried around the house lighting each of the room candles, a
procession is then lead around the house and outside into the gardens and property covering all
the grounds, carrying the Thurible of burning incense and the Ceremonial Bell. Once this has
been completed still in procession all now spiral back into the centre of the home, and invoke
the Lords and Ladies of the Quarters saying:

Warden of the East:

*"Mighty Euras, Great Ruler of the tempest storms and whirlwinds of time and space.
Master of the divine breathe of life and light,
Prince of the powers of Air. Come forth from the Shadows,
Be present we pray and take hold to guard this home of all perils approaching from the East".*

Warden of the South:

*"Mighty Notas, Great Ruler of the fiery realms of the Great Solar orb,
Master of the Salamanders, and Prince of the Powers of Fire.
Come forth from the Shadows be present we pray and guard this
home from all perils approaching from the South".*

Warden of the West:

*"Mighty Zephyrus, Great Ruler of the Watery Abyss,
Guardian of the deep bitter sea, Prince of the Powers of Water.
Come forth from the Shadows and take hold and guard this
home from all perils approaching from the West".*

Warden of the North:

*Mighty Bureaus, Great Black Goat of the North, O Horned One. Great Ruler
of the mountains and fertile fields, Prince of the Powers of Earth.*

Come forth from the Shadows and take hold and guard this
home from all perils approaching from the North".

The processional forms again spiralling out of the circle and out into the front garden at the very front of the property where a special place has been dug for the placement of the Hertha Box. All form a ring around the HPs and the Consecrated Box is placed into the ground as they Invoke Mother Earth saying:

"Great Mother Hertha, Goddess and Mother of all life, the living source of the Divine
Light of our Sun and the very fruits of the land. We know you as the Transformer of
Chaos into divine Creational life. For it is right that you are called the Great Mother.

Great Mother Hertha, bless this sacred Box and that it be a beacon to your
Light and Love to magnify your blessings of our house and home, to be a sacred
Shield of Light to protect and guard this home and all within always".

The Hertha Box is covered over, and a small Lavender or Rose bush planted on top. The ground is sealed.

"By the Power of Mighty Hertha, this home and all within are truly
guarded and truly blessed, as this is my Will, so mote it be".

THE THEBAN ALPHABET
LANGUAGE OF THE WICCES

A B C D E F

G H I,J K L M N O

P Q R S T U V W

X Y Z

The end.

FIF-FATH DOLL
MAGIC

We have all heard about the infamous Voodoo Dolls of the Voudoun priests and priestesses, who jab waxen images with pins for varied reasons, usually something sinister. But this is not the case; Voodoo Dolls have been used for a myriad of reasons, for healing, removing foreign objects and for love as well. Fif-faths are what Wicces call them, and they are a form of Sympathetic Magick, other words if something looks the same, then it will act the same if it is charged with Magickal energy. We use Fif-faths or lovingly called Dolly Magick for healing, love, and protection and for binding. Fif-faths can be made from poppets, wood, wax, clay or these days even plasticine.

When making your Fif-fath you will also need some items from the person you are making the doll in the image of, such as clothing, hair, nails, blood, urine, jewellery, and a photo. Get all your ingredients that you need to make your Fif-fath and have them all at hand ready for your ritual. When ready, in your Magick Circle do the LBRP, then cast your Magick Circle. Have all your items and tools on a side Altar ready to commence.

Start by moulding your base ingredient such as wax etc. into making your desire form.

1. Firstly, smash it and warm it with your hands, bash it and make it into a pulp.

2. Place all your items that belong to the person such as nails etc. (except for the photo as this gets placed on your doll last) into the clay and again mix it and bash it making sure it mixes well with your ingredients.

3. Now with your mind as if you were within the Great Womb of creation, create with your hands and breath an egg form and slowly giving it life, form it into an embryo.

4. Slowly form the dough into the desired sex whether male or female.

5. When the doll has been given shape and you feel there is no more you can add into it.

6. Take up the photo of the persons face and place on the head of the doll, and place your clothing on it.

7. Now place the doll on your Altar Pentacle and consecrate it with water and salt in the name of the desired person. Watch the doll carefully and give it life and breath. Focus

Magickly on your breathing of life into it, watch as its chest rises and falls, and see it become alive. When you know you have succeeded your Fif-fath is ready for your main purpose or ritual.

BRINGING LOVERS TOGETHER

This ritual should be done of the Day of the Goddess Venus, the day of Love, which is a Friday, her sacred number is 7, and her Seal is the 7-pointed Star. So, the seventh day, at the seventh hour, and this ritual is done for seven days. On each one of these days you should light a new virgin red candle, which should be anointed and Consecrated with Love Oil. During each Rite in your Thurible burn Frankincense with red 7 Rose petals. You will have already made two Fif-faths one for each of the lovers. They too must be blessed and Consecrated with their real birth names.

Place the two Fif-faths on your Altar about 18 inches apart, their heads facing the North. Between their bodies place a red cloth or paper heart shaped large enough to wrap the two dolls up together. The anointed candle is placed at the Northern most tip of the heart shape. Allow the candle to burn for 7 minutes each day at the designated time of 7 am or 7 pm. whilst it is being burnt chant the following Spell:

> *"Awaken beautiful lovers and awaken your hearts,*
> *Never to let these lovers part.*
> *If your love is true, then be as one, as beats your heart.*
> *Daily will I draw you near; closer the space between you will disappear,*
> *For when it is done, know that you will be dear.*
> *Make your hearts burst with illumined fire; let passion ignite your deep desire.*
> *Never more shall you parted be, if you are truly by love meant to be.*
> *Foot to foot, and lip-to-lip, heart and heart,*
> *May you never part?*
> *So never more shall parting be, as I do Will so mote it be".*

Each day at the end of your Ritual, move the dolls closer by more than an inch towards one another. On the seventh day place the male on top of the female and enfold them in the red heart. Place seven drops of Love Oil on the sealed parcel and tie them closed with red cotton. Bury in your garden under a Rose bush and say:

"As they do meet, in sweet desire, grow in the garden of loves desire.
Never more shall you parted be, as I do Will so mote it be".

ENTER THY
TEMPLE OF
OLD INITIATE!

"Of ancient times humanity sought to make its gain amongst the STARS.
The mortal sought the IMMORTAL that so deluded her.
BOUND to life so she might be free from the SPIRAL staircase of REBIRTH.
Down through the AEONS through SPACE and TIME and in a succession of lives,
YOU the SEEKER did come!

And in those AEONS the SEEKER found that the 'INITIATED DOER
IN THE BODY' and the conscious 'THINKER IN THE MIND',
and the I am that I am 'KNOWER IN THE SOUL'.

In the Great WOMB OF ETERNITY, she felt the pangs of REBIRTH, the
ordeal of the MYSTERIES of INITIATION, The pangs of LOVE. The art of
SACRIFICE and the PURIFICATION of DEATH, which makes a lifetime.
She was BOUND as all are by a cable tow of UMBILICUS at REBIRTH.
Her MEASURE of INITIATION prepared her for the BONDS of the
SACRED MARRIAGE consummate, and in the FIVE-FOLD SALUTE of
SACRIFICE, offered with her last BREATH a DIRGE TO DEATH.

And in the AEONS, the 'INITIATED DOER IN THE BODY', and the conscious
'THINKER IN THE MIND' and the I am that I am 'KNOWER IN THE SOUL'.

Took up the Magickal SWORD OF ENDEAVOUR and PIERCED THE CROWN.
Full of LIGHT it split the HOLY VEIL, and gained her a place amongst the STARS.
Having drunk from the OCEAN OF ETERNITY, the WOMB OF WONDER,
the 'INITIATE IN THE MIND', the sacred TEMPLE of the night whose
LIVING ALTAR is the body and soul of which she cried her PRAYER!
'Quicken the Blood, mingle the Soul. Come together as did the Gods of old.
To you the SACRIFICE I make is one, let thy SPIRIT UNITE and be won.

And in the AEONS, the 'INITIATED DOER IN THE BODY', and the conscious
'THINKER IN THE MIND', and the I am that I am 'KNOWER IN THE SOUL'.

Found that the MAGICKAL SWORD OF ENDEAVOUR was the SLAYER,
the CREATOR of TIME AND SPACE, and from it is taken the SACRED
POINT, for it is the CENTRE POINT that is the 'FIRST CAUSE', the
ultimate cause of ALL, the infinite potential Unmanifest within ALL.

The Sacred SWORD ENDEAVOUR defines the point, which has NO MAGNITUDE in SPACE, has POSITION but exists beyond the BOUNDS OF TIME AND SPACE. From this SACRED POINT the ENDEAVOUR SPINS A MAGICKAL WEB that is our NINE-FOLD MAGICK CORD that casts our MAGICK CIRCLE that has FORTY for its number.

There is but ONE GREAT MYSTERY and that MYSTERY is the GODDESS. Render the VEIL and dispel the FEAR, and at PEACE so shall you ever be for all ETERNITY. BLESSED BE!"

THE CHARGE OF
THE GODDESS

"I am the Mother of great and unconditional Love,
I am the Mother also of fear and hope.
Know that I have no beginning, and that I have no ending,
For I am time and space.
Within me is all Grace and Light, and within me is the Knowledge of the way and of
the Truth that is also within me is all Hope of Life and of virtue and of Rebirth.
I am the earth, the Moon, the Sky, the Wind, and the Stars are my crown.

I am Fire and Ice, I am Male and Female, I can create, and I can destroy.
For all glory is in my love and beauty. Come unto me you that desire me, and be filled
with my fruit, for my Spirit is sweet above honey and the Honey Comb.
Fear me!
For ultimately, I take as much as I give. Come unto me and give me fealty.
I shall share my secrets and my Mysteries with you.
Loving me you shall know freedom and exaltation, peace of mind and deep contentment.

My memory is unto everlasting generations, and those that Harken unto me
shall have sin not, and those who explain me shall everlasting life.
If you seek to part yourself from me, know that you will be a lost Soul mourning for home.
Those that have never known the rapture of Love, that doubt, can never appal.
Dare you seek me out and make me your Mistress! Think well!
For I am She who men call Nature, and mine is the Spell that binds forever.
Come now unto me, and learn from our teachings how true is Love, such as ours.
Learn now from us to choose that pathway that leads to Love and to Joy Divine.
To that fulfilment of life which is perpetual Happiness,
For there is None Greater!"

WICCES CALENDAR

JANUARY:

World Peace Day	1 January
Sir James Fraser, author of "The Golden Bough".	
Fiesta of the Black Nazarene (the Philippines).	1-9 January
Nativity of The Goddess Inanna, Sumerian Goddess of Heaven and Earth 2 January	
Advent of Isis from Phoenicia	
Earth is at Perihelion to the Sun, closest to the Sun than any other time of the year.	
Women's Fertility Festival, Pueblo Deer Dancers	3 January
Aquarian Tabernacle Church Australia by Lady Tamara Von Forslun 4 January 1994	
Day of the Goddess Isis and Hathor	
Doreen Valiente	4 January 1922 - 1 September 1999 *
Sir Isaac Newton	4 January 1643 - 31 March 1727
Eve of the Epiphany of Kore and Paeon.	5 January
Ritual to the Goddess Venus	
Feast of the God Poseidon	
Night of La Bafana who brings gifts to children, lump of coal if they have been bad	
Day of the Sacred Triune, Maiden, Mother and Crone	6 January
The Beatific Vision of the Goddess 6 January	
Arrival of the magi to Christs Manger in Bethlehem	
Joan of Arc	7 January 1412 -
Decrees of the God Sokhit and the Goddess Sekhmet (Justice and Law)	

Magical Day of the Seven Herbs	
Magical Day for healing with Herbs	
Old Druids New Year's Eve	8 January
Samuel Macgregor Mathers	8 January 1952 - 19 November 1918
Day of the Goddess Justicia, bringing justice to the world	
Day to Honour all Midwives	
Day of Antu - Isis searches for Osiris	9 January
Day to gather Yarrow to dry for insect sachets for dog's collars	
Dirge to the Goddess Isis and Nephthys	
Plough Day - until 1980 it was illegal to plough the fields before this day	10 January
Securitas - Invoke when threatened	
The Juturnalia	11 January
Day of the Goddess Carmenta - Goddess of childbirth	
Day of the African Mother Goddess Oddvdva	12 January
Basant Panchami Day - Day of Wisdom and Art	
Day of the Goddess Sarasvati	
Final Witchcraft Law Repealed in Austria in 1787	13 January
Festival of the God Faunus (St. Valentine's Day)	
Day to bathe for purification in the Ganges River	13 January
Blessing of the Vines dedication to the Gods of Wine	14 January
Official Confession of error, made in 1606 by the Jurors of Salem Witch Trials 14 January	
Hindu Festival - Makar Sankranti	14 January
World Religions Day	15 January
Day of the Goddess Vesta	
Feast of the Ass	
Day of the Goddess Concordia	16 January
Honour the Gods of the Eight Winds	
Day of the Queen of the Universe in France	16 January

Day of Rest and Peace - dedicated to the Goddess Felicitas	17 January
Women's Festival Honouring the Goddess Hera	18 January
Dorothy Clutterbuck	19 January 1880 - 12 January 1951
Day of Honouring the Goddess Minerva	19 January
Blessing of the Waters	
Dorothy Clutterbuck who Initiated Gerald Gardner	
Blessing of the Waters and all Water Goddesses	
Grandmothers Day	20 January
Festival of Peace and Harmony	
Feast of the Goddess Hecate	21 January
Day of St. Agnus	
Day of the Goddess Yngona (Denmark)	
Day of Visions	
Sir Francis Bacon - Philosopher	
Rasputin's Birth	
The Herb Mullein to be infused in olive oil for ear drops	22 January
Day dedicated to the Goddess Mawu	
Beginning of Aquarius	
Marija Gimbutas	23 January 1921 - 1994
Day to honour the Goddess Hathor by having a milk bath	23 January
Day of the Goddess Venus	
Sementivae Honour the Earth Goddess Terra	24 January
Blessing of the Candle of the Happy Women	
Tu Bi-Shivat - Hebrew holiday showing respect for trees and growing things 25 January	
The Shekinah - Sarah and Esther	25 January
Celebration of the Triple Moon	26 January
Day of the Goddess Cerridwen and Copper Women	
Day of the God Alacita, god of Abundance	

Dedicated to the Goddesses of the Grain and
Harvest

Gamelion Noumenia honouring all Deity	28 January
Up Kelly Aa (Scotland) Norse derived fire Festival to sacrifice to the Sun	
Peace Festival	29 January
Day of the Goddess Hecate	
Feast of the Goddess Charites	30 January
Dedication of the Altar of peace and Harmony	
Purification ceremony dedicated to the Goddess Yemaya	
Zsusanna Budapest Witch and author	30 January 1940 - 14 March 2008
Dr Frian - Alleged HP of North Berwick Witches, executed in Scotland in 1591	31 January
Feast of the Goddess Aphrodite	31 January
Candlemas Festival	
Festival of the Goddess Brigid	
Day of the Goddess Hecate	

FEBRUARY:

Festival of Lughnasadh Southern Hemisphere	1 February
Festival of Imbolg Northern Hemisphere	
Festival of the God Dionysus	
Festival of the Goddess Februa	
Ethnic Equality Month	2 February
Original Ground Hog Day	
Day of the Goddess Ceres and Proserpine	
Day Dedicated to the Horned Gods	
Lesser Eleusian Mysteries	3 February
Day dedicated to the Goddess Demeter and Persephone	
Halfway point of Summer in the Southern Hemisphere	

Lantern Lighting Ceremony Festival	4 February
Day of the Goddess Maat	5 February
Day to Honour Air Spirits	
H. R. Giger	5 February 1940 - 13 May 2014
Feast of St. Agatha - Patroness of Fire Fighters	
Day of the Goddess Maat - Goddess of Wisdom and Truth	
Festival of the Goddess Aphrodite	6 February
Day of the Goddess Artemis	
Day of the Goddess Selene	7 February
Stuart Farrar passed into the Summerland's 2000	
Death of Thomas Aquinas 1274 - whose writings refuted the Canon Episcopi	
Day to honour all Moon Goddesses	
Chinese New Year	8 February
Eliphas Levi	8 February 1810 - 31 May 1875
Celebration of the Goddess Kwan Yin	9 February
Day of the Goddess Athena	10 February
Festival of Toutates	
Feast of Our lady of Lourdes - visitation of the Goddess	11 February
Day of the Goddess Persephone	
Day of St. Gobnat	
Day of the Goddess Diana	12 February
Day dedicated to the Ancestors	13 February
Day of the Goddess Vesta	
Betrothal Day (later adopted by Christians and changed to St. Valentine's Day)	14 February
Women's plea to the Goddess Diana for children are granted this day	
Heinrich Cornelius Agrippa	14 February 1486 - 18 February 1535
Day of the Goddess Rhiannon	15 February

Pope Leo X issued the Bull Tonsured - that secular courts would carry out executions of Witches condemned by the Inquisition in 1521.

Day dedicated to the Goddess Juno Februata

Day of Lupa - The She-wolf

Day of Honouring Light	16 February
Christ accepted as the God Quetzalcoatl in South America	17 February
Festival of Women - dedicated to the Goddess Spandermat	18 February
Birthday of Ramakrishna - Hindu Mystic	
Day of the Wicces Sacred Tree - The Ash	
Day of the Goddess Minerus	19 February
Birthday of Copernicus - Astronomer	
Day of the Silent Goddess Tacita - averter of harmful gossip	20 February
Healing Day of the Goddess Kwan Yin	21 February
The Sun enters into Pisces	
Holiday of St. Lucia - Goddess of Light	22 February
Sybil Leek	22 February 1917 - 26 October 1982
Day of Blessing Land Boundaries	23 February
The Regigugium -	24 February
Flight of Kings, when the Year King is sacrificed, and successor crowned by the Goddess	
Day of the Goddess Nut	26 February
Shrove Tuesday - the first day of Lent	
Day of the Goddess the Morrigan	27 February
Time of the Old Woman	
Anthesterion Noumenia honouring all Deity	
The Great Wicces Night	28 February
Sabbatu - cakes and wine offered to the Goddess for Prosperity and Luck	

Leap Year - when women rule the Earth and can ask
men for marriage 29 February
Day of the Goddess St. Brigid

MARCH:

The Golden Dawn Founded	1 March 1888
The Covenant of the Goddess Wiccan Church was formed in 1975	
Day of the Goddess Hestia	
First Day of autumn	
Bale Fires are lit to bring back the Sun	
Festival of the Goddess Rhiannon	2 March
Day of the Goddess Spider Woman	
Women do not work on this day or the Goddess will send storms to destroy	
Doll Festival for young girls	3 March
Founding of the Church of All Worlds First Wiccan church to Incorporate in USA	4 March 1968
Festival of the Goddesses Artemis and Diana	
Feast of Flowers dedicated to the Goddess Flora and Hecate	
All Souls day – Greece	
Navigum Isidis of the Goddess Isis who opens the seas to navigation	5 March
Laurie Cabot Official Witch of Salem	6 March 1933 *
Junoalia — Celebration of matrons and young girls	
David J Conway author	6 March 1939
Day of the Goddess Ishtar	7 March
Ceremony of Peace	
Day of the Goddess Juno	
Birthday Celebration of Mother Earth	8 March
Day of the Goddess Ilmatar	
International Women's Day	

Mothering day - original Mother's Day	9 March
Feast of the Year Goddess - Anna Perenna	10 March
Day of Our lady of Lourdes - appearance of the Goddess Persephone 11 March	
Festival of the God Marduk	12 March
Day of the Goddess Demeter	
Discovery of the Planet Uranus - 1781	13 March
Bale Fires are lit to call in the Rain	
Birthday of Ronald Hubbard - Creator of Scientology	
Jacques de Molay - Head of the Knights Templar	14 March
Festival of the Goddess Ostara	15 March
Pete Pathfinder becomes the first Wiccan Priest elected as President of the Interfaith Council, 1995.	
Day of the Goddess Levannah	16 March
Day of the Goddess Morrigan	17 March
Feast of Liberalia - Women's Festival of the God Bacchus and the Maenads	
Festival of the God the Greenman	
Sheelah's Day - The Goddess Sheelah-na-gig of Sexuality	18 March
Birthday of Edgar Cayce	
Manley Palmer Hall	18 March 1901 - 29 September 1990 *
Marriage of the Goddess Kore to the God Dionysus	
Quinquatrus Festival of the Goddess Minerva`	19 March
Lesser Panathenacea - dedicated to the Goddess Athena	
Criminal Witchcraft Stature enacted under Queen Elizabeth - 1563	
Day of the God Aries	20 March
Day of the Goddess the Morrigan	
World Forest Day	21 March
Day of the Goddess Athena	

Day of the Autumnal Equinox Southern
Hemisphere

Mandate of Henry VIII against Witchcraft enacted
in 1542, repealed in 1547

Birthday of the Goddess Athena   22 March

Rev. Pete Pathfinder Founder of the Aquarian
Tabernacle Church 22 March 1937 - 2 November
2014

Day of Fasting   23 March

Day of the Goddess Ishtar

Day of the Goddess Bellona - Witches Power day   24 March

Lady Day - Feast Annunciation of Mary   25 March

Pope Innocent III Issues the Bull establishing the
Inquisition in 1199

Day of the Goddess Ceres (named for cereals)   26 March

Feast of Esus the Hunter

Day of the Goddess Ceres, who lends her name to
breakfast cereals

Day of the Goddess Hecate   27 March

Birthday of Rudolph Steiner

Elaphabolion Noumenia honouring all deity   28 March

Death of Scott Cunningham in 1993

Birthday of Kwan Yin Goddess of Mercy -
Healing Day

The Delphinia - dedicated to the Goddess Artemis   29 March

Festival of the Goddess Athena   30 March

Anita Festival

Festival of the Goddess Aphrodite and the God   31 March
Hermes

Last Witch trial in Ireland in 1711

Day of the Goddess Hilaria

Day of the Goddess Rhaeda

APRIL:

Veneralia Festival of Peace	1 April
Day of the Goddess Hathor	
April Fool's Day	
Feast of Ama - Goddess and Patroness of Fishermen	2 April
Birthday of Hans Christian Anderson	
Descent of the Goddess Persephone into Annwyn	3 April
Day of Ceralia - Seed Day	
Day of the Goddess Ceres	
Descent of the Goddess Persephone into Annwyn	
Honouring of Aesculapius, The Great Healer	4 April
Day of Megalesia of the Goddess Cybele	
Day of Fortune	5 April
Birthday of Kwan Yin	
Birthday of Harry Houdini the Magician	6 April
Stanislas de Guaita Occultist and author	6 April 1861 - 19 December 1897
World Health Day	7 April
Church of All Worlds Founded in 1962 in the USA	
Day of Mooncakes	8 April
Day of the Goddess Ata Bey's	
Empowering of Women day	9 April
Day of the Amazon Goddess of Women	
Day of the Goddess Bau - Mother of Ea (The Earth)	10 April
Day of Kista - Spiritual Knowing	11 April
Day of the Goddess Ceres	
Day of the Goddess Anahit - Armenian Goddess of Love and the Moon	
Anton La Vey Founder of the Church of Satan USA	11 April 1930 - 20 October 1997 *
Day of the Goddess Chy-Si-Niv Niv	12 April
Festival of Change	
First Confession of Witchcraft by Isobel Gowdie in 1662	13 April

Blessing of the Sea

Festival Honouring all Nordic Deity   14 April

Adoption of Principles of Wiccan belief at the 1974 Gnostica Witch Meet

Day of the Goddess Venus

Birthday of Elizabeth Montgomery (Bewitched)   15 April

Bernadette sees the Goddess at Lourdes

Day of the Goddess Luna, Tellas and Venus

Day of the Goddess Luna   16 April

Margot Adler Author and HPs of Wicca   16 April 1946 - 28 July 2014

Day of the Goddess Isis (Aset)   17 April

The Chariot Festival

The Rain Festival

Day of Honouring the Air Element   18 April

Day of Temple Offerings to the Goddess in Bali   19 April

Day of the Goddess Hathor, Isis and all Horned Goddesses   20 April

Astrological Beginning of Taurus

Feast of the Goddess Pales   21 April

Roma Dea Roma

Day of the pastoral Goddess the Perilya

Earth Day   22 April

The Rlenteria

The First day of winter

Clothes Washing Day

Festival of the God the Greenman   23 April

Pyre Festival of the Goddess Astarte, Tanith, Venus and Erycina

Birthday of actress Shirley MacLaine   24 April

Children's Day

First Seasonal Wine Festival of Venus and Jupiter

Day of The Goddess Robigalia of Corn and harvest   25 April

Passover originally dedicated to the God Baal

Day of the Goddess Yemaya	26 April
Birthday of William Shakespeare	
Mounikhion Noumenia Honouring of all Deity	
Feast of St. George originally derived from the God Apollo, the twin of Diana	27 April
Festival of the Goddess Florala (Flora)	28 April
The Ploughing Ceremony	29 April
Women's Day in Nigeria	
Walpurgis Nacht (The Wicces Night)	30 April
Samhain (Halloween) Southern hemisphere	
Beltane (Northern Hemisphere)	
Remembrance Day	

MAY:

May is dedicated to and named after the Goddess Maia.	1 May
May Day and Samhain day dancing with the Maypole for fertility to the Earth	
Day of the Goddess Maat The Goddess of Truth	
Day of Moon Goddesses Asherah, Damia, Latona, Bona Dea and Dea Día	
Day of Ysahodhara the Wife of Buddha	2 May
Festival of the Goddess Bona Dea for public welfare	3 May
Chloris Tarentia	
National Day of Prayer	4 May
Festival of the Goddess Cerridwen	
Veneration of the Sacred Thorn (Moon Tree)	
The beginning of Hawthorn Moon	
Rain Ceremony	5 May
Day of the Goddess Maat of Truth	
Birthday of Sigmund Freud	6 May
The Goddess visits Mut, Mother of Gods and Goddesses	

Festival of the Earth Spirits	7 May
Hathor Visits Anukis the Goddess of the Nile	
Festival of the God Apollo	
Furry Day	8 May
Morris dancing for Maid Marion originally the Goddess Flora	
Day of Honouring the Great White Mother	9 May
Joan of Arc canonised 1920	
Day of Ascension	
Day of Tin Hau the North Star	10 May
Celebration of the Goddess Anahit	
World Nations Reduce Greenhouse Emissions	
Day of Russali, the Triple Goddess - Ana, Badb and Macha	11 May
Shashti - The day of the sacred Forest	12 May
Founding of the Church of Wicca in Australia by Lady Tamara Von Forslun 13 May 1989	
Procession of our lady of Fatima	
The Goddess as a Young Maiden (Persephone, Athena, Artemis and Diana)	
Time of the Midnight Sun	14 May
The Panegyric of Isis - Her finding Osiris	
Honouring the Great Stag	15 may
Honouring the Queen of Heaven	16 May
Festival of the Goddess Hathor	17 May
Goddess with Child	
Festival of the Horned God	18 May
Feast of the Horned God Cernunnos	
Day of Nurturance	
Day dedicated to the Goddess Pallas Athena	
Festival of the God Pan	19 May
The Goddess Hathor arrives at Edfu in Neb	
Festival of Springs and Wells	

Beginning of Gemini

Day dedicated to Night and Day being Equal	20 may
Birthday of the Bard Gwydion Penderwen	21 May
Biological Diversity Day	22 May

Adoption of the Earth religion Anti-Abuse Act 1988

Day of the Rose	23 May
Celebration of the Birthday of the Goddess Artemis	24 May
Festival of the Triple Goddess	25 May

Sacred Day of St. Sarah for Gypsies

Thargelion Noumenia honouring all deity 26 May

Day of the Warrior

Morning Glory Zell HPs and author of Wicca 27 May

Night Time Healing Ceremony

Scourge of Pythia - Seer at Delphi, the Delphic
Oracle of the Goddess 28 May

Feast of the Oak Apple 29 May

Family Day

Blessing of the Fields 30 May

Death of Joan of Arc 1431

Thargelia Honouring the Goddess Artemis and the 31 May
God Apollo

Honouring of Joan of Arc in Commemoration
1412 –1431 (19yrs of age)

Pucelle of the Goddess

JUNE:

June named after the Goddess Juno. 1 June

Festival of Opet in Egypt

Feast of the oak Nymph

Day of Epipi the Goddess of darkness and Mysteries

Festival of the Goddess Ishtar 2 June

Birthday of Alessandro of Cagliostro Alchemist and
Heretic

Marion Zimmer Bradley author Mists of Avalon	3 June
Buddhist Blessing for young girls	
Free Women's Festival Skyclad (nudity)	5 June
Alex Sanders King of the Witches	6 June 1926 - 30 April 1988 *
Leave Cakes at Crossroads for the Goddess Artemis for luck	
Vestalia Festival of the Goddess Vesta	7 June
World Oceans Day	8 June
Day of the Goddess Rhea	
Mater Matuta Festival honouring all Mothers	9 June
Day of the Goddess Venus	10 June
Lady Luck Day	11 June
Dolores Ashcroft-Nowicki HPs and author	11 June 1929
Grain Festival to the Goddess Ashtoreth	12 June
Gerald B. Gardner Founder of Gardnerian Witchcraft 13 June 1884 - 12 February 1964	
William Butler Yeats author	13 June 1865 - 28 January 1939
Day of the Goddess Epona The Horse Goddess	
Day of the Muses	
Starhawk HPs and author	14 June 1951
Lesser Quinquatrus of the Goddess Minerva	
Day of Our Lady of Mount Carmel	15 June
Feast of the Water of the Nile	16 June
Night of the Goddess Hathor	
Day of the Goddess Eurydice the Goddess of the Underworld	17 June
Day of the Goddess Danu	18 June
Birthday of King James 1st of England	19 June
Day of all Hera's Wise women dedicated to the Goddess within	
First day of Cancer	20 June
Midwinter Solstice (Southern Hemisphere)	21 June
Midsummer Solstice (northern hemisphere)	

Festival of the God Herne the Hunter	22 June
Final law Against Witchcraft Repealed in England in 1951	
Day of the Faerie Goddess Aine	23 June
Day of the Burning Lams at Sais for the Goddess Isis and Neith	24 June
Janet Farrar Alexandrian HPs and author	24 June *
Day of Praises to the Goddess Parvati	25 June
Skirophorion Noumenia honouring all Deity	26 June
Stuart Farrar Alexandrian HP and author	26 June 1916 - 7 February 2000 *
Day of honouring all Corn Mothers	27 June
Scott Cunningham HP and author	27 June 1956 - 28 March 1993
Birthday of the Goddess Hemera the Daughter of Ayx	28 June
Day of the Sun God Ra	29 June
Day of Aestas the Goddess of Corn	30 June

JULY:

Named after Julius Caesar.	**1 July**
International Save the Species protection day	
Day to Honour all Grandmothers	
Day of the Goddess Selene	
The Coldest Day of the Year	2 July
Day of the Witch Gaeta	
Day of the God and Dogstar Planet Sirius	3 July
Ceremony of the Mountain Spirits	4 July
Earth is at the Perihelion to the Sun-the Furthest between the Earth and the Sun 5 July	
Day of the Goddess Hera	6 July
Running of the Bulls in Spain	
Day of the Goddess Hera	
Day of the Goddess Hel Goddess of the Underworld	10 July
Let Fete de la Magdalene (Mary Magdalene) the Sacred harlot	11 July

Day of Justice

Honouring of all Children

Day of Forgiveness

Dr. Margaret Murray HPs and author   13 July 1863 - 13 November 1963

All Souls day honouring the Spirits of Ancestors   14 July

Festival of the Sacred Rowan Tree   15 July

Day of the Goddess Carmen Healer and Midwife   16 July

Day of the Goddess Freya   17 July

Birthday of the Goddess Nephthys Goddess of Death   18 July

Lady Sheba HPs and author   18 July 1920 - 2 March 2002

The Opet Festival of Egypt the marriage of Isis and   19 July
Osiris

Day of the Dragon   20 July

Pope Adrian VI issues the Bull

Day For Binding the Wreaths for Lovers

Mayan New Year   21 July

Feast of the Forest Spirits

Beginning of Leo   22 July

Day of the Goddess Amaterasu

Max Heindal Author and leader of the Rosicrucians   23 July 1865 - 6 January 1919

Day of Salacia The Goddess of Oceans   23 July

Hekatombaion Noumenia honouring all deities

Day and the Games of the God Lugh   24 July

Day of the Serpent Goddess   25 July

Birthday of Omar Kha

Death of Pope Innocent VIII   25 July

Feast of St. Anne   26 July

Sacred day to all Buffalo Gods and Goddesses

Dr Carl Jung Occult psychiatrist   26 July 1875 - 6 June 1961

Day of the Goddess Hatshepsut Healer Queen and   27 July
Architect

Procession of Witches in Belgium

Day of the God Thor   28 July

Voudoun Sacred Day for Ceremonies	29 July
Day of the God Jupiter	30 July
Eve of Imbolg the Festival	31 July

AUGUST:
Named after the Emperor Augustus.

Imbolg Festival (southern hemisphere)	1 August
Lughnasadh Festival (northern hemisphere)	
Day of the Goddess Taitu	
Fiesta of Our Lady of Angels	2 August
Day of Saoka	
Day of the Dryads dedicated to Maiden Spirits of the Woods and Water 3 August	
Day of the Goddess Hathor	4 August
Day of the Lady of Snow	
Day of the Goddess Mara	5 August
Day of the Benediction of the Sea	
Day of the Cherokee Corn Dancers	6 August
Gaia Consciousness Day	7 August
Breaking of the Nile	
Day of the Goddess Nut	
Birthday of the Virgin Mary	8 August
Festival of the Goddess Venus	9 August
Festival of the Spirits	
Day to Honour the Star Goddesses	10 August
Holy day of St. Claire	11 August
Lychnapsia the Festival of Lights for the Goddess Isis	12 August
Helena Blavatsky occultists and author	12 August 1831 - 8 May 1947
Birthday of the Goddess Aradia Queen of the Witches Born in Volterra in 1313 13 August	
Celebration of the Goddess Diana and Hecate of the Moon	
Day dedicated to the Goddess Selene	14 August

Day of the Goddess Tiamat	15 August
Birthday of Charles Godfrey Leland	
Celebration of the Goddess Dea Syria	
Day of Giving	16 August
Feast of the Goddess Diana	17 August
Day of Healing the Past	18 August
Vinalia Thanksgiving	19 August
Day of Vinalia Rustica Venus of the Grape Vine	
Birthday of HP Lovecraft	20 August
Sacred Marriage of Heaven and Earth	
Harvest festival	21 August
Metagetnion Noumenia Day to honour all Deities	22 August
Beginning of Virgo	
Festival of the Furies	23 August
Festival of the Goddess of Fate Nemesis	
W. E. Butler author and occultist	23 August 1898 - 1 August 1978
Festival of the Opening of the Mundas Cereris the Womb of the Labyrinth to the Underworld of Demeter	24 August
Opseconsia the Harvest Festival Ritual of Thanksgiving	25 August
Feast day of the Goddess Ilmatar	26 August
Birthday of the Goddesses Isis and Nut	27 August
Opening the World Parliament of Religions	28 August
Birthday of the Goddess Athena	
Birthday of the Goddess Hathor	29 August
Egyptian New Year's Day	
Charistheria The Thanksgiving ceremony	30 August
Raymond Buckland HP and author	31st August 1934 – 27th September 2017

SEPTEMBER:

Awakening of the Women's Serpent Power Life Force	1 September

Ostara - First day of spring (southern hemisphere)

Festival of the Vine dedicated to the Goddess
Ariadne and the God Dionysus 2 September

Day of the Goddess Polias and the God Zeus

Women's Healing Ceremony for the Four Directions	3 September
Pilgrimage to test One's Soul	4 September
Day of the Goddess Cybele	5 September
Day of the Goddess Artemis	6 September
Day of the God Bacchus	7 September
Birthday of the Goddess Yemaya	8 September
Feast of the Shepherd	
Birthday of the Goddess Yemaya	
Day of Mercy	
Te Veilat the Gathering of the Fruit	9 September
Reunion Festival	10 September
Marie Laveau Queen of the Voudoun	10 September 1801 - 16 June 1881
Day of Honouring all Queens of Egypt	11 September
Day of the God Bel	12 September
Day of the Goddess Nephthys	13 September
Ceremony for the Lighting of the Fire	
Day of Honouring the Black Madonna	14 September
Day of the Goddess Kore	15 September
The gathering of Initiates	
International Day of Democracy	
Goddesses Ascent from Annwyn	16 September
Holade Mystai the Ritual bathing in the Sea	
Day of St. Sophia	17 September
Day of Faith, Hope and Charity	
Feast of St. Hildegarde	
Stephen Skinner author	17 September 1932 - 24 September 1997
Giving of Grain and Food to the Poor	18 September
Blessing of the Rain Goddesses	19 September

Boedromion Noumenia Day to Honour all Deities	20 September
Festival of Epopteia the day of Initiation	
Spring Equinox (southern hemisphere)	21 September
Autumn Equinox (northern hemisphere)	
Feast of Honouring the triple Aspect of Maiden, Mother and Crone	
Festival of Mabon the Wicces Thanksgiving	22 September
Day of the Goddess Demeter	
Beginning of Libra	23 September
Genesia Day to make offerings to the Dead	24 September
Day of Mercy	
Birthday of the Goddess Sedna	25 September
Day of Atonement	26 September
Birthday of the Goddess Athena of Knowledge	27 September
Day of Saleeb the Cresting of the Nile at its greatest height	28 September
Feast of Michaelmas (honouring archangel Michael)	29 September
Day of the Goddess Meditrinalia of Medicines and Healing	30 September

OCTOBER:

Day to Forgive Your Enemies	1 October
Neville Drury author	1 October 1947 - 15 October 2013
Isaac Bonawitz Druid and author	
Power Day for Arachnids	
Day of the Goddess Rhiannon	2 October
Feast of the Guardian Spirits	
Rosaleen Norton witch and author	2 October 1917 - 5 December 1979
Arthur Edward Waite witch and author	2 October 1857 - 19 May 1942
St. Dionysis Transformation of the Pagan God of Wine into Christianity 3 October	
Oddudua The Santeria Mother of the Gods and Goddesses	4 October

Fasting day for the Goddess Demeter	
Byzantine day of the Holy Spirit for the Goddess Sophia	5 October
Wine festival for the God Dionysis	
Day of the Goddess Artemis	6 October
Day of the God Bau	7 October
Francis Barrett occultist and author	7 October 1872 - 21 February 1941
Oschophoria The bearing of Green Branches to commemorate Theseus Return 8 October	
Day of the God Horus	9 October
The Eye of the God Festival	
Day of White Buffalo calf Woman	10 October
Thesmophoria of the Goddess Demeter	11 October
Aleister Crowley occultist and author	12 October 1875 - 1 December 1947
Day of Women's Prayers	
Day of the God Eros	13 October
Victory day of Good over Evil	14 October
Day of Lady Godiva	15 October
Day of the Goddess Gaia and Nymphs day	16 October
Festival of Fortune	
Day of the Goddess Isis	17 October
Day of Clean Water	18 October
St. Luke's day The Great Horn Fair Honouring Horned Gods Day	
Day of Good Luck	19 October
Pyanepsion Noumenia Day to honour all deities	20 October
Birthday of Selena Fox HPs and author	
Day of the Virgin Mary	
Kite Flying festival	
Day of the Goddess Aphrodite	22 October
Sacred day of the Willow Tree	
Timothy Leary	22 October 1920 - 31 May 1996
Day of the Goddess Aphrodite	

Beginning of Scorpio	23 October
Day of the Goddess Lilith	24 October
Feast of the Spirits of Air	
Day of the God Ge	25 October
Proerosia Festival Harvest	
Festival of the Goddess Hathor	26 October
Honouring the Womb in all Female Life	27 October
Patricia Crowther HPs and author	27 October 1927 - 5 February 2009
Day of the Goddess Isis	28 October
Feast of the Dead	29 October
Day of the God Osiris	30 October
Day to Remember the Burning Times	31 October
Beltane Festival (southern hemisphere)	
Samhain (northern hemisphere)	
Wicces Remembrance Day	

NOVEMBER:

Day of the Banshees	1 November
Rebirth of the God Osiris	3 November
World Communication Day	
Stag Dances	4 November
Birthday of the Goddess Tiamat	6 November
Day of the Goddess Leto	7 November
Sacred day of Elphane	11 November
World Tolerance Day	16 November
Day of the Goddess Ereshkigal	
Israel Regardie author and witch	17 November 1907 - 10 March 1985
Maimakterion Noumenia Day to honour all Deities	18 November
Day of the Goddess Ishtar	21 November
Thanksgiving	23 November
Elders Day of Respect	
Lady Tamara Von Forslun Elder HPs and author	23 November 1956*
Day of the Goddess Cerridwen	26 November

Day of the Goddess Sophia	27 November
Oberon Zell Witch and author	30 November *

DECEMBER:

Franz Bardon occultist and author	1 December 1909 - 10 July 1958
World Aids Day	1 December
Day of the Goddess Pallas Athena	
Day of the Goddess Arachne	2 December
Day of the Goddess Bona Dea	3 December
Day of the Goddess Bride	5 December
Dione Fortune author and occultist	6 December 1890 - 8 January 1946
Day of the Goddess Tara	9 December
Day of the Light Bringer	13 December
Day of the Goddess Sapientia	16 December
Festival of Saturnalia	17 December
Poseidon Poumenia	18 December
Day of Saturnalia	
Day of the Goddess Kwan Yin	
Day of Opalia	19 December
Day of the Goddess Selene and the God Janus	20 December
Festival of Evergreen Trees	21 December
Birthday of the God Mithras	22 December
Mid-Summer Solstice (southern hemisphere)	
Mid-Winter Solstice (northern hemisphere)	
Day of the Goddess Hathor	23 December
Festival of the Goddess Freyr and the God Freyja	25 December
Festival of the of Poseidon	25 December
Birthday of the God Horus	26 December
Birthday of Buddha	
Birthday of the Goddess Freya	27 December
Day of the Goddess Artemis	29 December
Festival of Father Time	31 December
Day of the Sun God Ra	

EPILOGUE

This book is the second of my series "Complete Teachings of Wicca", subtitled from Book One through to Book 6. This book is for the Wiccan who seeks to learn of the ancient Craft and become a Wicce. You notice that the spelling of the word Witch is different, as this detracts from the Judaic word Witch, and the original word was Wicca taken from the Anglo-Saxon word Wicce (to shape and bend). It was from here a short debasement to the word Wicca and Wiccecraft.

This book will help you lead up to and prepare for working within the Magick Circle, and within the deeper understanding and teaching of Wicca as a Wiccan. Wicca has changed very much over the last 60 years but the essence and the basis behind its rituals and structure are all the same. The journey of the Wicce is one starting from bewilderment with the Magickal, into the knowledge of the Natural principals of what Wicca is truly all about, into the more in-depth knowledge of the Old Religion and its Mysteries and the ways of the Goddess and God and the Magickal Patterns of nature.

It takes you next into the deeper understanding of the Priesthood, that works with the community, guiding and assisting where it is needed as chaplains in hospitals and prisons, marriage celebrants, psychologists, psychics, spiritual guides, healers, teachers and mentors, and medical practitioners.

The Higher level is that of the High Priesthood, that of the High Priests and High Priestesses, who are the Clan mothers and fathers and run their own covens, circles and Churches, with the assistance of the Priesthood and the community. They are the Elders of the Wiccan community and respected as such. Once a High Priest or High Priestess retires from office, they still become an active member of the Wiccan community but as Elders, the Crones and Magi of the highest rank, who work together as a committee known as the "Grand Council", as advisors to all the covens and their respective leaders.

But this Book takes you through from Wiccaning up to the known requirements to be an Initiate of the Goddess and God and become a Wicce. My next Book "Complete teaching Of Wicca – Book Three – Tarot and Internal Alchemy", takes you through the deeper meanings and trainings of the Wicce up to Priesthood. It uses the Tarot cards as a system of Magickal Portals that take you into a deeper understanding and knowledge of all the 21 systems of Magickal areas that is required to become a Priest or Priestess of the Wiccan community. This level is very in-depth with much training and practice required.

This book teaches you all the methods in Properly Preparing your Magick Circle, the Temple of the Wicces. Starting from the clearing and purification of your sacred space whether it is indoors or outdoors, to the correct Preparation of the Opening of the Portals and Protective Shields to protect the Magick Circle.

Followed by the "Self-Blessing Ritual" and then the "Lesser Banishing Ritual of the Pentagram", which is performed at every Circle gathering. It then takes you through the stages of visualization and the creating and casting of your Magick Circle by using the Elemental system, and how to invoke and banish certain powers and energies that you work with safely.

"May the Goddess hold you safely in the palms of Her hands and always close to Her heart".

The Witch of Oz

Aquarian Tabernacle Church

PO Box 409

Index, Washington 98256 USA

E-mail: ATC@AquaTabCh.org

www.AquaTabCh.org.

Pagan Federation

BM Box 7097

London, WC1N 3XX England

Covenant of the Goddess

Box 1226

Berkeley, California 94701 USA

Pagan Alliance

PO Box 823

Bathurst NSW 2795 Australia

Buckland Museum of Witchcraft & Magick

www.buckland museum.org

Email: toni@bucklandmuseum.org

316 Linwood Avenue

Columbus, Ohio 43205 USA

Fellowship of Isis

www.fellowshipofisis.com

Foi_info@fellowshipofisis.com

Clonegal Castle, Enniscorthy Eire

Printed in the United States
By Bookmasters